CRIPPEN

CRIPPEN

A CRIME SENSATION IN
MEMORY AND MODERNITY

Roger Dalrymple

THE BOYDELL PRESS

First published 2020
The Boydell Press, Woodbridge

ISBN 978-1-78327-508-3

The Boydell Press is an imprint of Boydell & Brewer Ltd
PO Box 9, Woodbridge, Suffolk IP12 3DF, UK
and of Boydell & Brewer Inc.
668 Mt Hope Avenue, Rochester, NY 14620–2731, USA
website: www.boydellandbrewer.com

A catalogue record of this publication is available
from the British Library

This publication is printed on acid-free paper

Typeset by BBR Design, Sheffield

Printed and bound in Great Britain by TJ International Ltd, Padstow, Cornwall

In memory of Martin Fido

Contents

Illustrations

Every effort has been made to trace the copyright holders of the illustrations; apologies are offered for any omission, and the author and publishers will be pleased to add any necessary acknowledgement in subsequent editions.

Acknowledgements

This book was written in Oxford in the befuddling era of Brexit, but I suspect it really started life in The Green Man, Sutton in the late 1950s. From those pub regulars who shared a post-war interest in popular criminology, their dependable landlady, my grandmother, gleaned a host of true crime anecdotes which I would encourage her to recount to me some twenty-five years later. Patrons would claim to have rubbed shoulders or exchanged innocent pleasantries with John Reginald Halliday Christie, the killer of Rillington Place; others would recall encounters with 'acid bath murderer' John George Haigh, whose crimes had been committed in the neighbouring town to my birthplace – 'He drank blood!' had come the appalled (and misinformed) grandmaternal whisper. And some would even share reminiscences of the Crippen case of 1910, when a seemingly respectable North London doctor poisoned his wife, buried her body in the cellar, and fled overseas with his mistress disguised in drag, before his capture, trial at the Old Bailey, and hanging at Pentonville. I'm sure I heard this last tale in the spring of 1980 on my first visit to the Chamber of Horrors, Crippen's original wax effigy before me. So, my first thanks are due to those unknown pub patrons, and to their publican for balancing my childish fervour for mystery with reminders of the very real tragedies behind true crime stories – something I have sought to keep in view in each line of this book.

My more immediate debts for the genesis of this book lie with Caroline Palmer, Michael Middeke, Megan Milan, Lizzie Howard, and the anonymous reader of Boydell & Brewer whose probing questions and insightful feedback have shaped the scope and focus of my attempt to produce a full account of the literary and cultural legacy of the Crippen case. Colleagues at Oxford Brookes have generously shared insights, contexts, and rationalisation for a writer ambivalent about discoursing on murder, particularly Patrick Alexander, Joanne Begiato, Dominic Corrywright, Jacqui Dearden, Anne-Marie Kilday, Chris Rizza, Nick Swarbrick, and Cassie Watson. Christie scholars have modelled creative approaches to inter-relating criminological text and context, especially Mark Aldridge, Jamie Bernthal-Hooker, and Rebecca Mills. Nicholas Connell, surely the foremost authority and most accessible writer on Crippen, has generously shared his expertise throughout the project, as has Martin Edwards, current President of the Detection Club, who signposted much of the terrain of 'literary Crippen'. I am also indebted to Sgt Paul Gathercole, expert guide and finest of companions to the Museum of London's 'Crime Museum Uncovered' exhibition of 2016, where we inspected Crippen's shovel and Belle's hair curlers; Tony Grand, who, Poirot-like, identified many a bibliographical avenue from his armchair; James Helling who compiled the index; Russell Inglis and Pakeeza Rahman, who kindly advised on Edwardian legal process; Bonnie McGill at Boydell Press; Andrew Millichip, who has suffered lengthy updates on the book's progress through many a conference; Martin Nichols, who signalled many an Edwardian intertext; Carrie Parris, who very kindly shared her excellent unpublished work on the Crimes Club's enthusiasm for discussing Crippeniana; Michael Plater, who was completing his Ripper-themed Ph.D. thesis in parallel (and who crossed the line first!); Zoe Richards of the Madame Tussaud's archive; David James Smith; Susannah Stapleton; the respective staffs of the Museum of the Mind Archive in Beckenham; the Museum of London; the National Archives in Kew; and the Wellcome Library.

Dr Matthew Pearson has generously offered insights and encouragement through all stages of the project.

Above all, Sean, Freya, and my wider family have patiently tolerated the doctor as a houseguest for more years than can have been healthy for any of us.

Finally, this project was immeasurably enriched by discussion and correspondence with the late Martin Fido, contributor of the *Dictionary of National Biography* entry on Crippen. Martin's ranging between literary and criminological subjects over the course of his prolific career offered precedent and inspiration for others tempted to venture out of their disciplinary homes and to write at the intersection of literary and criminological history. He also held a rare talent for writing about true crime without ever losing sight of its human cost. This book is dedicated to his memory.

PART ONE

THE CASE
AND ITS CONTEXT

CHAPTER ONE

ACCOUNTING FOR CRIPPEN

Crippen and the Ripper – in the annals of English crime perhaps only Jack the Ripper and Dr Hawley Harvey Crippen have truly crossed the boundary from historical personage to *dramatis persona*, haunting the popular imagination well beyond the Victorian and Edwardian periods in which they respectively gained their notoriety. More than a century since sensational press reports first broadcast their deeds of 'murder and mutilation' to an aghast reading public, the Victorian Whitechapel Murderer and the Edwardian 'North London Cellar Murderer' have been remembered and revisited in a broad range of literary and cultural forms.[1] For over a century, posterity has memorialised both malefactors in crime history, fiction, film, and even two ill-judged attempts at musical theatre.[2] The anonymous Ripper and the 'mild mannered' domestic murderer Crippen even figured on the London tourist's itinerary for close on a hundred years: effigies and *realia* associated with both criminals were included in that once reliable barometer of crime sensations, Madame Tussaud's Chamber of Horrors, where the Ripper's East End was

---

1   The Crippen case straddles the reigns of Edward VII and George V with 'Bertie' dying two months before the discovery of a body in Hilldrop Crescent. Nevertheless, the case is generally associated with the Edwardian age, the coronation of George not taking place until June 1911, and for the purposes of this study Crippen and his contemporaries will be referred to as Edwardian.

2   For the Ripper musical, see Ron Pember and Denis de Marne, *Jack the Ripper: A Musical Play* (London: Samuel French, 1976). The 1961 musical *Belle* is discussed in Chapter Six.

reconstructed and Crippen's effigy stared out from the prisoner's dock until the Chamber's closure to the public in 2016.[3]

The endurance of the figure of Jack the Ripper is more readily explained. Never brought to justice for the murder and mutilation of at least five women in autumn 1888, the Whitechapel Murderer's escape into the East End backstreets and the shadows of history allowed his swift transformation into enduring myth. Over the ensuing 130 years, the Ripper story has become, in the words of Judith Walkowitz, 'an enigmatic thriller that continually reverberates and reconstructs itself over time'.[4] An unbroken thread of speculation as to the Ripper's identity extends from the contemporaneous press reports, through the later reminiscences and memoirs of the investigating detectives and officials, beyond the appearance of the first full-length book on the subject in 1929, to the thriving publishing industry on the subject that continues to the present day.[5] This tradition has seen a seemingly never-ending parade of Ripper suspects proposed – some drawn from the historical record as persons known to be of interest to the police at the time; others (the majority) plucked seemingly at random from the available contemporaneous cast of great or inglorious Victorians. A random selection of these suspects indicates the exuberance and poetic licence of the tradition of 'Ripperology' which has offered up such outlandish candidates as Queen Victoria's physician Sir William Gull; her grandson Prince Albert Victor, Duke of Clarence and Avondale; impressionist painter Walter Sickert; philanthropist Dr Barnardo; Cambridge scholar and cousin of Virginia Woolf, J.K. Stephen, and Oxford-based children's author Lewis Carroll. The London fogs which were once popularly imagined to have encircled the Ripper may now have been dismissed as poetic fancy, but aided by such fabrications and elaborations, the unfathomable heart of the Jack the Ripper mystery endures.[6]

3   Throughout the twentieth century, Crippen's name was sufficiently well known that it could be described as a 'byword' in Ursula Bloom's *The Girl Who Loved Crippen* (London: Hutchinson, 1955), p. 1.
4   Judith Walkowitz, *City of Dreadful Delight: Narratives of Sexual Danger in Late-Victorian London* (London: Virago, 1992), p. 201.
5   For a systematic bibliography on the Ripper down to 1973 see Alexander Kelly, *Jack the Ripper: A Bibliography and Review of the Literature* (London: Association of Assistant Librarians, 1973).
6   The fog-less weather conditions on the nights of the Ripper murders are detailed in *The Mammoth Book of Jack the Ripper*, ed. Maxim Jakubowski and Nathan Braund (London: Robinson Publishing, 1999), p. 474.

The Ripper remains, in more ways than one, still *at large* – looming in our collective memory like folk demon predecessor, Spring-Heeled Jack.[7]

Accounting for the enduring memory and legacy of Edwardian doctor Hawley Harvey Crippen, the project of this book, is altogether more challenging. It is less obvious why the domestic metropolitan drama of Dr Crippen's poisoning of his wife Cora, his concealment of her dismembered remains in the cellar of their suburban house, 39 Hilldrop Crescent, North London, and his doomed attempt at escape overseas with his cross-dressed mistress should have arrogated to itself a cultural resonance approaching to that of the Whitechapel Murderer. Why, when Crippen was executed at Pentonville Prison in November 1910, should this single Edwardian uxoricide have passed into enduring memory, even attaining a place in the criminal pantheon, as Catharine Arnold has suggested, 'among the immortals, alongside Jack Sheppard, Dick Turpin and Jack the Ripper'?[8]

To the best of our knowledge, Crippen killed but once.[9] Though the first of his two wives also predeceased him in 1892, insinuations that she too might have died at his hand seem only to have been tentatively raised in 1910 and were never substantiated.[10] Other homicides of the era claimed a far greater tally of victims, as witness the example of 'Brides in the Bath' murderer George Joseph Smith in 1915; they employed more devious methods, as witness the

---

7 The standing of historical studies of the Whitechapel Murders has been bolstered by Walkowitz's *City of Dreadful Delight* and Judith Flanders, *The Invention of Murder: How the Victorians Revelled in Death and Detection and Created Modern Crime* (London: Harper Press, 2011). On the cultural significance of Spring-Heeled Jack, see Karl Bell, *Spring-Heeled Jack: Victorian Urban Folklore and Popular Cultures* (Woodbridge: Boydell, 2012). Spring-Heeled Jack's own eighteenth-century forebear is chronicled by Jan Bondeson, *The London Monster: Terror on the Streets in 1790* (Stroud: Sutton Publishing, 2003).

8 Catharine Arnold, *Underworld London: Crime and Punishment in the Capital City* (London: Simon and Schuster, 2012), p. 220. The suggestion of immortality for Crippen's name is perhaps overstated; straw polls conducted during the writing of this book among undergraduate lecture audiences, even those studying forensic linguistics or criminal history, indicated waning recognition.

9 John Boyne notes this is against popular expectation: 'Common perception seemed to have placed him as a vicious serial killer' – *Crippen: A Novel of Murder* (London: Black Swan, 2011), p. 505.

10 Chapter Three will explore the circumstances surrounding the death of Crippen's first wife, Charlotte Bell.

tangled webs woven by poisoner and fraudster Frederick Seddon in 1912; or they did their own part to court active notoriety and infamy, as witness the case of an earlier doctor-poisoner, Thomas Neill Cream, who at his 1892 execution for a series of strychnine poisonings in Lambeth is reputed to have exclaimed from the scaffold, 'I am Jack the – !'.[11] All of these broadly coeval crimes received a degree of sensational press coverage, with the details of investigation, trial, conviction, and execution all drawing sustained public interest and leaving a lasting imprint on the collective memory of lurid crime. Yet it is impassive and self-effacing Dr Crippen, 'surely the mildest mannered murderer that ever stood in the dock' according to one early biographer, or an 'insignificant little man' as arresting officer Detective Chief Inspector Walter Dew styled him, whose name has loomed larger than these more nefarious counterparts for more than a century, its profile waning only since the turn of the millennium.[12]

The notoriety of the Crippen story in its own time is in part accounted for by those many sensational and luridly gothic elements which the present study will have cause to elaborate in detail. There were two 'ladies in the case' (Crippen's wife, Cora, alias music hall soubrette 'Belle Elmore', and his long-term mistress Ethel le Neve); there was a concealed dark secret in a quasi-respectable London townhouse (Crippen poisoned Cora and buried portions of her dismembered body in the cramped and dark coal cellar); there was an audacious disguise involving Ethel cross-dressing and masquerading as Crippen's son; there was a picaresque but doomed attempt at escape by steamship played out against Atlantic vistas; and there was the famous novel deployment of wireless telegraphy, the ship-to-shore transmission from Captain Henry Kendall prompting international pursuit by Scotland Yard's Chief

11   The *Notable British Trials* series chronicles the trials of Smith and Seddon: *The Trial of George Joseph Smith*, ed. Eric R. Watson (London: William Hodge, 1922); *Trial of the Seddons*, ed. Filson Young (London: William Hodge, 1914). The most comprehensive scholarly account of the Cream case is provided by Angus McClaren, *A Prescription for Murder: The Victorian Serial Killings of Dr Thomas Neill Cream* (Chicago: University of Chicago Press, 1995).

12   Harold Eaton, *Famous Poison Trials* (London: Collins and Sons, 1923), p. 157; Walter Dew, *I Caught Crippen* (London and Glasgow: Blackie and Son, 1938), p. 12. Dew's description of Crippen is anticipated, and perhaps influenced by, Filson Young's description of Crippen in his edition of the trial proceedings as 'an entirely unremarkable little man': *The Trial of H.H. Crippen*, p. xiv.

Inspector Walter Dew, who boarded a faster steamship, overtook and arrested Crippen, putting an end to the doctor's vision of a new life in the New World, and leading him instead to the condemned cell and the hanging shed at Pentonville.

The sum of these macabre and dramatic elements was a curiously theatrical true crime story, whose potential was rapidly recognised and exploited in reportage from the earliest stage of the 1910 investigation and which was to leave an enduring imprint on the public memory of the crime. Yet there were also silences, lacunae, and secrets taken to the grave – the kind of riddles that would keep the case at the centre of speculative criminological opinion and lay commentary for the subsequent century. Had Crippen acted alone in the murder of his wife? How far had Ethel le Neve been privy to the crime or even complicit in its execution? What indeed was the immediate motive for the murder? Had the death in fact been an accident, a misadministration of sedative drugs by the quack doctor? Since Crippen continued to protest his innocence at his trial and went to the scaffold without making any confession, the discursive vacuum at the heart of the story left room for speculation and hypothesis, something plentifully afforded in the reportage and commentary of the day and in crime histories and fictionalised retellings in subsequent decades. Speculations as to motive, the degree of impulsion in the crime, the nature of the criminal mind, and the contrast between the callous and calculated murder and the ostensibly affable and personable perpetrator have provided a continuous strain of commentary since 1910 and illuminate why 'Crippen continues to jostle among a select few contenders for the title of Britain's most famous murderer'.[13]

Likewise, a degree of posterity might anyway have been expected for the Crippen story given its embodiment of signature features which crime historians have noted as germane to crimes of 'classic status'. Martin Fido's wide-ranging survey of London murders helpfully draws together those signatures of the 'classic' crime which, from the Victorian era onwards, were increasingly codified, drawing instant recognition and interest amongst the newspaper-reading public: 'The Victorian murderer won classic status by unusual violence or the mutilation of his victim; by disappearing and sparking a widely publicised manhunt; by the prominence of his victim or his own

---

13   Julie English Early, 'A New Man for a New Century: Dr Crippen and the Principles of Masculinity', in George Robb and Nancy Erber (eds), *Disorder in the Court: Trials and Sexual Conflict at the Turn of the Century* (London: Macmillan, 1999), p. 209.

respectable status.'[14] The Edwardian Crippen drama fits this description well and indeed exhibits four of the five signature features that Fido predicates as intrinsic to the classic murder cases of this period: bodily mutilation, a murder hunt, a middle-class murderer, and sex. Only in the further category of 'Many victims' does Crippen fail to conform to type, though as we shall see, the first-wave press accounts of his crime certainly sought to cast him as the actual or potential perpetrator of further murders.

A second schema, proffered in Yvonne Jewkes's sociological study of media and crime, also helps us in accounting for Crippen as a media sensation in its time.[15] Jewkes identifies the distinctive characteristics of those stories of violent crime which are most likely to command a 'news value' in the modern age. While drawn up with the media of 'a new millennium' in mind, many of Jewkes's identified features were clearly already enshrined in journalistic practice at the time of the Crippen drama. These are:

THRESHOLD (where the story quickly reaches a certain level of perceived importance among the reading public);

PREDICTABILITY (where the story's development largely conforms to an established pattern of crime reporting and reader expectation);

SIMPLIFICATION (where the story is easily reducible to a minimum number of parts or themes and crucially enables an associated moral simplification);

INDIVIDUALISM (where personalised and individual responses to the crime are privileged over more complex cultural and political explanations for criminal behaviours and actions);

RISK (where the story conveys a sense of imminent danger to the public, especially where a dangerous criminal is designated as being 'at large');

SEX (where implications of sexually motivated murder invariably receive substantial and sensational attention and provoke corresponding interest);

CELEBRITY OR HIGH-STATUS-PERSONS (where an existing high profile for killer or victim accentuates the story's interest);

PROXIMITY (where readers are prompted to reflect on both the physical

---

14   Martin Fido, *Murder Guide to London* (London: Weidenfeld and Nicolson, 1986), p. 11.
15   Yvonne Jewkes, *Media and Crime*, 3rd edition (London: Sage, 2015), pp. 49–69.

propinquity of a murder taking place 'on the doorstep' [despite the timeless averral of the scandalised voice on the street that 'one wouldn't expect such a thing to happen here'] and the perceived relevance to their own lives);

VIOLENCE OF CONFLICT (in the nature of the murder or murderous attack);

VISUAL SPECTACLE AND GRAPHIC IMAGERY (where all aspects of the murder including crime scene, victim's body, and murder weapon can command prurient and appalled interest);

CHILDREN (whose involvement will tend to elevate the news profile of a crime story still further); and

CONSERVATIVE IDEOLOGY AND POLITICAL DIVERSION (where the crime narrative concludes with reinforced assumptions regarding the need for deterrence, sanction, punishment and even retribution).

Again, it is striking just how neatly the Crippen crime maps onto this taxonomy of criminological interest. A focus upon the selected domains of THRESHOLD, RISK, SEX, and VISUAL SPECTACLE AND GRAPHIC IMAGERY is instructive. The first of these, threshold of public interest, was instantly achieved in this story by victim Belle Elmore's associations with the London stage. While she appears to have enjoyed only very modest success as a light entertainer in music hall, her subsequent role as Treasurer with the Music Hall Ladies' Guild had made her sufficiently prominent in fashionable London society to warrant special mention in *The Era*'s report of the Guild's Second Annual Dinner in October 1909. Presented, 'amid great enthusiasm', with a gold bangle, a basket of flowers and a box of gloves, 'in recognition of her services', Belle is reported as acknowledging the honour in a speech which poignantly appeals to a futurity that was more limited than she could have known: 'I can only say that as long as I am permitted I shall do in the future as I have done in the past, and, as we all learn by experience, I hope to improve upon the work I have done, and further the interests of the Guild to the best of my ability.'[16] Likewise, as will be shown in Chapter Three, there is also evidence that Crippen had attracted a certain level of profile before the murder story broke by virtue of his aggressive marketing of patent remedies and from the appearance in print of at least two exposés of his dubious practice by 1910.

16   *The Era*, 2 October 1909.

Moving from THRESHOLD to RISK, it is clear that while Crippen's murderous activity was confined to uxoricide in the domestic sphere, early reportage did indeed magnify the perceived sense of social danger. Press coverage emphasised the mutilation of the body in the cellar, implying the disordered impulsions of the lust-murderer (when instead Crippen's dismemberment of his victim appears to have been entirely motivated by a desire to obliterate all evidence of the crime). Cultural anxieties regarding murderous medical men were also pressed into service, with allusions to Crippen's medical training reviving Victorian anxieties around the figure of the doctor as a potential somatic and social oppressor. Whilst Edwardian advances in medicine and public and community health had gone some way to diminish this archetype of gothic imagination, there remained a 'paranoid fascination with the idea that regulators of health may themselves by unhealthy'.[17] The dread was intensified by fears that a doctor might use medical knowledge to attempt the 'perfect' or undetectable crime by means of poison and 'trying by every cunning means to out-fox the toxicologists by using drugs which couldn't be detected at post mortems'.[18] Apparent social progress and urbanisation appeared to increase rather than diminish this fear. Indeed, as Burney has observed, homicide by poison appeared a particularly apposite means of murder in the urban modern environment: 'As poison was thought to leave no marks directly accessible to the eye, its victims could be construed as characteristically "modern" in presenting to the world an inscrutable façade masking an inner reality.'[19]

Jewkes's suggestion of SEX as intrinsic to the newsworthy crime needs little justification and finds plentiful expression in the Crippen case. The trial brought revelations of not only Crippen and Ethel le Neve's affair but an alleged liaison between Cora Crippen and American entertainer Bruce Miller. Moreover, Ethel's cross-dressed masquerade, something played down by both fugitives as an innocent 'adventure in boy's clothes', created a discursive space in which ambivalence regarding gender and identity categories might be recognised and the possibility of counter-normative sexuality confronted.

This leaves VISUAL SPECTACLE AND GRAPHIC IMAGERY from our sample of

---

17 J.C. Bernthal, *Queering Agatha Christie: Revisiting the Golden Age of Detective Fiction* (London: Palgrave Macmillan, 2016), p. 176.
18 Arthur Kent, *The Death Doctors* (London: New English Library, 1974), p. 9.
19 Ian A. Burney, 'A Poisoning of No Substance: The Trials of Medico-Legal Proof in Mid-Victorian England', *Journal of British Studies* 38:1, pp. 59–92 (p. 70).

Jewkes's schema. Both were plentifully afforded by the exhumation of the remains in Crippen's coal cellar – an event which drew crowds to Hilldrop Crescent and which commanded columns of press coverage during the inquest in Islington, the committal proceedings at Bow Street, and the trial at the Central Criminal Court. The leafy enclave of Hilldrop Crescent became a focus for 'dark tourism' from the summer of 1910 onwards and the assembled crowds proved sufficiently troublesome that by January of the following year a group of local residents were petitioning the council for a change of street name.[20] 'Murder tours' of London still take in the address as part of a North London itinerary, though the site of Crippen's house is now occupied by a block of flats.

Mapping the case against Fido and Jewkes's criminological schemas helps to locate some of the drivers of press and public interest in 1910. It also goes some way to account for Crippen's notoriety in the immediate years after his trial and execution, attested by fluctuating accounts in the regional press down to at least 1920 of the name 'Crippen!' being bandied about in street scuffles and brawls as a term of opprobrium.[21] Yet the question remains why this particular story should have endured well beyond the point where Crippen's near contemporaries had long faded from popular memory. While the case histories of Henry Wainwright (d.1875), Charles Peace (d.1879), and Frederick Seddon (d.1912) were to become the province of criminologists and crime historians within decades of their executions, Crippen was to remain a household name, a bogeyman figure to be name-checked as a casual point of cultural reference when shorthand evocation of the criminous was required.[22]

The present study argues that in order to account for the endurance of Crippen, we must acknowledge two distinct phases in the case's reception

---

20 *Kilburn Times*, 6 January 1911.
21 For example, *The Belfast Telegraph* of 20 February 1911 relates how Patrick M'Greecy charged James Gorman, a farmer, with threatening and abusive language. 'On one occasion in the public streets he had shouted "Crippen!" at him in the presence of a number of persons, and he had also called him a rover and a rogue.' In the case of 'Brides in the Bath' murderer George Joseph Smith, landlady Mrs Crossley, banishing Smith from her property after the suspicious death of his wife under her roof, shouted 'Crippen!' after Smith as he left the house: Gordon Honeycombe, *The Murders of the Black Museum* (London: Hutchinson and Co, 1982), p. 84.
22 An indicative popular culture reference is supplied by *The Radio Times* synopsis of a 1990 episode of soap opera *EastEnders*: 'Dot [Cotton] cannot decide if her son is truly a reformed character or the worst thing since Dr Crippen', *Radio Times*, 19–25 May 1990.

history, representing two starkly distinct renditions of Crippen. The first, instated by the press reportage of 1910, rendered the story as a familiar melodramatic script whose outlines had precedent in a long-established tradition of crime sensations. The second, led by criminological and fictional reinterpretation of the case from the 1920s onwards, took Crippen as a case study of modern murder, highlighting the insufficiency of settled narratives of criminal deeds and their motivations. Treatments in this second phase of Crippeniana were obliged always to negotiate and interrogate the iconic bogeyman figure history had bequeathed them, resulting in an enduring cultural impression of Crippen as forever poised between memory and modernity.

My starting point is thus the recognition that the Crippen story is both throwback and presage. Its narrative lines stem first from a Victorian melodramatic tradition which portrayed domestic murder in sensational terms, regarding it, as Richard Altick, Rosalind Crone, and Judith Flanders have found, as 'spectacle'.[23] This tradition remained highly recognisable to that portion of an expanded reading public who had benefited from the Education Act of 1870 and who in 1910 were approaching or upward of middle age.[24] These readers would have recognised the tendency of the Victorian press to trope new murder cases on the paradigm of past crimes, 'weaving together a culture of violence in the popular imagination'.[25] The Edwardian reception of the Crippen story (and as I am to show, elements of its inception) can only be fully understood by restoring certain 'classic' Victorian crimes to our understanding of the story and appreciating how, for a significant portion of the Edwardian reading public, the story represented an intensive collation of earlier crime narratives. To restore this context is to unearth a striking instance of wilful nostalgia in late Edwardian culture while going some way to account for Crippen as a true-crime sensation.

This 'first phase' Crippen is neglected in studies of the case to date. While an

---

23   Richard D. Altick, *Victorian Studies in Scarlet* (London: Dent, 1970), p. 10; Judith Flanders, *The Invention of Murder: How the Victorians Revelled in Death and Detection and Created Modern Crime* (London: Harper Press, 2011) p. 466; Rosalind Crone, *Violent Victorians: Popular Entertainment in Nineteenth-Century London* (Manchester: Manchester University Press, 2012), p. 10.

24   Roy Hattersley, *The Edwardians* (London: Abacus, 2004), p. 419.

25   Crone, *Violent Victorians*, p. 103.

CENTRAL NEWS.

1. Crippen and Le Neve in the dock at Bow Street Police Court.

element of cultural nostalgia has been recognised, in agreement with Richard Altick's view of murder trials as 'an almost unexcelled mirror of an epoch's mores',[26] the images invoked have been of the Edwardian twilight: Crippen's reported delight at a catchy music hall ballad sung aboard the *Montrose*; his predilection for taking tea at the height of his trial;[27] Ethel hiding her face from the crowds outside the Old Bailey 'behind an open umbrella';[28] 'tariff reform, HMS Dreadnought; Marconi, Home Rule for Ireland, Doctor Crippen' as James Hilton's *Goodbye Mr. Chips* has it.[29] This book argues that in fact we must extend this backwards perspective a good deal further. The Crippen story represents not simply a time capsule of Edwardian England but rather an echo chamber of the crime sensations that had compelled public interest in the preceding century. Its enduring posterity depends not only upon its embeddedness in its own epoch but in part upon the journalistic formation of Crippen on the model of a still older context of Victorian crime sensations extending at least as far back as the 1850s.

The book's argument thus begins with study of 'classic Crippen' – the first phase rendition which linked the case with Victorian crime sensations and which reached its apotheosis with installation of an effigy of Crippen in the rogues' gallery of the Chamber of Horrors, the hawking of execution broadsides on the streets of London, and the appearance of a bogus confession in the press shortly after the execution. By such means was the Crippen story first held in cultural memory.

Attention then turns to 'second phase' Crippen, the re-imagining and remaking of the character in modernity. Within a decade of the execution, the appearance of the first edition of the Crippen trial proceedings, the burgeoning of interest in popular criminology, and the dawn of the literary epoch now known as the 'Golden Age of crime fiction', meant the Crippen case was revisited and re-imagined by writers, criminologists, and lay

---

26   Altick, *Victorian Studies in Scarlet*, p. 12.
27   Ibid., p. 139.
28   Ibid., p. 146.
29   James Hilton, *Goodbye Mr. Chips* (London: Hodder and Stoughton, 1934, rep. 1958), p. 68. Richard Whittington-Egan remarks how the Crippen story 'somehow contrives to embrace the entire atmosphere of the vanished world in which it was played out. The sudden verdure of the respectable Holloway residential enclave. Crumpets for tea. The muffin man's bell echoing through the afternoon streets': Connell, *Doctor Crippen*, p. 11.

commentators. These reappraisals of the case promptly showed how Crippen in fact departed fundamentally from the template murder stories to which he had been yoked in Edwardian imagination. These earlier sensations tended to exemplify a predictable pattern where murder was done from transparent motives and where the malefactors were to go to their deaths contrite or at least having confessed to their crime.[30] The Crippen drama, in which there was no confession, stubbornly resisted this pattern, even as it raised deep and troubling questions as to the motivations of the criminal, the potential complicity of Ethel le Neve, and ultimately, the limits of knowledge in relation to the modern criminal mind. Crippen troubled and haunted criminological and literary minds in the years following the First World War. He seemed to epitomise the 'terra incognita' that H.B. Irving detected at the heart of every criminal act, 'which, unless we could enter into the very soul of a man, we cannot hope to reach.'[31] His motivations obscure, his guilt unacknowledged, Crippen becomes a contextually contingent figure, 'constructed in multiple narratives'.[32] He represents a complex criminological character study at a time when literary, artistic, and cultural preoccupation with constructed identity and character was emerging as a signature concern of modernity. 'In or about December, 1910, human character changed' asserted Virginia Woolf in an essay whose theme of novelistic preoccupation with character might equally describe the Edwardian reading public's obsession with Crippen that same year:

> [T]here is something permanently interesting in character in itself. When all the practical business of life has been discharged, there is something about people which continues to seem to them of overwhelming importance [...] The study of character becomes to them an absorbing pursuit.[33]

Journalist and criminologist Filson Young's 1920 edition of the trial proceedings was instrumental in provoking interest in Crippen as character study. Young's

---

30 Judith Flanders notes how 'Confessions were an integral part of the emotional narrative of trial, conviction and execution.' *The Invention of Murder*, p. 237.

31 H.B. Irving, *A Book of Remarkable Criminals* (London: Cassell, 1918), p. 27.

32 Julie English Early, 'A New Man for a New Century: Dr Crippen and the Principles of Masculinity', in *Disorder in the Court: Trials and Sexual Conflict at the Turn of the Century*, ed. George Robb and Nancy Erber (London: Macmillan, 1999), pp. 209–30.

33 Virginia Woolf, 'Character in Fiction', *The Criterion* II (1924), 409–30 (412).

introduction claimed a principal interest 'in the characters of the people concerned' while a short case-history of three years later pronounces it to be 'impossible to define the mental processes which drove him to commit this deed'.[34] If all this suggests that Crippen seems a rather congenial criminal subject for an emerging modernist mentality, T.S. Eliot's decision to attend a fancy-dress party attired as the Doctor rather confirms the impression.[35]

The second phase of this book's reception history of Crippen thus explores the ways in which literary and criminological re-imaginings wrested the case free from the wilful nostalgia of the Edwardian first-wave presentation to open instead onto the preoccupations and anxieties of modernity. These re-imaginings substitute a 'queer Crippen' for a 'classic Crippen', recognising the 'deep cultural preoccupations'[36] embodied in the story. These included gender (where the strains and violence of the Crippen marriage and murder might be seen to encode a crisis of Edwardian masculinity); sexuality (where Ethel le Neve's cross-dressed masquerade might threaten to expose the performativity of gender); and social identity (where Crippen's own masquerading as an authentic doctor, despite his dubious qualifications; his adoption of the alias Peter Franckel; and the contrasting onstage and offstage lives of Belle Elmore/Cora Crippen threatened to uncover the instability and non-essential nature of identity).

This competing image of Crippen in modernity was patently more open to exploring those truly eccentric and outlandish features of the story which had been downplayed in 1910. As George Orwell wrote, 'No novelist would dare to make up [...] Crippen's flight across the Atlantic with his mistress dressed as a boy.'[37] Prurient public interest in this feature of the story was indulged but contained in 1910 – Ethel's drag act was recreated *post hoc* in some posed photographs for the daily newspapers. But as we shall see, it was only with later literary re-imaginings of the case that serious scrutiny was afforded to

---

34 Young, *The Trial of H.H. Crippen*, p. xiii; Harold Eaton, 'The Case of the Century: Crippen and the Belle Elmore', in *The Fifty Most Amazing Crimes of the Last 100 Years*, ed. J.M. Parrish and John R. Crossland (London: Odhams Press, 1936), pp. 102–19 (p. 119).

35 Peter Ackroyd, *TS Eliot: A Life* (New York: Simon and Schuster, 1984), p. 143.

36 A.N. Wilson, *After the Victorians: The World Our Parents Knew* (London: Arrow, 2006), p. 75.

37 'The Decline of the English Murder', in *George Orwell: Essays* (London: Penguin, 2000), pp. 345–8 (p. 346).

the way in which the cross-dressed masquerade might have intersected with cultural anxieties regarding shifting identities and gender roles in Edwardian England. Only in the 'second wave' rendition of Crippen did explorations of the case anticipate any of the tensions and contradictions recognised by contemporary theory, such as the performativity of gender or the notion of masculinity existing only in relationship to oppositional concepts of the other or the non-normative.[38]

Awareness of the performative dimensions of the Crippen case, where so many of the principal players were 'clearly not what they wished to seem',[39] is suggested by the professions and preoccupations of some of the spectators at Crippen's trial, including actor H.B. Irving; dramatist W.S. Gilbert; and no lesser a crime novelist than Sir Arthur Conan Doyle, observing proceedings from a prime seat behind the Bar benches facing the jury box. Many of these eminent spectators would go on to make their own contribution to the rewriting of Crippen in subsequent decades.

Before setting out these two competing versions of Crippen, Part One of this book sketches background and context. In Chapter Two, the 'year of Crippen' is revisited, with particular reference to Edwardian London, its press, policing, and criminal justice system. In Chapter Three, the histories of the key players in the case are outlined, while in Chapter Four an objective account is assayed of the Crippen drama of January to November 1910.

Part Two of the book then explores respectively 'The Making of Classic Crippen' and 'Crippen Rewritten', contrasting the project of cultural nostalgia which enfolded the case in 1910 with the re-imagining of the case that took place in the years immediately following the First World War, galvanised by the 1920 publication of the Crippen trial proceedings and the inauguration of new imaginative engagement with crime and criminality at the dawn of the Golden Age of crime fiction. This 'second phase' Crippen involves a broad chronological sweep, taking us to the London stage musical 'Belle or the Ballad of Dr Crippen' in the early 1960s and through to recent crime fiction of the early

---

38   Judith Butler, *Bodies that Matter: On the Discursive Limits of 'Sex'* (New York: Routledge, 1993); Eve Kosofsky Sedgewick, *Epistemology of the Closet*, 2nd rev ed. (Berkeley: University of California Press, 2008).

39   Julie English Early, 'Technology, Modernity, and the "Little Man"', *Victorian Studies*, 39:3, p. 313.

twenty-first century where Crippen (or at least the Crippen case) remains a centre of literary preoccupation.

Finally, Chapter Seven provides a short afterword, charting the gradual diminution of the profile of Crippen in recent memory as a new age of post-war serial killers obtruded itself onto public notice and was recognised and accommodated in less sensational and more sociologically nuanced accounts of criminal behaviour and social danger.

This book thus assays a cultural and literary account of the endurance of the Crippen story, seeking to illuminate the reasons for its curious longevity and resonance. 'I Caught Crippen!' crowed Inspector Walter Dew in 1938. Catching Crippen's *meanings*, in historical understanding, fiction, and culture, is the accompanying task of the present study.

CHAPTER TWO

THE BACKDROP

It is a central thesis of this book that many ostensible facts in the Crippen drama are inseparable from a matrix of literary, criminological, and journalistic tropes that shaped its reception in Edwardian imagination and posterity. As later chapters will demonstrate, the case resonated deeply with earlier crimes. It exhibited, in Orwell's phrase, a 'family resemblance' to an established group of Victorian-Edwardian crime sensations – pattern texts which had left an abiding imprint upon the popular imagination.[1] As we shall see, it is possible to imagine that these criminological forebears even shaped the contours of the story, with the concealment of a body in the cellar and the fugitive's flight in transgressive disguise revealed as established motifs in the shared inheritance of crime stories which preceded Crippen. Add to this mix the medico-legal speculation as to what really took place at 39 Hilldrop Crescent (Crippen maintained a dogged silence until the end), and the lines between fact and fiction are truly blurred.

To peel away the resulting *grand guignol* filter from the plain facts can be a challenge. Even within the official documents, including the imposing Home Office, Metropolitan Police, and Central Criminal Court files held at the National Archives, this interpenetration of criminological, literary, and journalistic discourses is apparent. For example, a significant portion of one of the Home Office files is given over to Home Secretary Winston Churchill's mission to expose the professional malpractice of Crippen's solicitor, Arthur Newton, who spread rumours of a Crippen confession and fed the press apocryphal

---

1   'The Decline of the English Murder', in *George Orwell: Essays* (London: Penguin, 2000), pp. 345–8 (p. 345).

exclusives from the condemned man's cell. Likewise, another official dossier among the police papers is effectively a scrapbook of Crippen curios. Bringing together a substantial array of press cuttings, the book collates not only trial coverage but such legacy cuttings as a 1926 article on a visit to London of spiritualist medium Etta Bledsoe, whose 'name became known in this country some years ago by reason of her warning to the notorious murderer, Dr Crippen'.[2] Even these most sober of archival sources thus reflect how the lines between documentary record and imaginative elaboration of the Crippen legend were blurred from the beginning.

Some of this conflation of fact and fiction must be attributed to Crippen himself. Many of the oft-cited details of his life with Cora, their unhappy marriage, and their final days together at Hilldrop Crescent derive from his police statements and court testimony alone – something that has been insufficiently noted in many of the case histories where the particular image Crippen retailed of his wife as a blowsy, over-bearing, and demanding domestic tyrant has for too long been rehearsed without scepticism or question.[3] Practised, as we shall see, in rhetorical persuasion via his patent remedy businesses, Crippen has had a significant share in his own posterity.

With these caveats in mind, Part One of this book seeks to present as objective an account as possible of the North London Cellar Murder of 1910 with recourse to the contemporary documentation including the official files. Clearing the ground in this way enables sharper insight on the subsequent construction of the Crippen legend by London editors, before the case was re-imagined and rewritten by Golden Age detective novelists and their followers.

The present chapter thus outlines the backdrop to Crippen, considering the character of late Edwardian London, its people, press, and policing, before the ensuing two chapters recount the key episodes of the case from Hilldrop Crescent to the Pentonville scaffold, in those nine dramatic months in 1910.

---

2   HO144/1719/195492.
3   M. Constantine Quinn's *Doctor Crippen* (London: Duckworth, 1935) and Tom Cullen's *The Mild-Mannered Murderer* (Boston: Houghton Mifflin, 1977) are the case histories most responsible for sustaining this view; the best corrective to date is David James Smith's *Supper with the Crippens* (London: Orion, 2005).

Edwardian London

The London of 1910 was a fast-growing city, its population steadily increasing since the turn of the century and now passing seven million.[4] This population growth was fuelled by the twin sources of convergence from rural areas and immigration from overseas, even if the provisions of the 1905 Aliens Act had made the process of settlement rather more administratively burdensome than before.[5] As the seat of a still extensive if now declining empire, London in 1910 was a city of contrasts. Horse-drawn carriages and omnibuses shared the roads with an increasing number of motor cars and trams, while beneath the ground a growing electrified network of underground trains was operating.[6] New communication channels were also increasingly in evidence, with communication by telephony and telegraphy speeding the pace of progress. The interpenetration of these different technologies was remarked, in a rather ambivalent tone, by the *Illustrated London News* in December of that year in a piece on 'The Telephone: Two of its More Unusual Uses Today'. The paper reported on the versatility of the increasingly familiar technology, noting how it conflated work and leisure: 'For those who must work and eat at the same time – table telephones in use at a restaurant. For those who must work and travel at the same time: telephoning from a Pullman car'.[7]

Not that these new technologies and commodities were open to all; perhaps the sharpest contrast in this Edwardian backdrop was the capital's continued legacy of a thriving West End abutting a still impoverished and overcrowded East. While the East End docks were the effective gateway to a still extensive empire, their environs retained much of the squalor and poverty bewailed since

4   Donald Read, *Edwardian England 1901–15: Society and Politics* (London: Harrap, 1972), p. 27.
5   Under the provisions of the Act, immigrants were now asked eleven questions including: 'What means have you in your possession'; 'What prospects have you of decently supporting yourself in the United Kingdom'; and 'Have you been convicted of any crime?' An immigration agent interviewed in the *Pall Mall Gazette* at the inauguration of the Act considered that its most useful clause 'will be found to be the Extradition clause, by which actual criminals may be sent back to their country'. *Pall Mall Gazette*, 30 December 1905.
6   On the Edwardian expansion and electrification of the London underground network, see Peter Ackroyd, *London Under* (London: Vintage, 2012), pp. 112–37.
7   *Illustrated London News*, 17 December 1910.

the 1880s. The ongoing Edwardian need for charitable missions to the East, alongside such exposés and surveys of working-class conditions as George R. Sims's *How the Poor Live* (1883), Charles Booth's *Life and Labour of the People of London* (1889–1903) and Jack London's *People of the Abyss* (1903), continued to highlight how the West and the East 'were two different worlds, though linked by commerce'.[8] The East End's employment sectors, including dockyard labouring, tailoring, boot-making and cabinet-making, were insufficient to provide consistent occupation for all, and they furnished meagre means for those whom they did employ: Priestley cites an example weekly wage bill which details the sums of 8 to 12 shillings for making artificial flowers; 9 to 11 shillings for bookbinding; 8 to 15 shillings for brushmaking; and 10 to 18 shillings for manufacturing umbrellas.[9] As for those Edwardian Londoners without any work at all, Hattersley relates how 'out of work families sometimes spent as little as a penny per day per person on food'.[10] While the potential for social mobility had broadened in the Edwardian period, such a context of prolonged deprivation limited the prospects for the younger generation to better themselves; Jack London noted how labouring jobs requiring a healthy constitution went to 'invading hordes from the country. The railway men, carriers, omnibus drivers, corn and timber porters, and all those who require physical stamina, are largely drawn from the country; while in the Metropolitan Police there are, roughly, 12,000 country-born as against 3,000 London born.'[11]

The divide between rich and poor may have been most starkly apparent in the contrast between West and East, but the distribution of wealth was no respecter of geographical boundaries and pockets of indigence could certainly be found in the fashionable West. A 1908 *London Evening Standard* investigative article on poverty found seventeen people sharing a single room in Camberwell, a family in Stoke Newington sharing their cramped home with a menagerie, 'while in Marylebone, a woman's flesh was made hideous by

8   J.B. Priestley, *The Edwardians* (London: Heinemann, 1970), p. 74.
9   Ibid., p. 74.
10   Roy Hattersley, *The Edwardians* (London: Abacus, 2004), p. 77.
11   Jack London, *The People of the Abyss* [1903] (London: Journeyman Press, 1977), p. 26. Chief Inspector Walter Dew reflects this rural demographic in the Edwardian composition of the Metropolitan Police, hailing from Far Cotton in rural Northamptonshire.

vermin, and the very bread and butter on the table turned grey by insects'[12] while other reportage reminded readers that London slums might be found 'within sight of the great Houses of Parliament, and beneath the shade of Westminster Abbey'.[13] Celebrated chronicler of Victorian and Edwardian London George R. Sims roamed these and other mean streets of the city gathering material for his 1906 book *The Mysteries of Modern London*. In his account of time spent in a common lodging house, Sims looks beyond the blanket classification of 'the poor' to distinguish the different sub-groups sharing the doss house: 'The thieves do not care to mix with the honest folks; the tramps and vagabonds look down upon the workers, and the men of the working-class look askance at the wreckage of the black coat brigade.'[14]

While political interventions to address low wages and long working hours repeatedly stalled over policymakers' insistence on a distinction between the 'deserving' and 'undeserving poor', philanthropy and social action sought to bring some interim relief to London's poor. In briefly bringing the capital's two worlds together, these charitable initiatives bequeathed some poignant vignettes to the historical record. Examples from 1910 include a winter visit by the Lord Mayor and Archbishop of Westminster to the Providence Row Night Refuge in Spitalfields ('the poorest, lowest-rented, most over-populated area in the metropolis');[15] the ministrations of Mrs Leverton Harris's Needlework Guild for Poor Women of Stepney, which employed 'about 200 women for six or eight months when their services, owing to the course of trade and fashion in London, would be very infrequently called upon';[16] and, most poignantly, the charitable staging of a flower show in Plaistow in August 1910 where many of the 700 competitors 'were factory girls earning a paltry wage in a factory, who had given up their spare time on Saturday afternoons to tend their plants which they reared in allotments belonging to the church. [...] The primary object of the show to advance a step in the direction of relieving by the cultivation of

12   'Children withered by the street', *London Evening Standard*, 21 August 1908.
13   'London as seen from the East End', *Tower Hamlets Independent and East End Local Advertiser*, 13 February 1909.
14   George R. Sims, *The Mysteries of Modern London* (London: C. Arthur Pearson Ltd, 1906), p. 32.
15   *Daily Telegraph and Courier*, 18 February 1910.
16   *Daily Telegraph and Courier*, 11 April 1910.

flowers the dreariness of life in the East End'.[17] Such piecemeal interventions and initiatives could bring only limited relief; even approaching twenty years after Crippen, the 'New Survey of Life and Labour in London' would find 8.7 per cent of Londoners still living in poverty.[18]

The Scene from Kingsway

This image of an Edwardian London in transition between old and new is evocatively captured in a 1910 photograph of Kingsway, Holborn (a very particular part of our backdrop for it was here that Crippen operated one of his many business ventures). Taken five years after the opening of Kingsway as a new flagship north-south thoroughfare for the modern metropolis, the photograph shows a tram bound for Tower Bridge emerging from the Kingsway tunnel, flanked by two electric lampposts. A horse-drawn carriage proceeds in the opposite direction while another waits at the side of the road, and a cyclist and pedestrians on opposing sides of the highway wait for this novel form of transport to pass so that they might cross. This frozen historical moment forms an evocative visual complement to *The Globe*'s 1905 leader on the opening of the thoroughfare by Edward VII: 'as regards all forms of locomotion we are in a transition era. The competition of tramways, tubes, electric and mechanical street vehicles of all sorts, has doomed horsed traffic; but nobody can prophecy as to which particular mode of conveyance will win the day, or what modifications may be necessary.'[19]

The monarch for whom Kingsway was named went some way himself to epitomise this admixture of the old and the new. While King Edward VII, or 'Bertie', had revived certain monarchical traditions that had fallen away during Victoria's reclusive latter years (not least restoring the seat of monarchy to London and reviving the State Opening of Parliament) he equally embodied 'a new kind of king'[20] and even 'a new age in which the old standards were despised and abandoned'.[21] Since his accession in January 1901, Bertie had been quick to show an enthusiasm for such modern fashions as racing, yachting,

---

17   *East London Advertiser,* 13 August 1910.
18   Peter Ackroyd, *London: The Biography* (London: Vintage, 2000), p. 604.
19   *Globe,* 18 October 1905.
20   Priestley, *The Edwardians,* p. 84.
21   Hattersley, *The Edwardians,* p. 33.

LONDON. - Kingsway

2. Kingsway in 1910, where Crippen's office with the
Aural Remedies Company was based at 129 Craven House.

and motoring; descriptions of the king, his motor car, and his companion fox terrier Jack are constant calling cards in the press accounts of his reign.[22] These interests, and Bertie's willingness to foreground other members of the royal household as 'the royal family', were congenial for the expanded reading public following the exploits of the monarchy in an increasingly affordable daily press (the editors of which were circumspect enough to keep the king's many romantic intrigues and dalliances out of the public domain).

The new king was also a political animal. Despite an apparently limited interest in affairs of state during his time as Prince of Wales, upon accession the king's modernity extended to much greater political engagement than Victoria had shown in the latter years of her reign. Bertie pronounced on – and perhaps sometimes even interfered in – a range of the defining issues of the era. Related by birth to most of the royal houses of the continent and a speaker of German, French, Italian, and Spanish, he was well placed to comment on foreign policy in an increasingly militarised Europe. During his nine-year reign he was also to engage to a greater or lesser extent with questions of free trade, the emergence of the social service state, Irish nationalism, House of Lords reform, and women's suffrage. On the latter issue, Bertie tended to show a conservatism that was at odds with his modernity in other quarters. He consistently opposed the movement, upbraiding Liberal Prime Minister Campbell-Bannerman for his support of the 1907 Women's Franchise Bill, refusing to receive a 1909 deputation from the Women's Freedom League so that they might present a petition,[23] and more than once criticising the direct action taken by the suffragettes for whose cause he had 'no sympathy'.[24]

The king had rather more sympathy for the poor and destitute of the metropolis, to whose plight he had been acutely sensitive since at least 1884 when, as Prince of Wales, he had been appointed to the Royal Commission on the Housing of the Working Class. His role on the commission had included an element of fieldwork, which he undertook disguised in rough clothes and with a discreet Scotland Yard chaperone, amongst deprived areas around St Pancras and Holborn. The experience appears to have impressed him

---

22   cf. the account of Bertie's meeting with the Tsar at the Cowes Regatta in August 1909: 'The king, in his motor, passed over the Medina on board the ferry. His majesty was nursing his favourite fox terrier, Jack.': *Globe*, 5 August 1909.

23   'The King declines to receive suffragettes', *The Globe*, 8 July 1909.

24   Jane Ridley, *Bertie: A Life of Edward VII* (London: Vintage, 2012), p. 403.

deeply, resonating in a speech delivered in the House of Lords: 'I can assure your Lordships that the condition of the poor, or rather of their dwellings, was perfectly disgraceful.'[25] Accordingly, Edward involved himself in a range of charitable missions and interventions on his accession – and here another vignette from the aforementioned Kingsway is illustrative. In November 1905 royal support was given to a Church Army initiative to erect temporary 'King's Labour Tents' on one side of Kingsway: 'Three working tents and two for cooking purposes will be erected. Any destitute man can obtain a ticket from the clergymen, guardians, Church Army officers, or other philanthropic people to whom they will be furnished.'[26] Ticketholders were assigned a day's manual work in one tent so that they might receive some remuneration and provisions in the other.

Policing Edwardian London

Edward's short reign also saw him taking keen interest in another important metropolitan constituency in our backdrop to Crippen, the police. At the start of the century, the ranks of the Metropolitan Police were understaffed by some two thousand constables, though the modernisation efforts of Sir Edward Henry as Assistant Commissioner (Crime) and subsequently Commissioner would see improvements in pay, conditions, and training.[27] After a successful coronation procession and ceremony in which the part played by the police received royal commendation and coronation medals for the officers involved,[28] Edward signalled his own support for the Metropolitan force by conferring the Royal Victorian Order on two senior policemen from Scotland Yard and London's A division: 'the first [occasion] in the history of the police on which any officer who has risen from the ranks has received a Royal decoration of the kind.'[29] Royal appreciation of the work of the capital's other force, the City Police, was also conveyed with coronation medals and by events ranging from a 'demonstration of life-saving and rescue from drowning' by City officers before

25   Ibid., p. 237.
26   *Morning Post*, 11 November 1905. Bertie was also patron of the Ragged School Union among other ventures.
27   Hattersley, *The Edwardians*, p. 144.
28   'King congratulates the police', *London Daily News*, 13 August 1902.
29   *London Daily News*, 16 August 1902.

a royal audience in June 1903; Edward's patronage of the Metropolitan and City Police Orphanage; and the pomp and ceremony that attended the royal opening of the Central Criminal Court, the Old Bailey, in February 1907.[30] Of the other shows of royal favour and appreciation for the police during Edward's reign, the most enduring was to be the establishment in 1909 of the King's Police Medal: 'for his Majesty cannot but be greatly interested in a body of men who are unsurpassed in efficiency and integrity by any other body of men in the United Kingdom.'[31] A press encomium to the Metropolitan force, published to mark the medal's inauguration, paints an evocative picture of London policing on the eve of the Crippen drama:

> What society owes to the police in big cities like London it is hard to realise and impossible to express. We see the police in the streets, regulating the tides of traffic, which but for them would collapse into anarchic confusion; we see them rule by a lifted hand, the unacknowledged masters of the crowd; we see them helping the inform, protecting the young, directing the stranger. Or we see them strolling leisurely round on their beats at nights, testing the fastening of doors, and keeping watch while the city sleeps. [...] but every day the murderer is arrested or the armed burglar confronted and caught. There are more than a thousand "habitual criminals" at large in the Metropolis every year; a thousand more are under police supervision; and the number of others who are "known to the police" is enormous.[32]

As this vignette indicates, policing London in 1910 showed some of that distinctive Edwardian conflation of old and new remarked above. The establishment of the Metropolitan Police Fingerprint Bureau in July 1901, the installation of telephones in divisional stations, and even the widespread adoption of typewriters at Scotland Yard all spoke for modernity, but other aspects of London policing showed the persistence of older traditions: 'The *Police Gazette*, which circulated details of wanted men, illustrated the descriptions with woodcuts long after photographs could have been used to improve the

---

30 'Coronation Medal for the City Police', *St James's Gazette*, 14 August 1902; 'King and the City Police', *London Daily News*, Wednesday 24 June 1903; *Morning Post*, 28 February 1907.
31 *Daily Telegraph and Courier*, Wednesday 21 July 1909. The encomium was of the Metropolitan Police specifically.
32 *Daily Telegraph and Courier*, 9 July 1909.

prospects of identification. Until about the time Churchill arrived at the Home Office, the telegraph was preferred to the telephone because of the fear that operators might overhear the conversations.'[33] Likewise, a sample list of crimes for which prisoners were to be indicted at the opening of the September 1909 sessions of the Central Criminal Court shows how, for all the novelty of the rebuilt Old Bailey premises, many of the crimes investigated by the police and brought before the magistrates would have been equally familiar a century before. These included two cases of incendiarism; three of bigamy; four of burglary, thirteen of counterfeiting; fourteen of conspiracy to defraud; two of throwing corrosive fluid; eleven of forgery; eight of fraud; twelve of house-breaking; twenty-two of larceny; seven of libel; three of manslaughter and three of murder; five of attempted murder; two for demanding money with menaces; four of violent robbery; and eleven of wounding.[34]

The London Press

The pronounced public appetite for details of the investigation and prosecution of such crimes was ably met by the last constituency in our Edwardian metropolitan backdrop requiring attention: the London press. In 1910 the capital's readers had a plethora of London titles to turn to for their news and recreation. The daily papers included the *Citizen*, the *Express*, the *Graphic*, the *Mirror*, the *News*, the *Pall Mall Gazette*, the *Sketch*, the *Telegraph*, the *Morning Leader*, *Morning Post*, and *The Times*.[35] For weeklies, they might turn to *Lloyd's Weekly News*, the *News of the World* or, for crime stories in particular, *The Illustrated Police News* (a weekly lurid round-up of criminality in the metropolis, without any formal affiliation to Scotland Yard). Demonstrating strong continuities with the Victorian period, this was a press 'which specialised in sensation'.[36] When it came to the reporting of crime, this press retained the Victorian tendency noted by Judith Walkowitz to 'glory in intensifying terror'.[37] The

33 Hattersley, *The Edwardians*, p. 145.
34 *Daily Telegraph and Courier*, 8 September 1909.
35 See Matthew Engel, *Tickle the Public: One Hundred Years of the Popular Press* (London: Indigo, 1997).
36 Hattersley, *The Edwardians*, p. 144.
37 Judith Walkowitz, *City of Dreadful Delight: Narratives of Sexual Danger in Late Victorian London* (London: Virago, 1982), p. 218.

avid metropolitan readership for such tales of terror had only grown since Victoria's reign. Indeed, the expansion of the Edwardian press reflected the relative successes of the 1870 Elementary Education Act which had seen a newly literate younger readership of the 1870s and 1880s cutting its teeth on much maligned 'penny dreadfuls' and other forms of sensation literature.[38] If those same readers, now in late middle age, savoured heightened reports of real-life metropolitan crime, it was at least clear how their taste had been nurtured.[39]

The modes of journalism and reportage in Edwardian London were also more expansive than hitherto. Pre-eminent press baron of the era, Alfred Harmsworth (Lord Northcliffe from 1905) shaped the emergence of a new popular press in which heightened reportage and amplified news stories were the order of the day. Advances in mechanical typesetting and in the output of printing presses supported Northcliffe's ambition to establish an expanded base of popular titles. To meet the needs of a growing lower middle-class readership, he launched the *Daily Mail* in 1896 and the *Daily Mirror* in 1903. To reach the established middle class, Northcliffe could leverage a controlling interest in *The Times* by 1908. From such a position, Northcliffe would come to exert a profound impact on both the journalism and the political opinion of the Edwardian age while, in a manner then novel but now entirely characteristic of the dailies, Northcliffe's mode of journalism both reported and *created* content: 'anything to keep up the excitement – stunt races and competitions, chances of large prizes, and, what was far more dangerous, impassioned challenges, revelations, campaigns for sudden irrational "causes".'[40]

Northcliffe's titles and their competitors thus confirmed a direction of

---

38   On penny dreadfuls and Victorian juvenile literacy see John Springhall, '"Pernicious Reading?" The Penny Dreadful as Scapegoat for Late-Victorian Juvenile Crime', *Victorian Periodicals Review* 27:4 (1994), 326–49 and '"Disseminating Impure Literature": The "Penny Dreadful" Publishing Business Since 1860', *Economic History Review*, n.s. 47:3, 567–84.

39   A literary example of one such middle-aged Edwardian reader is protagonist Bunting in Marie Belloc Lowndes's *The Lodger* (1912). Much of the book's first chapter is taken up with Bunting's internal dialogue, rationalising the expense of a one penny paper so that he can read about the latest 'Avenger' murder alongside 'the vast world of men and women who take an intelligent interest in such sinister mysteries'. *The Lodger* (Oxford: Oxford University Press, 1996), pp. 7–8.

40   Priestley, *The Edwardians*, p. 178.

journalistic travel instated in the later Victorian period, when journalists of the school of *Pall Mall Gazette* editor W.T. Stead (1849–1912) had practised a 'new journalism' which was high on sensational content, steeped in an awareness of an expanded and curious reading public, and alert to the sensibilities and anxieties of an urban context where large numbers of readers lived, worked, and consumed their news in close proximity to one another. As the advocates of the 'new journalism' recognised, such a scenario made urban readers into potential spectators, well placed to observe and even inform on the events of the metropolis around them.[41] The age of 'urban spectatorship' and the 'universal interview' had arrived whereby the urban citizenry were all potential spectators and commentators on the news of the day. The sensational reportage of Stead and his followers was initially deployed in a reforming cause, offering exposés of abuses, scandals and malpractice, with the intention of prompting reform on behalf of an outraged reading public.

As critics of this journalistic school would later point out, a reforming agenda was often less obvious when it came to stories of crime. Here, it seemed that lurid and sensational details were included (especially after the 1888 Whitechapel Murders) as a means of selling papers rather than to draw attention to reformist causes such as the plight of crime victims or the social circumstances impinging on criminal behaviours. Some commentators were also concerned at the capacity of the cheap dailies of this school to form and lead opinion based on scant and speedily assembled copy: G.K. Chesterton remarked that 'when a fire, a murder or an interrupted wedding occurs, very few can immediately see it, while millions immediately read about it. But the result is that millions have a conventional picture in their minds which is as different as possible from the real picture, but which nevertheless colours their sentiments'.[42]

Many of the principal newspapers that would feature so prominently in the Crippen case were long-established daily publications whose circulations

---

41 An assessment of the impact of the 'new journalism' is supplied by Joel H. Wiener (ed.), *Papers for the Millions: The New Journalism in Britain, 1850s to 1914* (London: Greenwood, 1988). For an account of reactions against the 'new journalism' and the attempt to supply a more critical journalism to the Edwardian era and particularly the pre-war years, see Nelson Ritschel, *Bernard Shaw, W.T. Stead, and the New Journalism* (London: Palgrave Macmillan, 2017).

42 *Illustrated London News*, 8 January 1910.

had been retailing the lurid details of crime sensations since the days of the Whitechapel Murders and indeed earlier. These included Northcliffe's *Daily Express* (founded 1900); *The Daily Mail* (1896); *The Daily Telegraph* (1855); and *The Times* (established 1785). A fashion for highly illustrated content characterised many of these papers, as witness such representative titles as *The Graphic*, *The Sketch* and *The Mirror*. The Crippen drama, by turns gothic and picaresque, lent itself well to this highly visual format. Perhaps the most sensational among the weekly publications was *The Illustrated Police News*, which had been established by proprietor George Purkess in 1864, just in time for the notorious Dr Pritchard poisoning trial of the following year.[43] For the graphic and pictorial elements of its presentation, the publication took as its template *The Illustrated London News* which had been established early in Victoria's reign.

The narrative templates for *The Illustrated London News* had older roots in the disparate group of publications that have come to be known collectively as 'The Newgate Calendar', comprising a wide corpus of chapbooks, broadsheets, and more formal publications including J. Cooke's three-volume *Newgate Calendar* of the 1770s, *The Malefactor's Register* of 1799, and *The Criminal Recorder* of 1804.[44] With a pronounced focus on the lives and deeds of the criminals rather than on a paradigm of detection and apprehension of the malefactors, the Newgate Calendar tradition emphasised sensation and shocks – a tradition perpetuated by *The Illustrated Police News* despite its title. Where police officers and detectives are presented in its iconic illustrations it is characteristically in scenes of discovery, revelation or dramatic conflict, the emphasis remaining firmly on the criminal protagonists and their acts. The ghastly discovery of a corpse or uncovering of a grave was a vignette tailor-made for such depiction, accounting for the lurid presentations of both the Jack the Ripper and Crippen cases in its pages. Indeed, the *Police News* depiction of the Ripper murders in particular – police constables shining their bullhorn lanterns into the dark corners of Whitechapel – is most likely the strongest visual influence on the popular imagination of the Ripper crimes. The combination of gothic illustrations and the distinctive font of *The Illustrated Police News* ultimately amounted to a memorable and distinct aesthetic, aptly

---

43 It ceased publication in 1938, the year Walter Dew was to publish *I Caught Crippen*.
44 Rayner Heppenstal, *Tales from the Newgate Calendar: True Stories of Crime and Punishment* (London: Futura, 1983), p. 11.

defined by Sinclair McKay: 'the frozen, captured moment of violence or terror, the captions written in a stylised, florid hand. It is real-life given the patina of drama or fiction: knowing and brashly entertaining.'[45]

A second prominent weekly in the reporting of Crippen would be *Lloyd's Weekly News*. Another long-established paper by 1910, *Lloyd's* had been founded in 1842 by young compositor Edward Lloyd, trading initially as *Lloyd's Illustrated London Newspaper*, the identification with the capital being dropped six years later as railway expansion extended both the readership and the scope to cover regional stories. *Lloyd's* carved a defining place for itself in the coverage of Crippen, running extensive copy on the discovery of the cellar crime, the arrest, and the fugitives' return to England. The paper would even claim a share of the credit for the couple's capture: 'Their carefully-laid plans of escape have been defeated by means of press publicity and the wireless telegraph.'[46]

There was certainly scope to read about murder in the London press in the year leading up to the Crippen case. A search of selected London dailies in the twelve months preceding Mrs Crippen's exhumation from the Hilldrop Crescent cellar reveals twenty-one metropolitan murders between July 1909 and July 1910.[47] In true 'new journalism' style, many of these murders are ascribed memorable titles such as the 'Music Hall Murder'; 'Sweetheart Murdered'; and 'The Fog Murder'.[48] The first of these crimes, which was to dominate the papers that year, was more accurately an assassination – the murders of Sir William Hutt Curzon Wyllie, an official of the British Indian Government, and Dr Cawas Lalcaca, both shot down by Madan Lal Dhingra, an Indian independence activist, at the Imperial Institute (now part of Imperial College)

---

45 Sinclair McKay, *The Lady in the Cellar: Murder, Scandal and Insanity in Victorian Bloomsbury* (London: White Lion, 2018), p. 306.

46 *Lloyd's Weekly News*, 31 July 1910.

47 For the purposes of this study the search was confined to reports carried by the *Daily Telegraph and Courier* and the *London Daily News* of London homicides. Limitations of space prevent consideration of these papers' coverage of murders outside the capital though, suggestively for the Crippen story, some of the contemporary instances outside London include bodies discovered in cellars in Liverpool and Paris: *Daily Telegraph and Courier*, 9 July 1909; Monday 12 July 1909.

48 'Music Hall Murder' – *London Daily News*, 30 April 1910; 'Sweetheart Murdered' – *Daily Telegraph and Courier*, 24 August 1909; 'The Fog Murder' – *London Daily News*, 12 November 1909.

in South Kensington. Prompting both political and criminological comment, the story stayed in the papers for much of the year and well beyond the execution of Dhingra at Pentonville in August 1909. Of the other London murders occurring in the year preceding Crippen, a striking number are domestic tragedies, often involving out-of-work or lightly employed husbands killing their spouses and young families when desperate poverty overtook them. Such domestic tragedies are reported with tragic frequency in the year under review, the names of Thomas Saunders, Henry James Higginbottom, carman, and William Thomas Gregory memorialised in the historical record for the most tragic domestic crimes. These household assailants were not always male: in March 1910 Hannah Walker suffered fatal injuries from a woodchopper at the hands of Fanny Watson, her daughter-in-law. Appearing before the magistrate at the Central Criminal Court in June, Fanny, 'who appeared to be in weak health', entered a plea of not guilty. In a pattern that repeats across these 1910 domestic murders, diminished responsibility was recognised in the sentencing that followed: Fanny was convicted but the jury deemed her 'not responsible for her actions at the time'.[49] Such sentencing implies the alertness of jurors and magistrates to the fragile mental health of many of the domestic murderers brought before them; those who did appear had often attempted suicide – and indeed, of the domestic tragedies occurring in the 'year of Crippen', a pattern of murder and suicide is recurrent. Likewise, it will be worth recollecting, when we come to consider Crippen's crime, that in none of these domestic murders is there any attempt at concealment of the crime; instead, in further sign of their desperation, the perpetrators generally turn their violence upon themselves or offer themselves up immediately to the judgement of the law. The contrast with Crippen's calculated covering of his tracks is marked.

Similarly frequent in this sample year of Edwardian tragedies are double deaths of young lovers. Some of these appear to be suicide pacts between young lovers driven to desperate action when their relationship and prospect of future happiness appeared blocked by parental prohibition, economic blight or some other obstacle. Others are 'sweetheart murders', such as the killing of May White by John Bee in South Acton in August 1909. Previously engaged to Bee, White was murdered 'at the gate of her father's house' by Bee, a grocer's assistant who then cut his own throat.[50] In the same month a parallel case

49   'Wood Green Axe Tragedy', *London Daily News*, 3 June 1910.
50   'Acton Love Tragedy', *London Daily News*, 11 August 1909.

occurred in Enfield when Sidney Bunyan, aged 22, cut the throat of his partner, Lucy Smith of Harringay. 'It is stated that the couple agreed to die together, and that if he did not kill himself he was to surrender to the police. The murderer went to a constable and gave him intimate details of the tragedy, afterwards conducting him to the spot where the unfortunate young woman was lying dead.'[51] In March 1910 a further example occurs: the 'Kings Cross Double Tragedy' which saw Henry George Ryan, 27, and Kate Martha Durrant, 24, poisoned by prussic acid. Clearly familiar with the pattern of such cases, Ryan left a suicide letter addressed to none other than the district's coroner: 'This is not a case, as it may at first appear, of two persons agreeing to take poison together, but it is one of suicide and poison. I put the poison into her beer unseen by her. I watched her drink, and waited for the consequences.' The question of whether this was in fact a double suicide with a subsequent attempt to protect one partner's reputation, rather than a murder, is perhaps raised by the letter-writer's protesting too much: 'I have a reason for committing this mad act but I shall not disclose it. No blame should be attached to the girl. She was entirely under my influence, and absolutely innocent of any real intention.' The inquest jury accepted Ryan's version of events, returning verdicts of respective murder and suicide.[52]

There is evidence, then, of a disturbing trend in 'sweetheart murders' and suicide pacts in the year of Crippen, with other examples recorded beyond the capital in August 1910 in Heamoor in Cornwall, and in October in Sparkhill, Birmingham. As we shall see, the contrast between these tragedies of young lovers and the novel alternative narrative supplied by the middle-aged Crippen and his younger mistress must have been pronounced in that summer of 1910.

While the London editors in particular tended to present murder stories in sensational terms, Edwardian press coverage was beginning to devote column space to more sophisticated criminological commentary and to the role of forensic science in murder cases. This relatively new player in murder trials could lead to some unpredictable courtroom verdicts, in both directions. For an example of a shock acquittal, newspaper readers in 1910 need only have cast their minds back three years to 'the Camden Town Murder', when in a widely

---

51 'Sweetheart Murdered', *Daily Telegraph and Courier*, 24 August 1909.
52 'Kings Cross Double Tragedy', *Daily Telegraph and Courier*, 23 March 1910. Ryan's enigmatic suicide note even concludes with a quotation of Sydney Carton's words from the guillotine in *A Tale of Two Cities*.

publicised trial, young artist Robert Wood was acquitted of the murder of Emily Dimmock. The acquittal had been achieved by the eloquent and fastidious defence presented by young QC Edward Marshall Hall. Hall had so laboured the insufficiency of the circumstantial evidence against Wood (sightings of Wood with Dimmock on the night of her death and an inconclusive bloodstain on his clothing) that even the judge was prompted to issue a strong steer to the jury before their final deliberations commenced: 'you must not find a verdict of guilty against the accused unless no loophole is left by which he can escape. In my judgment, strong as the suspicion is in the case, I do not think that the prosecution has brought the case home near enough to the accused.'[53] So avidly was the trial followed by the public that when the news of Wood's acquittal issued from the court later the same day, a cheer went up from Newgate Street to Ludgate Circus.

Likewise, for a prosecution based on circumstantial evidence that had gone the other way, the 1910 reading public had very recent memory of the trial of John Alexander Dickman, convicted earlier in the year of the murder of John Innes Nisbet on a train in Newcastle. While the identification evidence provided at Dickman's trial had been enough to prompt a unanimous guilty verdict from the jury, Dickman protested his innocence until the last and extensive popular disquiet was expressed in the press as to how safe the conviction truly was.[54] The resulting debate about the nature of circumstantial evidence and the risks of miscarriages of justice was being played out in the press during the summer of 1910 as the tail end of the Dickman trial and the start of the Crippen case overlapped. The very day before the papers were to carry banner headlines proclaiming the discovery of the body in Hilldrop Crescent, the socialist *London Daily News* was carrying details of Dickman's planned appeal: 'A petition is being prepared, and will be sent out immediately, praying for a reprieve. Amongst other things the petition will point out that, with the exception of Dickman having once been fined, there is nothing against his character, and that the evidence given at the trial was purely circumstantial and incomplete.'[55] Likewise, while Crippen was making his way back from Canada

---

53 David Napley, *The Camden Town Murder. Great Murder Trials of the Twentieth Century* (London: Weidenfeld and Nicholson, 1987), p. 146.

54 The most thorough treatment of the case is provided by Diane Janes, *Edwardian Murder: Ightham and the Morpeth Train Robbery* (Stroud: Sutton Publishing, 2007).

55 *London Daily News*, 14 July 1910.

under extradition order on the eve of Dickman's execution on 9 August 1910, a letter in the same paper from one J.C. Arnold was expounding further on the 'old question as to how far such [circumstantial] evidence can be held to justify a verdict of guilty in the most serious cases'. Troubled by the Dickman verdict and by historical cases where misidentified human remains had led to the supposed victim appearing alive and well after sentence and execution had been carried out on their putative murderer, Arnold looks ahead to the coming Crippen trial with trepidation and uncanny foresight:

> As anyone who has studied the case knows, the trial of Dr Crippen for the murder of his wife will turn entirely on the identification of the body found in the cellar of his house, and it seems a hundred chances to one that the doctors will be thrown back upon some such circumstantial identification [...] and the whole result of the trial may depend on their cross-examination as to this point.[56]

While these developments showed growing recognition of the uniqueness of each crime case, with crucial determinations of guilt or innocence often resting on ambivalent identification evidence or forensic evidence, there remained a simplifying tendency in the London papers to report new crimes as if they were echoes of previous murder sensations. This temptation to stereotype was compounded by simple demography and the editors' knowledge that the majority of their readers would have long memories: the 1911 census revealed that the majority of the Edwardian population was in middle or older age; over two-thirds of the population was aged over 20.[57] Thus a May 1910 report of a Metropolitan police officer's retirement could confidently allude to his involvement in the 'notorious case' of Mary Pearcey's 1889 murders of a woman and a child, safe in the knowledge that most readers would recollect the crime.[58] The memory of the 1888 Jack the Ripper murders was also kept alive and well in Edwardian London journalism. In George R. Sims's 1906 compendium *The Mysteries of Modern London,* the post-Dickensian connoisseur of urban gothic speculates that the Victorian Ripper may have traversed the capital on the early tube network with which Edwardian passengers were now

---

56 *London Daily News,* 8 August 1910.
57 Donald Read, *Edwardian England 1901–15: Society and Politics* (London: Harrap, 1972), p. 23.
58 *Daily Telegraph and Courier,* 16 May 1910.

so familiar: 'Probably on several occasions he had but one fellow-passenger in the compartment with him, and that may have been a woman. Imagine what the feelings of those travellers would have been had they known that they were alone in the dark tunnels of the Underground with Jack the Ripper!' Of a piece with the endurance of the gothic in contemporary Edwardian fiction, Sims's writing shows the comfortable endurance of the figure of the classic Victorian bogeyman into the conspicuously modern Edwardian age: 'there are maniacs of the Ripper type still at large' he avers. 'There have been several crimes of the Ripper character committed in low lodging-houses during recent years, and the perpetrator has always succeeded in making his escape and in retaining his liberty.'[59]

And indeed, early in the year of Crippen, the *Daily Telegraph and Courier* reported on 'a strange individual, who must certainly be a madman' who was 'trying to emulate the exploits of Jack the Ripper in the Fifteenth Arrondissement of Paris, with the difference that he chiefly attacks men and boys at night, instead of women, and does not entirely succeed in killing his victims.'[60] If these differences in *modus operandi* rather differentiated this attacker from his Victorian forebear, the press temptation to follow Sims in stereotyping and invoking the shadow of the Ripper seems to have been irresistible. Less of a stretch was required in July 1909 when, in a chillingly authentic echo of the Ripper, a young woman was murdered in Spitalfields within yards of the spot where the final Ripper victim had been murdered two decades before:

GHASTLY MURDER IN SPITALFIELDS

The East End of London has once again been the scene of a brutal murder, the victim being a young woman named Kitty Ronan, twenty four. [...] The scene of the tragedy was the top apartment of a two-roomed house. [...] Two doors away on the right-hand side near the entrance to the court, is the house

---

59   The Ripper's place in the public mind had been heightened in 1910 by the serialisation of Dr Robert Anderson's memoirs in *Blackwood's Magazine*, prior to their publication as *The Lighter Side of My Official Life* (1910). The memoirs included reminiscences of Anderson's time as Assistant Commissioner of the Metropolitan Police and officer in charge of the Whitechapel Murders investigation from October 1888 until the unsuccessful conclusion of the Ripper investigation in 1892.

60   'French Jack the Ripper', *Daily Telegraph and Courier*, 9 February 1910.

in which one of the last "Jack the Ripper" murders was committed, the victim being Marianne [sic] Kelly.[61]

The same report also notes how 'the crime recalls in its circumstances the Bloomsbury murder, when Esther Prager was killed in her room by a man who has never been brought to justice'. This instinct to interweave each new case with an established lineage of previous crimes was to play a crucial role in the cultural formation of the Crippen story. Indeed, the tapestry of urban gothic reportage woven by editors and journalists of the schools of Stead and Sims established the most vivid part of our backdrop to Crippen. Writing a mere four years before the Crippen drama, Sims turned his prose to tales of disappearances in London, writing prophetically, 'Every year a certain number of men and women disappear suddenly from their homes, from their accustomed haunts, from the circle of their friends and acquaintances...The secret of many a mysterious disappearance lies buried in the earth, sometimes in the cellars, behind brick walls, beneath the flooring of a kitchen or an outhouse, in the garden.'[62] Sims might almost have been writing the prologue to the story that would play out as 'the North London Cellar Murder' four years later. His words certainly helped to ensure that the headlines of July 1910 would resonate immediately for the Edwardian readership.

MYSTERIOUS MURDER IN CAMDEN TOWN
WOMAN'S BODY BURIED
DISCOVERY IN CELLAR

Last night a terrible discovery was made at a house in Hilldrop-crescent, Camden Town, the body of a woman being found buried in a coal-cellar. All the circumstances point to one of the most atrocious crimes known in the long record of the metropolis, having been committed there.[63]

Whose was the body in the cellar and how had it come to be there? The principal players in the Crippen tragedy, their biographies and how they came to follow the 'road to Hilldrop Crescent' forms the subject of the following chapter.

---

61   *Illustrated Police News*, 10 July 1909.
62   Sims, *The Mysteries of Modern London*, p. 99.
63   *Daily Telegraph and Courier*, 14 July 1910.

CHAPTER THREE

THE ROAD TO HILLDROP CRESCENT

Against the backdrop sketched in the previous chapter, January 1910 found Dr Hawley Harvey Crippen navigating the streets of the metropolis each weekday to pursue three professional endeavours. First, he had some remaining business to complete for Munyon's Homeopathic Remedies Company, an American pharmaceutical agency which dispensed patent medicines through the post and with which Crippen had been connected since 1894. This would be the doctor's last month with homeopathic field-leader Munyon's. Since November of the previous year his role had diminished from London manager, receiving £3 per week, to mere agent working on commission and his connection with the firm was to cease completely at the end of January 1910.[1]

Crippen's second venture operated from the same premises as Munyon's in Albion House, New Oxford Street. Here Crippen was also partner in a dental practice with fellow American Dr Gilbert Rylance, the pair operating under the name 'The Yale Tooth Specialists' and offering a 'painless dentistry' clinic. From Rylance's subsequent witness testimony it appears their partnership agreement, formed in 1908 and renewed as recently as March 1910, ascribed

---

[1]   The professional relationship had weathered some difficult chapters, including a suspension for Crippen in 1899 for moonlighting as his wife's theatrical manager. At Crippen's trial, Marion Curnow confirmed that when she assumed the role of manager on 1 February 1910 'his connection with Munyon's ceased'. *The Trial of Hawley Harvey Crippen*, ed. Filson Young (London: William Hodge, 1920), p. 27.

to Rylance the greater knowledge of dentistry: 'Dr. Crippen agreed to put £200 into the business, and I was to put in my experience, knowledge and skill.'[2]

If Rylance's description rather cast Crippen as the sleeping partner in the business, perhaps his proper specialism was better reflected in his third line of employment: since the autumn of 1909, operating from a small office in Craven House on the aforementioned Kingsway, Crippen had also been acting as 'consulting physician' to another patent chemist operation, the Aural Remedies Company, where he prescribed and dispensed remedies through the post for deafness and 'head noises' or tinnitus. To lend gravitas and market edge to this venture, Crippen had even published a short pamphlet, *The Otological Gazette*, which claimed the efficacy of his deafness cures and sported testimonials from apparently satisfied customers.[3] Masquerading as a special issue of an established periodical (while actually a *sui generis* publication cooked up by Crippen and his business partner Eddie Marr), the *Gazette* was widely advertised in the London press in November 1909 and free copies were despatched to correspondents who expressed interest in the Aural Remedies Company's treatments and cures, together with a letter from Crippen typically offering discounts, 'try-now-pay-later' opportunities, and other incentives.[4]

These business activities offer insight on Crippen's facility with rhetorical persuasion outside of the deceptive fictions he would shortly be weaving for the friends and family of his missing wife and for the Scotland Yard detectives who would soon come calling at Albion House and Hilldrop Crescent in search of her. In a letter dated 9 June 1910 – a mere month before his flight from justice – Crippen writes from the Aural Remedies Company offices, commending his *Otological Gazette* to the recipient's notice, offering a through-the-post consultation that places the patient 'under no obligation whatsoever' and pursuing the hard sell in urging prompt action to avert increasing deafness: 'May I urge you in your own interests to give this matter your serious and immediate

2   *Trial*, p. 29. Rylance elsewhere described Crippen as his advertising and business agent: *Daily Mail*, 16 July 1910.
3   A small number of copies of this publication remain in circulation. One is retained at the Madame Tussaud's archive in London.
4   'Are You Deaf?', *The People*, 7 November 1909. An even more exclamatory piece followed in the 21 November issue trumpeting 'A marvellous discovery … which adds one more victory to the many triumphs of science over disease. The Deaf can hear!!!' See also the advertisements appearing in the *London Daily News*, 25 January 1910 and 9 March 1910.

THE AURAL REMEDIES COY.

Consulting Specialist.
H. H. CRIPPEN, M.D.
(U.S.A. 1884)

OCULI ET AURIS CHIRURGIS.
(N.Y. OPHTHALMIC HOSPITAL COLLEGE 1887.)

Craven House.
Kingsway.
London. W.C.

9/6/10.

Dear Sir,

In reply to your favour I have much pleasure in sending you here-
with a copy of the "Otological Gazette", containing full particulars of
my simple home-treatment for Deafness and Noises in the Head.

The accompanying sheet of testimonials gives you a faint idea of the
remarkable success which has attended my new method of Treatment, especially in severe chronic cases of long standing which had previously been regarded as absolutely incurable.

I naturally infer that your enquiry is prompted by some Ear Trouble
from which you are suffering. I am, therefore, enclosing an Analytical
Form on which a series of questions are printed, covering every symptom
of Ear Disease which may be present.

If you will carefully fill in your answers to each question and return the Analytical Form in the enclosed envelope, I shall be most happy
to make an exhaustive study of your symptoms, and will send you, free of
all charge, my opinion on your condition, together with my advice as to
the special Treatment necessary. Kindly note that this places you under
no obligation whatsoever.

May I urge you in your own interest to give this matter your serious
and immediate consideration. Deafness is a progressive ailment and each
single day means a firmer hold of the disease. At the same time, may I
point out the necessity for giving complete and accurate answers to the
questions in the Analytical Form, as it is upon these that I base my report on the cause, history and special features of each individual case.

Yours faithfully,

E/A.

3. Letter from Crippen as consulting specialist for the Aural
Remedies Company written one month before his flight.

consideration. Deafness is a progressive ailment and each single day means a firmer hold of the disease.'[5]

The character of Crippen's 'Aural Remedies' letters closely mirrors those of contemporary Holborn-based homeopath 'Professor Keith Harvey', whose 1907 advertisement for the 'Keith-Harvey' system appearing in the *Penny Illustrated Paper* similarly cautioned: 'To neglect ear trouble is the greatest folly, for deafness is a disease that grows more serious as days progress.'[6] The resemblance is not accidental, for 'Professor Harvey' was in fact the aforementioned Eddie Marr, financial backer of the Aural Remedies Company. Marr, a particularly shadowy figure who also went by the aliases of Scott Hamilton and Elmer Shirley, oversaw an extensive portfolio of homeopathic and patent remedy businesses across London. According to a police paper filed in July 1910 by Sgt William Hayman, and later testimony by Crippen's long-term associate William Long, Crippen was a paid employee of Marr, working for him not only at Craven House but, for a period in 1908, at a separate office in Holborn. Here, under the alias of Peter Franckel, Crippen would answer correspondence and place advertisements for Harvey's remedies under the banner of the spurious 'Imperial Press Agency'.[7] He would use the same rhetorical strategies to drive business to his shared dentistry practice at Albion House. A 1908 *London Daily News* advertisement for 'The Yale Tooth Specialists', clearly

5   Examples of Crippen's Aural Remedies Company letters survive in various locations, including the National Archives and Madame Tussaud's archive. The company began trading in September 1909 but the surviving examples I am aware of are all dated 1910, suggesting they were retrieved from writing desks and drawers after Crippen became notorious. The letters provide excellent examples of Crippen's autograph though not of Ethel's typewriting – a different typist was employed at Aural Remedies.

6   *Penny Illustrated Paper*, 23 March 1907.

7   Statement of Sgt Hayman, MEPO 3/198; William Long's statement, *London Daily News*, Thursday 22 September 1910. Marr is elusive in the historical record: neither of the Edward Marrs identified as resident in the respective parishes of Kensington and Newington would appear to be the medicine man (though their stated professions of domestic coachman and printer's compositor may be misleading). The many aliases used by Marr provide a suggestive context for the disguises and impersonations of the Crippen drama. David James Smith describes Marr as 'probably the leading patent medicine huckster in the country' at this time: *Supper with the Crippens* (London: Vintage, 2005), p. 44. *The Northern Whig* of 28 February 1908 carried an advertisement for a book of 'Frankel's remedies': 'Readers of the *Northern Whig* can obtain the book free by post from M. Frankel, publisher, 61 New Oxford Street, London, W.C.'

penned by Crippen, promises: 'you need not feel the least obligation to have any work done on your teeth. We only want "Daily News" readers to realise that the Yale Methods represent an entirely new departure, in the treatment of the teeth and gums, which has completely abolished the sufferings inflicted by the old-fashioned way of filling and extracting teeth.'[8]

Hastening between Kingsway and New Oxford Street each day to balance these three enterprises, it is clear that at this stage of his career, Crippen's prospects were uncertain, forcing him to hustle for business. With no steady traffic of regular patients driven by reputation and loyalty to the door of his New Oxford Street consulting rooms, he was obliged to carve out an uncertain portfolio career, the viability of which depended upon constant access to a new market for his patent remedies.

'An ever-varying panorama'

What had brought the American doctor to New Oxford Street and Kingsway and forced such a diversification of his talents? Crippen's story starts forty-eight years previously on a different continent and includes many blind spots in the historical record. In particular, the precise sequence of Crippen's early biography is difficult to fix, his later recollection of dates being either wilfully or unwittingly inexact and the fast-moving pageant of locations in his early life making an exact chronology of his travels difficult to assemble.

We know at least that Hawley Harvey Crippen was born in Coldwater, Michigan in July 1862, the only surviving child of dry goods merchant Myron Augustus Crippen and Andresse Crippen, née Skinner. A pioneering spirit seems to have infused the young Crippen's close family: his grandfather Philo had travelled from his native New York to Coldwater, Michigan and was to be described as one of the pioneers of that town, its population being between only five and six thousand inhabitants when he moved there in the mid-nineteenth century.[9] Myron and Andresse were to follow Philo's example, leaving Coldwater for the burgeoning prospects of California during the 1870s, apparently during the course of Crippen's early education. This would account for the picaresque

---

8   *London Daily News*, 2 December 1908.
9   In a notice of what appears to be remarriage in his mid-seventies, Philo is described as
      one 'of the pioneers of Coldwater' in *The True Northerner*, 19 February 1885.

sketch Crippen would later paint of this period in his statement to Chief Inspector Dew, mentioning Coldwater, Indiana, and California as the places where he was 'educated first'. This tallies with the 1880 US census record uncovered by David James Smith which shows 'Ardesse' Crippen, aged 44, and Hawley Crippen, aged 17, living in Santa Clara Street, San José.[10]

While that same census entry records the teenage Crippen as working in a canning factory, the young man's sights were set early on a medical career. In the early 1880s Crippen commenced a long and eventful course of homeopathic training, entering into a medical tradition which, since its foundation in the early nineteenth century by German physician Samuel Hahnemann, had attracted equivalent levels of interest and scepticism. In distinction to the allopathic tradition, 'the homeopathic vision focused inward on the body's organs and tissues and bones, as well as outward, encompassing the patient's feelings about his pain, his environment, his symptoms. Treatment was to be based on a delicate balance between symptoms defined objectively (by the physician) and subjectively (by the patient).'[11] Crippen's precise reasons for choosing homeopathy over allopathy are not known. It was perhaps a question of pragmatics and expediency. The threshold qualifications for homeopathy were not as onerous or expensive to acquire – or perhaps, as David James Smith has speculated, 'at the time, it seemed like the exciting future of medicine, the pioneers' end of the profession.'[12]

In any case, Crippen's training in the homeopathic tradition would be acquired over the course of the next five years at a striking number of institutions across the States. The first step involved studies for a Diploma at the University of Michigan, which had recently established a chair of 'eclectic medicine' and a dedicated School of Homeopathic Medicine.[13] Studying here 'until I was about twenty', Crippen then moved south to Ohio in 1882 to continue studies at the Homeopathic Hospital College at Cleveland, 'one

10 MEPO 3/198. David James Smith, *Supper with the Crippens* (London: Orion, 2005), p. 32. Myron Augustus is strangely absent from the entry and perhaps the couple were estranged at this point. He lived on until 1910, dying only days before his only son's execution.
11 Naomi Rogers, 'The Proper Place of Homeopathy: Hahnemann Medical College and Hospital in an Age of Scientific Medicine', *The Pennsylvania Magazine of History and Biography* 108:2 (1984), 179–201: 182.
12 David James Smith, *Supper with the Crippens*, p. 34.
13 *The True Northerner*, 18 March 1881.

of the oldest and best medical schools of the West' in the view of the *Chicago Daily Tribune* of October 1881.[14] Certainly his time at Cleveland appears to have provided the young Crippen with crucial networks and social capital for advancing his career. During his time there he had an opportunity to take up a short placement with the well-connected Dr Philip Porter of Detroit, a leading light of Michigan's burgeoning homeopathic movement, who had been elected Vice President of the Homeopathic State Convention (Michigan) in 1883[15] and who was highly active as editor of a number of homeopathic journals, particularly those concerned with homeopathic treatment of obstetric and gynaecological conditions. Porter clearly warmed to the young Crippen and was an enthusiastic sponsor of his career over the next few years, introducing him to homeopathic networks within Michigan, nationally, and in Europe. In an early sign of favour and approbation, Porter included in his published medical papers an acknowledgement of the assistance of H.H. Crippen in the performance of an ovariotomy 'in the fall of 1883'.[16] Shortly thereafter the older man appears to have encouraged Crippen to publish extensively in the many homeopathic journals which Porter edited, including the *Homeopathic Journal of Obstetrics, Gynaecology and Paedology* and the *American Homeopathic Journal of Gynaecology and Obstetrics.*

To gather material and to extend the range of his experience, Crippen travelled to London in 1883 where he 'attended various hospitals to see the operations' before he returned to complete his studies and graduate with a diploma from Cleveland in 1884.[17] Upon graduation his connection with Porter deepened further, now working as his assistant for 'three or four months'. Further building the young man's profile in print, Porter even conferred on Crippen the status of 'special correspondent' for the *American Homeopathic Journal of Obstetrics and Gynaecology,* sending him back to Europe in winter 1884/5 to gather further field notes and case studies of European homeopathy and medical sciences and to submit dispatches to the journal's readers from London, Paris, and Berlin.[18] Crippen's 'London notes', posted in January

14   *Chicago Daily Tribune*, 7 October 1881.
15   *Weekly Expositor*, 24 May 1883.
16   Phil Porter, 'Ovariotomy-Recovery', *The Medical Advance* 14 (1884), 275–6: 275.
17   Crippen's statement to Inspector Dew, MEPO 3/198.
18   Frustrating the effective cataloguing of Crippen's many medical writings, the proper nouns in this periodical's title are transposed from the third issue onwards and the

1885, report on a busy itinerary in a country which showed an ambivalent relationship with homeopathic medical practice. Crippen comments regretfully how 'the graduates from the homeopathic schools [are] obliged to graduate first from allopathic schools before the laws sanction their practice' yet he also notes the more favourable trend that homeopathic practitioners 'enjoy a large share of the patronage of the upper classes'.[19] This London trip involved visits to the London Homeopathic Hospital and Medical School which had operated since 1849 out of premises in Golden Square, Soho and the nearby Hospital for Women in Soho Square, where he attended a series of lectures on the cervix given by distinguished medic Richard F. Smith.[20] This lengthy stop on the itinerary was by no means accidental: for in a little-known aspect of Crippen's medical training, it is clear that at this stage of his career he was following Porter's interest and specialism in obstetric and gynaecological conditions and their potential influence and bearing on other aspects of bodily wellbeing. These aspects of Crippen's medical training and experience would later be carefully concealed by Crippen in cross-examination, anxious as he was to disavow the kind of medical expertise that would equip him to 'de-sex' a corpse.

During his time in London Crippen's scientific interests (and perhaps his imagination) were particularly piqued by the possibility that nervous disorders might be prompted by irregularities in the reproductive system. 'Flexions, versions, tumors, or over excitement of the generative apparatus', he wrote in February 1885, 'are a constant source of reflex irritation of the nervous system producing hypochondriasis and various forms of mania, to say nothing of motorial and functional disturbances.'[21] Crippen was testing this hypothesis and researching these putative connections in, of all places, London's Bethlehem Hospital, where he collated detailed notes and patient histories of hospital inmates in that dark winter of 1884/5. The resulting notes on the conditions

journal is thereafter known as the *American Homeopathic Journal of Gynaecology and Obstetrics*.

19 H.H. Crippen, 'London Notes: The Hospitals', *American Homeopathic Journal of Obstetrics and Gynaecology* 1:1 (1885), 141–45: 145.

20 In a later issue, Crippen separately relayed the abstract of a series of lectures on the cervix given at the hospital by Dr Richard F. Smith to the *American Homeopathic Journal of Obstetrics and Gynaecology* 1:3 (March 1885), 75.

21 H.H. Crippen, 'Diseases of Women as a Cause of Insanity', *American Homeopathic Journal of Obstetrics and Gynaecology* 1:2 (February 1885), 42–49: 46.

and reflections of confined patients read with more poignancy than Crippen and his peers may have noted at the time:

> Jan. 23 – The first examination revealed no hallucinations but delusions that her relatives are against her, that she is about to die, that she can not go to heaven etc.
>
> Jan. 25 – Incoherent, almost constantly talking nonsense. Knows where she is however, and wants to get out.[22]
>
> Feb. 28 – Not so noisy, except at night.

Given the gothic shudder that the doctor's name would later come to summon, this image of Crippen collating field notes on the distressed women prisoners of Victorian Bedlam is another of those aspects of his story that seems more redolent of sensation fiction than documented fact. The vignette invokes gothic anxieties surrounding doctors as potential oppressors, with free rein to banish patients to the dread asylum.[23]

Initially lighter in tone is Crippen's account of his trip to the continent early in 1885 when 'a delightfully spring-like morning tempted your correspondent to brave the dangers of seasickness and cross the English channel to France'. Crippen relates his train journey through the London suburbs and into the Sussex countryside:

> the train was soon rolling through the suburbs of London out into the splendid farming country towards Newhaven. From the window of the car, an ever-varying panorama could be seen, long stretches of green fields, dotted here and there with quaint old-fashioned houses, and a back-ground of brown hills, almost leading one to believe it a bit of landscape taken from our own Pacific coast.[24]

During a stop at Brighton Crippen and colleagues visited 'the Brighton

---

22 'Diseases of Women', 44.
23 On this persistent Victorian anxiety see Andrew Scull (ed.), *Madhouses, Mad Doctors and Madmen: The Social History of Psychiatry in the Victorian Era* (Philadelphia: University of Pennsylvania Press, 1981) and David Wright, 'Getting out of the Asylum: Understanding the Confinement of the Insane in the Nineteenth Century', *Social History of Medicine* 10 (1997): pp. 137–55.
24 *American Homeopathic Journal of Obstetrics and Gynaecology* 1:1 (1885), 102.

Aquarium and the Free Library' before a 'short uneventful trip by boat' the next day. Arriving in Paris, Crippen's party visited the Salpêtrière where Jean-Martin Charcot and followers were conducting landmark studies into hysteria.[25] Charcot was not on-site, but the image of Crippen standing in the physician's office, studying every detail of the setting, once again shows a startling coincidence of history, placing Crippen quite literally at the source of some of the dominant medical discourses of the late nineteenth century: 'we penetrate to the study of M. Charcot, but much to our regret do not find the great alienist at work. Evidences of his life's work are scattered around, histological and pathological specimens of nerve tissue, making up a valuable laboratory.' Crippen in Bedlam; Crippen in Salpêtrière. Only a visit to a renowned Viennese psychologist is missing from this astonishing pageant of travels into the wellsprings of late-nineteenth-century neurophysiological, pathological, and psychological thought.

The last of Crippen's 'special correspondent' letters series is penned not from Vienna, however, but from Berlin, where he contrasts the favourable weather with the 'cloudy, damp, and smoky atmosphere of London'.[26] This account offers less vivid detail, relating some observations on the still relatively novel antiseptic technique in performing operations, and bemoaning the lack of Prussian governmental support for homeopathic practice, despite the irony that 'here is where Homeopathy was first given to the world'.[27] In contrast to the image of outdated medical practice that would be invoked at his trial, Crippen's interest in the patient histories and case studies of Bedlam, the pathological samples in Charcot's laboratory, and indeed the whole thrust of his fact-finding European travels, shows his openness to a 'modernised' homeopathy in which the medical sciences might be integrated rather than held as oppositional. It also shows an interest, awareness, and level of surgical experience that he would wholly disavow in the witness box.

This 'ever-varying panorama' of Crippen's early life means that a comprehensive mapping of his travels eludes us. There are missing years and details not easily reconciled. For example, any written testimony showing that

25 On the influence of Charcot see Ruth Harris, *Murders and Madness: Medicine, Law and Society in the fin de siècle* (Oxford: Oxford University Press, 1989), p. 159.
26 'Our Berlin Letter', *The American Homeopathic Journal of Gynaecology and Obstetrics* 1:8 (August 1885), 242–4: 242.
27 Ibid., 244.

4.   N.L. Merrill's previously unpublished portrait of Crippen.

Crippen's travels took him north of New York into Vermont has yet to be found, but we know from a recently discovered and previously unpublished portrait of a young Crippen that he was photographed by N.L. Merrill of Johnson, Vermont in the early 1880s. In a striking contrast to the images of the middle-aged, bespectacled Crippen that would later become immortalised in the international press, this early portrait shows an urbane and assured younger Crippen, the signature moustache already in place, the head of hair fuller, and the piercing and prominent eyes as yet unscreened by those famous gold-rimmed spectacles. A world away from the iconic image of a deflated Crippen in the dock at Bow Street Magistrates Court taken over thirty years later, the countenance conveys a confidence, ambition and latent energy.

    No doubt Crippen more closely resembled this portrait than those later iconic images when he returned to America, well-travelled and well-published, in 1885. Here there was a further qualification to be gained (this time from the

New York Ophthalmic Hospital as an ear and eye specialist); more surgical work and publication activity with Dr Porter; and next an internship at New York's Hahnemann Homeopathic Hospital. Established in 1869, the hospital had garnered sufficient public confidence and benefactions to move to new premises on the east side of Fourth Avenue in the mid-1870s. 'The officers, directors and medical board are among the most prominent and philanthropic of our citizens and physicians' averred the *New York Herald* in August 1872: 'The success that has attended the treatment of the suffering sick under the homeopathic system has set at rest all doubts as to its excellence.'[28] Attesting to his success at the hospital, *The Hahnemannian Monthly* of August 1887 lists Crippen as a member of the Bureau of Ophthalmology, Otology and Laryngology.[29]

The First Mrs Crippen

It was while he was working at the Hahnemann that Crippen met the woman who was to become his first wife, Charlotte Jane Bell. An Irish immigrant, Charlotte was completing her nurse training at the Hahnemann. The couple's courtship resulted in a marriage held in Detroit at the residence of Crippen's mentor, Dr Porter, on 13 December 1887. One of Porter's many homeopathic journals reported on the nuptials as follows: 'The happy couple have selected San Diego, California for their future residence. The best wishes and congratulations of the OBSTETRICAL JOURNAL will accompany them to their new home.'[30] And indeed, the next phase of the 'ever-changing panorama' was in the offing, the newlyweds moving to the Pacific Coast where Crippen appears to have held roles of increasing responsibility. Still writing for Porter's journals, his 1889 contribution on 'Hygiene of the Eyes of Children' gives his affiliation as Surgeon in Charge of the San Diego Optical Institute – though the effect is perhaps rather diluted by his adding 'Eye and Ear Surgeon to the San Diego Free Dispensary, and to the Good Samaritan Hospital'.[31] Twenty years before he would be juggling his London businesses, Crippen seems already to have developed (by choice or necessity) a portfolio approach to medical practice.

---

28 *New York Herald*, 25 August 1872.
29 *The Hahnemannian Monthly*, XII:8 (August 1887), 518.
30 *Homeopathic Journal of Obstetrics, Gynaecology and Paedology* 1 (1888), 65.
31 'Hygiene of the Eyes of Children', *Homeopathic Journal of Obstetrics, Gynaecology and Paedology* 1889, 528–37: 528.

The couple settled long enough in San Diego for the birth of a son to be recorded there – Otto Crippen being born on 19 August 1892. Already however the next phase of Crippen's peripatetic career was in the offing. The young family relocated to Salt Lake City, Utah where, in a pattern that paralleled Crippen's professional relationship with Dr Porter, he now found the favour of a second senior figure in the homeopathic community, Dr James Dart.[32] A Civil War veteran and President of the Utah Homeopathic Medical Association, Dart had trained at the New York Homeopathic Medical College in the early 1870s and had moved to Salt Lake City as a practising homeopath in 1885.[33] The two men appear to have met soon after Crippen's entrance to the Utah homeopathic community, living only one block apart from one another. In May 1892, Crippen is reported as being present at the inaugural meeting of the Utah Homeopathic Medical Association, giving an address to Dart and the assembled audience on the 'Therapeutics of Acute Conjunctivitis'.[34] The paper was presented by a man not long out of mourning. For on 24 January, Charlotte Bell, the first Mrs Crippen, had died at the family home, attended by her husband. *The Salt Lake Tribune* carried a short death notice the following day: 'CRIPPEN – On January 24th, Charlotte J., beloved wife of Dr H.H. Crippen. Funeral from residence 565 South Street at 10 o'clock a.m., Tuesday.'

What is to be made of Charlotte's sad demise in the light of future events? Whether there were any suspicious circumstances surrounding Charlotte's death is a question that divides historians of the case, though the weight of opinion so far has been against suggesting foul play. Martin Fido's *Dictionary of National Biography* entry for Crippen simply records the fact of Charlotte's death without speculation, while Tom Cullen's 1977 case history relates the position of the official record: 'she died suddenly of apoplexy;'[35] and Katherine Watson likewise asserts: 'There is no reason to suppose that her death was in

---

32   This under-researched phase of Crippen's career has recently been illuminated by Jonathan Menges, who also collates the different sources of rumour and innuendo surrounding the death of Charlotte Bell: Jonathan Menges, 'Connective Tissue: Belle Elmore, H.H. Crippen and the Death of Charlotte Bell', *Ripperologist* 158 (2017), 11–16: 13.

33   Obituary of James Monroe Dart, *The Roxbury Times*, 10 January 1925.

34   The *Salt Lake Herald*, 4 May 1892.

35   Tom Cullen, *The Mild Murderer: The True Story of the Dr Crippen Case* (London: Houghton Mifflin, 1977), p. 34. Cullen suggests Charlotte 'was within two or three days of giving birth to another child' but the accuracy of this detail is uncertain.

any way unnatural.'[36] More recently, Jonathan Menges has reassessed the 1910 press speculation about Charlotte's death and has compared the conflicting details included in reports which variously ascribed Charlotte's demise to apoplexy or heart failure and in some instances intimating that the death took place while she was pregnant (or even after the birth of a child of whom there is no historical record).

The press reports, most of them appearing in that feverish summer of 1910, are certainly suggestive. 'Dr Crippen's first wife died under mysterious conditions 18 years ago' related Iowa's *Ottumwa Tri-Weekly Courier*. 'Apoplexy and paralysis were given as the cause of death, which occurred soon after the birth of a child. Neighbors were suspicious, but there were not sufficient grounds for an investigation.'[37] If this reportage appeared based largely on unfocused rumour and suspicion, more revealing and suggestive detail had been unearthed by *The Washington Times* a month earlier. Under the headline 'DR. CRIPPEN'S FIRST WIFE SLAIN, SAYS BROTHER', the article features quotations attributed to W.R. Bell, Charlotte's brother. It is from Bell that the suggestion arises that Crippen 'got into trouble' in New York and was obliged to relocate to California and then Salt Lake City, where Crippen 'posed as a dentist and optician'. To substantiate a claim that Crippen was performing forced operations on his sister, Bell then quotes a letter from Charlotte apparently written soon after the birth of Otto: 'My husband is about to force me to the knife again and I feel that this will be the last time. I want my relatives to know that if I die it will be his fault.'[38] This disturbing suggestion of enforced medical experiments in the domestic setting, an image deeply resonant with *fin de siècle* cultural anxieties about murderous medical men, might just have some basis. Certainly, one wonders if Crippen was reporting on his pregnant wife as case study when he is cited by Dr Philip Porter in the *Homeopathic Journal of Obstetrics, Gynaecology and Paedology* in 1889: 'Dr. H.H. Crippen of San Diego has also verified the symptom of pain in the left ovarian region during pregnancy, more particularly where there was pain as if the left ovarian region were pressed on by the enlarged uterus.'[39]

---

36   Katherine D. Watson, *Dr Crippen* (London: The National Archives, 2007), p. 12.

37   *Ottumwa Tri-Weekly Courier*, 6 August 1910.

38   *Washington Times*, 16 July 1910. An article appearing later the same month in the *Dundee Courier* further quotes Bell as claiming that Crippen turned up in Dublin in 1893 to demand of Charlotte's mother 'certain small valuables' that had belonged to his wife.

39   *The Homeopathic Journal of Obstetrics, Gynaecology and Paedology*, 1889, 318.

These disturbing implications of a profoundly misogynistic Crippen, abusing his spouse and his medical training alike, are not to be set aside lightly. Indeed, a 1950 letter from Belle Elmore's half-sister Louise Mills adds to the picture of a predatory and dangerous man, quite distinct from the 'mild murderer' of later tradition.[40] Yet given that these claims were advanced only during the feverish manhunt of 1910 and that the same issue of the *Washington Times* also ran a piece on Crippen as diabolical mesmerist, it is perhaps more likely that the article rehearses generic cultural anxieties of doctor as potential oppressor, the spectre of which had certainly been raised by the Crippen story. The police of the day seem not to have found a case to pursue; the mooted investigation of Charlotte's death seems never to have taken place. Entrusting his son Otto to the care of the young boy's grandparents, Crippen returned to New York, where he assisted in the practice of Dr Jeffrey of Brooklyn.[41] It was here in July 1892 that Crippen was to meet the woman who was to become his second wife and the unfortunate victim in one of the most infamous murder cases of all time.

The Second Mrs Crippen

Cora Crippen was born in Brooklyn on 3 September 1873 as Kunigunde Mackamotzki. Her father, Polish immigrant Joseph Mackamotzki, had run a fruit stand in Brooklyn prior to his premature death. Her mother, German immigrant Mary, had taken a second husband, Frederick Mersinger, six years after Joseph's passing, and according to the *New York Tribune*, it was as Cora Mersinger that Kunigunde was known in Brooklyn during this period. Cora gained a half-sister, Theresa, by virtue of the Mersinger marriage, and seeking to naturalise and assimilate still further into Brooklyn society, was going by the name of Cora Turner when she met Crippen. Rather than disavow her European roots entirely however, Cora romanticised them, telling

---

40 Mills suggested that while staying at Hilldrop Crescent, 'Crippen always bothered me as soon as he was out of sight.' She also claims he was a drug addict, self-administering most of the narcotics he purchased. Nicholas Connell, *Doctor Crippen*, p. 157.

41 David James Smith's 2005 book published the listing of Crippen and his mother on the 1880 census return (listing them in Santa Clara Street, San Jose) and established that Myron and Andresse also had a daughter, Ella Sophia, who died in infancy in 1861: *Supper with the Crippens* (London: Orion, 2005), p. 32 *et passim*.

5. Crippen's second wife Cora, alias Belle Elmore, who has been much traduced in Crippen case histories since the trial proceedings were first published in 1920.

acquaintances that father Joe had in fact been a Polish baron and that she had an unclaimed title and property back in the family homeland.[42] This propensity for romanticism and imagination was perhaps the only talent that fitted her for the profession she was seeking to pursue when she met Crippen in 1892 – a life upon the stage.

It is difficult to establish exactly what Cora's circumstances were when she entered Crippen's Brooklyn surgery. The doctor's subsequent innuendo-laden police statement and trial testimony, presumably designed to question Cora's character, suggested that when they met, she was living 'under the protection' of an older man, a stove manufacturer called C.C. Lincoln.[43] Crippen suggested that Cora had previously co-habited with Lincoln but was now living alone in a room on which he paid the rent. Crippen's hints were of an affair and an unwanted pregnancy, suggesting that it was reasons relating to the latter that had brought Cora to the Brooklyn surgery in the first place. Details outside of Crippen's own claims are sketchy; an 1891 newspaper places a C.C. Lincoln, stove repairer, at 1207 Douglas Street, Omaha – a considerable distance from Brooklyn but perhaps this was the location to which Cora was being encouraged to relocate with Lincoln when Crippen relates 'she told me Lincoln wanted her to go away with him'.[44] This threat of an enforced separation appears to have focused the minds of the courting Crippen and Cora and, shortly afterwards, the doctor proposed marriage.

The protagonists in one of crime's most famous poisoning cases were thus formally allied in a Catholic ceremony on 1 September 1892 at St Paul's Church, Jersey City. Married life began with an early blow to any hopes of augmenting the family. Cora required an operation, probably an ovariotomy, that left her without prospect of motherhood but with a significant abdominal scar that was to loom large in the forensic evidence presented at Crippen's trial. Perhaps intensified by this curtailment of family life, Cora's ambitions for a career on the stage gathered pace just as Crippen's practice was increasingly failing. After a short spell in St Louis where Crippen served as a consulting physician to an optician, they returned to New York where Crippen was to begin his long connection with Munyon's patent remedies.

---

42 *The Mild Murderer*, p. 34. Cullen notes that Crippen capitalised on this exotic name of 'Baron Mackamotzki' to market one of his patent medicines.
43 *Trial of Hawley Harvey Crippen*, p. 88.
44 *Omaha Daily Bee*, 20 December 1891; CRIM 1/117.

By the mid-1890s patent medicine was an increasingly regulated but still thriving field, offering over-the-counter or through-the-post remedies for an assortment of ills. The nominal patent resided in the 'secret formula' employed in each preparation – in many cases allegedly derived from folk medicine or herbal remedies. Available without prescription, patent medicines formed one of the most prominent sectors of the nascent advertising industry in the late nineteenth and early twentieth centuries. Indeed, it is a striking irony of the case that, as a rule, any page of 1910 press coverage of the Crippen case will almost certainly carry an advertisement at its foot or periphery, advertising exactly the kinds of remedy the doctor traded in.[45] The remedies firm Crippen signed with in 1894 was a market leader. Established by James Monroe Munyon in 1885, the Munyon Homeopathic Home Remedy Company operated from headquarters in Philadelphia and had rapidly gained a firm foothold in the sector, bringing to market such staples as Munyon's pile ointment; Munyon's 'paw-paw pills' (avowedly alleviating constipation, dyspepsia and indigestion); headache remedy; Kidney Cure; Munyon's Asthma Cure; and even a Special Liquid Blood Cure that proposed to eradicate syphilis and scrofula. While the company was to sustain some reputational damage in the wake of the Pure Food and Drug Act enacted by Congress in 1906 (which was to expose some of the secret ingredients for these cures as being no more exotic or tutelary than white sugar, alcohol, and potassium iodide) Munyon's would prove a secure enough proposition to provide Crippen and Cora with a living for the best part of a decade.

Crippen's assignment to Munyon's in 1894 was to lead the New York office on East 14th Street near Sixth Avenue. This first posting was a family affair, with Cora assisting her husband as a cashier and the couple sleeping in a room above the office. The industrious doctor made a favourable impression on Munyon, who on the later occasion of Crippen's criminal celebrity was to reminisce to *The New York Times*: 'He was one of the most intelligent men I ever knew…[Crippen] was so proficient that I gave him a position readily, nor have I ever regretted it.'[46] Accordingly, Crippen was quickly advanced in 1895

---

45   For example, adjacent to *The Daily Mail*'s account of 'Crippen's Life in London' (30 July 1910) was an advert for a patent medicine for Rheumatism and Gout: 'Speedy relief and cure. Never known to fail. It has always proved to be a successful remedy in the most obstinate cases, it is a safe medicine, absolutely harmless, and never been known to fail.'

46   Cullen, *The Mild Murderer*, p. 38.

to serve as general manager of the Philadelphia office; then to open a Canadian branch in Toronto before returning to Philadelphia. These postings served to separate the couple for substantial periods: during the Philadelphia stint, Cora spent long stretches living away from her husband in New York while she undertook vocal training to support her theatrical ambitions. The couple persisted with this challenging domestic arrangement and costly investment, funded by the industrious Crippen, despite the fact that, by this time, any engagements Cora managed to acquire were running more to vaudeville than opera.

Yet a new opportunity extended itself to the couple in 1897 when Crippen was offered the post of manager of the London office on the substantial salary of $10,000 a year.[47] Crippen set off first, in April 1898, over a decade after those European travels he had so enthusiastically chronicled in the homeopathic journals. Cora, her ambitions refocused on the English music hall stage, was to follow him across the Atlantic within four months; the Crippens were bound for London.

The Crippens in London

The Crippens were to reside at a number of London addresses before ultimately settling at the address that was to become notorious. Crippen first took lodgings in South Crescent, St John's Wood and then in Guildford Street, but their most settled address prior to arrival at the notorious Hilldrop Crescent was in Store Street, Bloomsbury where, as Erik Larson notes, they would have shared the broad pavements with some of the guiding intellects of the era, including Chesterton, Wells, and Madox Ford.[48] Crippen's Munyon's office, described as 'palatial' by journalist and dramatist Adeline Harrison, was a short distance away at 121–123 Shaftesbury Avenue, where it stood opposite the Palace Theatre.[49] That he was well established there by August 1898 is attested by a press coverage of an unsuccessful prosecution of Munyon's 'consulting physician' James Edward Deane for irregular accounting and stock-keeping

---

47   Writing in 2006, Erik Larson calculated this sum as equivalent to $220,000 in twenty-first century dollars. Erik Larson, *Thunderstruck* (London: Bantam Books), p. 58.
48   Larson, *Thunderstruck*, p. 95.
49   'The Crippen Household – Intimate Friend Tells How They Lived', *Daily Express*, 15 July 1910.

practices at the London branch for which Crippen was manager. Appearing as a witness, Crippen was open about Deane's and his own dubious medical qualifications, but evasive about the contents of Munyon's remedies; asked by the judge, 'Can you tell me any other ingredient than sugar and water in these cures?', Crippen replied: 'I don't think I need answer that question.' It was suggested that Deane was dispensing his own remedies to patients under the Munyon's banner rather than the real article. Deane's colleagues 'Mr Crippen' and one Susannah Stopper are also cited in the article, albeit as ostensibly innocent parties.[50]

During their years at the Store Street flat, the Crippens broadened their social circle, acquiring some of the friends who would later depose testimony at Crippen's indictment and trial. Among these were Maud and Dr John Herbert Burroughs, who recalled first meeting the Crippens in 1902 in Store Street and who represented the couple's marriage as affectionate and the husband as keenly attentive. 'From my long knowledge of him', deposed Burroughs in 1910, 'I should describe him as a kind-hearted, well-mannered man. We looked upon him as a model husband, he always seemed anxious to do his wife some little service and shew her some attention.'[51]

Sure enough, at this early stage of their life in London, the couple appear to have been working in concert. Crippen was not only funding Cora's theatrical aspirations, he was even acting as her manager and enjoying some success in placing her on the music hall variety bills alongside 'jugglers, tumblers, dancers, comedians, male impersonators, female impersonators, soubrettes, ventriloquists'.[52] As a novel American vaudevillian, Belle was able to achieve a certain amount of traction in the early years of the century, and a fairly steady stream of variety appearances can be charted through the newspapers from 1900 until at least 1904, when the number of listings diminishes. The ultimate failure of Cora's stage career is well-documented, but it is less well known that at this early stage she was managing to earn some modestly favourable notices for both her appearances in London and the regions. Her early London

50 'Munyon's Medicines: Allegations as to Their Ingredients', *Western Mail*, 26 September 1898. The account of Deane's charging and remand in *Lloyd's Weekly Newspaper* of 21 August 1898 also mentions Crippen and co-worker Susannah Stopper as the personnel of the Munyon's London office.
51 CRIM 1/117, Deposition of John Herbert Burroughs at Bow Street, 6 September 1910.
52 Read, *Edwardian England*, p. 66.

appearances, at venues such as the Marylebone Music Hall, were under the name of Màcka Motzki and gave her affiliation as The Bright Lights Company 'from the principal American theatres'.[53] This exotic name soon made way for Cora's reinvention as 'Belle Elmore' and it is by this name that she is mentioned in the January 1901 *Music Hall and Theatre Review* as available for appearances in 'special concerts and smokers' and in a later issue the same year as 'rehearsing an entirely New and Original Sister Act'.[54] The notices of her appearances at this early stage are more varied than later tradition might have us expect. A review of her February 1902 appearance at The Balham Empire, for example, reports how Belle sang a 'song of the "Motor Car"' which the reviewer found 'has a captivating refrain which is vigorously chorused'.[55]

Encouraged by these early developments, Belle engaged the services of established music hall journalist and dramatist Adeline Harrison to enhance her self-penned sketch *An Unknown Quality*. Harrison later related how she was 'invited by a mutual friend to write the libretto' and initially scoped ideas with the Crippens over lunch at a fashionable restaurant where she quickly gelled with Belle while feeling repulsed by her doctor husband – or so she would later write with hindsight when the man was wanted for murder.[56] Described by Crippen biographer Tom Cullen as 'a feeble affair about blackmail' which exposed the limitations of Belle's singing voice, the sketch caused an early stir at the Marylebone Music Hall by virtue of its finale – an ill-judged piece of stage business in which Belle would hit a high C while throwing genuine bank notes at the feet of her co-star.[57] This had the effect of causing a mad competitive dash to the stage by audience members bustling to scoop up notes (almost certainly Crippen's own money) and imitation bank notes would be used in subsequent performances.

All the same, Harrison's workshopping of Belle's act appears to have paid other dividends; by the late summer of 1902, a Derbyshire weekly described Belle as 'a charming comedienne' and deemed *An Unknown Quality* to be 'a capital sketch' which was 'well acted on this occasion, a large audience giving

53   Jonathan Goodman, ed., *The Crippen File* (Allison and Busby, 1985), p. 25.
54   *Music Hall and Theatre Review*, 4 January 1901; 12 April 1901.
55   *The Era*, 8 February 1902.
56   *Daily Express*, 15 July 1910.
57   *The Mild Murderer*, p. 43.

it a splendid reception'.[58] By the autumn, Belle was appearing at the Park Hall, Hanwell where, in a reference which suggests she had not yet grown into the fuller body shape that was noted at the time of her death, she was characterised by one reviewer as 'a dainty soubrette' and received a double encore.[59] These relatively auspicious notices were sustained by an appearance in Portsmouth late the following year which prompted a reviewer to predict that 'Belle Elmore, comedienne, should make herself a great favourite'.[60]

Yet this early phase of Cora's short-lived music hall career was soon to bring a cloud over both personal and professional matters. First, Crippen's moonlighting as Cora's theatrical manager came to the notice of his employer James Munyon all the way back in Philadelphia. Shortly after organising and bankrolling his wife's short stint at the Old Marylebone Music Hall in 1899, Crippen found himself briefly recalled to Munyon's head office in Philadelphia for a reprimand that resulted in dismissal. While his connection with Munyon's would later be renewed, this was a considerable blow to the couple's fortunes and prospects, obliging Crippen to diversify his enterprises in a manner that was to become characteristic of the man by 1910. Then, to compound this professional setback, while Crippen was back in America being chastised by Munyon, Cora formed a close attachment and likely began an affair with a fellow American expatriate performer, Bruce Miller, whose person and whose indiscreet love letters to Belle signed 'love and kisses to brown eyes' would later be produced at Crippen's trial. Miller had traded his boxing career as a prize-fighter in Chicago for a spell in London music hall, where his act largely centred on performing as a one-man band.[61] In the early years of the century he was appearing in London and in coastal towns, also ranging further afield to the Paris Exposition of 1900. Here he was exhibiting the same 'Automaton Orchestra' that, as 'Professor' Miller, he would bring to Earls Court in September 1900, where: 'The movements of 11 figures, represented as playing various instruments, are directed by pneumatic tubings, connected to an organ played by Professor Miller.'[62] Miller would later recall how he had first met 'Mrs Crippen in a house in Torrington Square, London,

58 *Derbyshire Times and Chesterfield Herald*, 23 August 1902.
59 *Ealing Gazette and West Middlesex Observer*, 11 October 1902.
60 *Portsmouth Evening News*, 8 December 1903.
61 Larson, *Thunderstruck*, p. 112.
62 *Lloyd's Weekly Newspaper*, 30 September 1900.

in December 1899' while Crippen was absent in America, where he would
remain until the following spring.[63] The doctor would later describe to Chief
Inspector Dew the changed domestic situation that he found on his return.
Now routinely performing under the more exotic stage name 'Belle Elmore',
not only had Cora been reduced to 'singing at Smoking Concerts', a lower tier
entertainment it seems that Crippen would not have endorsed, it appeared that
Bruce Miller had been a frequent gentleman caller in Bloomsbury:

> She told me this man visited her, had taken her about and was very fond of
> her, also that she was fond of him.
>   I may say that when she came to England from America her manner
> towards me was entirely changed, and she had cultivated a most ungov-
> ernable temper, and seemed to think I was not good enough for her, and
> boasted of the men of good position travelling on the boat who had made a
> fuss of her, and, indeed, some of them visited her at South Crescent, but I do
> not know their names.
>   I never saw the man Bruce Miller, but he used to call when I was out, and
> used to take her out in the evenings.[64]

Thus, the destructive dynamic that drove the tragic events of 1910 was already
established by this early stage of the Crippens' life in London. Before ever
they had moved to the infamous 39 Hilldrop Crescent, a nexus of resentments
and grievances was already building within the Crippen marriage; Hawley
supporting the professional endeavours of Cora (at both fiscal and reputational
cost), and Cora channelling her professional disappointment and frustration
into at least one infidelity and, if Crippen's later account is to be credited, a
growing roll of criticisms and admonishments of her husband.

Compounding the difficulty of this growing domestic estrangement, Crippen
needed to find new employment following his dismissal from Munyon's. The
doctor now served a brief stint at a second patent medicine company, the
Sovereign Remedy Company near Tottenham Court Road. Promising 'No
quackery! No secret preparations!' and offering 'only remedies that can be
analysed', the company operated out of premises in Newman Street, off Oxford
Street.[65] Despite offering remedies for a whole range of ills from dyspepsia

63   *Trial of Hawley Harvey Crippen*, p. 20.
64   CRIM 1/117: Indictment file, ex.39.
65   *Penny Illustrated Paper*, 23 June 1900.

to headaches, sore throats and rheumatism, the company floundered in a crowded market and soon Crippen was again in search of work. This he found in early 1901 at the increasingly disreputable Drouet Institute for the Deaf, where he would work until the bankruptcy of the company in 1908. Based first at Regents Park and later at Marble Arch, Drouet's had been founded in 1888, establishing itself by means of a concerted press advertising campaign in which the benefits of the spurious 'Dr Drouet's' hearing apparatus would be expounded by quotation of the letters of satisfied customers. In a pattern later echoed by Crippen's *Otological Gazette*, a dedicated 'Drouet's Newspaper for the Deaf' was also offered 'gratis and post free' so that readers might learn the particulars of 'a large number of remarkable cures which have been accomplished under this treatment, many having been effected in cases of long standing and of a most serious nature'.[66]

When Crippen joined the Drouet Institute, it was doing a steady enough trade to warrant the employ of William Long, long-term assistant to Crippen and crucial player in his escape of 1910, and young, quiet, and reserved typist Ethel Clara Le Neve. Born in Diss, Norfolk on 22 January 1883, Ethel hailed from a large family of six children. Parents Walter and Charlotte Neave relocated the family to London seven years later, the 1901 census listing them as resident in Gayton Road, Hampstead and giving Walter's profession as dairy manager, eldest son Claud as junior clerk and sisters Adene ('Nina') and Ethel as typists. It was this secretarial skill, learned from a family friend, that was to bring the Neave sisters into contact with Crippen. Both joined the Drouet Institute in 1901, and when Crippen arrived soon after, according to Ethel's ghost-written reminiscences, all three became good friends, continuing to work together until 1903 when Nina left the business to get married. Ethel relates how 'I took her place as Dr Crippen's private secretary' and proceeds to paint a picture of an unlikely couple thrown together by mutual loneliness. Of a hypochondriac tendency (and reported as habitually replying to enquiries after her health with 'Not very well, thank you'), Ethel warmed further to her employer when he apparently cured her of a long-standing catarrh complaint. She professes to have thought him unmarried when they met, learning only later of Cora's existence from laconic comments from Crippen and a stormy appearance at the office by the lady herself: 'I was leaving the office for lunch

66   'To the Deaf', *St James's Gazette*, 24 May 1898.

when I saw a woman come out of the doctor's room and bang the door behind her. She was obviously very angry about something.'[67] This unfavourable first impression of 'Belle' does not seem to have deterred Ethel from later making a visit to Hilldrop Crescent on an errand and in her police statement to Chief Inspector Dew in the summer of 1910 she would even claim that Belle 'treated me as a friend'.[68]

The exact chronology of Crippen and Ethel's affair is another of those aspects of the story which is difficult to chart with precision, but according to Ethel's 1910 statement to Dew, she had been 'on intimate terms with Mr Crippen for between 2 and 3 years' and subsequent references in the love letters exchanged in the weeks before Crippen's execution suggest a first physical consummation in early December 1904. There are also references in Crippen's letters (though understandably not in Ethel's memoirs) of a miscarriage in the autumn of 1908.[69] Office assistant William Long reported a strained atmosphere between Crippen and Ethel at about this time – though whether this can be attributed to this specific event or simply reflected the strains of their clandestine relationship is unclear.

Despite these confirmations of a physical relationship, Crippen and Ethel's own writings present a companionate rather than passionate relationship – one in which the lovers sought comfort in one another and retreated from an increasingly hectoring and prying world into a sedate sphere of quiet conversation and company. Crippen's letter of 6 November 1910, penned from the condemned cell, is particularly evocative of this mood: 'I see ourselves in those days of courtship, having our dinner together after our day of work together was done, or sitting sometimes in our favourite corner in Frascati's by the stairway, all the evening listening to music.'[70] This picture of innocent leisure and shared recreation even seems to have featured in the pair's time as fugitives in July 1910. At his trial, Crippen suggested that rather than lying low at their Antwerp hotel amidst the hue and cry that pursued them that

---

67   *Ethel Le Neve: Her Life Story with the True Account of their Flight and her Friendship for Dr Crippen. Also startling particulars of her Life at Hilldrop Crescent* (London: Publishing Office, 1910), p. 9.
68   MEPO 1/198.
69   David James Smith has assembled suggestive evidence of a possible second pregnancy and discreet adoption within the Neave family: *Supper with the Crippens*, pp. 67–9.
70   Cullen, *The Mild Murderer*, p. 214.

380 LONDON. — Oxford Street and Frascati's. — LL.

6. Crippen and Ethel's favourite retreat at Frascati's in Oxford Street.

summer, the pair 'visited the Zoological Gardens and walked all over the place'. 'Enjoying yourselves?' exclaimed prosecuting counsel. 'Certainly', came the unabashed reply.[71]

Crippen's letters to Ethel particularly emphasise this more innocent construction of their affair, referring habitually to their relationship to one another with the somewhat infantilising endearments 'Hub and wifie'. An equivalent attempt at mitigation of the affair is found in Ethel's memoirs, where she reports having seen Bruce Miller's 'affectionate correspondence with Belle Elmore' and suggests how this diminished her misgivings about her own intimate relations with the married Crippen: 'He told me often that she was his wife only in name, and that I was everything to him. She went her way and he went his.'[72] Certainly by 1910 the relationship had matured and may well have provided the immediate catalyst for the tragic events that unfolded in the February of that year.

71 *Trial of Hawley Harvey Crippen*, p. 112.
72 *Ethel Le Neve: Her Life Story*, p. 12.

While Crippen's position at Drouet's initially seemed a very sound prospect, the institute was already gathering some unfavourable publicity by the time he joined the operation. A long-running libel trial between 1904 and 1907 saw Drouet's medical director Dr Dakhyl suing the publication *Truth* for having described him as 'a quack of the rankest species'.[73] Syrian-born Dakhyl held reputable medical qualifications from Paris and extensive clinical experience gained from many years' practice, but during the course of the libel case he found that he suffered from association with an institution 'whose work consisted in treating by correspondence patients with ear, nose, and throat troubles'.[74] The protracted *Truth* libel action affords a range of insights on the perception of quack doctors in the period, including allopaths' deep suspicion of patent remedies and their certainty that ear disease could not be diagnosed or treated through the post. At the climax of the case, the defence counsel for *Truth* waggishly suggested that while the jury had been furnished with examples of Dr Dakhyl's 'cures' they had 'no records of his failures, which were probably represented in the church yard'; the court broke out into laughter.[75]

By 1906 a number of adverse outcomes for Drouet patients were being reported, including the unfortunate death of one patient who had attempted to self-administer a dubious remedy. A subsequent exposé of quackery at Drouet's, undertaken by *Albion Magazine* editor Evan Yellon, serendipitously captures a vignette of Crippen at work in his consulting rooms in 1906 – though the portrait is hardly a flattering one. Having taken the unusual step of securing an in-person appointment with his prescribing physician (Drouet 'consultations' were generally conducted at a distance as per standard patent remedy practice), Yellon described his first impressions of Crippen's consulting rooms. He noted the prevalence of somewhat disconcerting pictures of anatomical subjects, and the prominence of a large operating chair. Yellon went on to describe his prospective physician in extravagant terms:

---

73 *Morning Post*, 8 March 1904.
74 'Action against *Truth*', *Daily Telegraph and Courier*, 5 November 1907.
75 *Globe*, 7 November 1907. The action seems to have provoked much merriment in court. When Dakhyl related how he had made £2000 in his first year of medical practice in Paris and was asked whether he had paid income tax on the sum, the presiding judge, Mr Justice Darling, weighed in: 'There is no income tax in Paris and I am thinking of going to live there. [Laughter]': *London Daily News*, 5 November 1907.

The man facing me was got up in a very fantastic fashion for a member of a learned and sober profession and an aural specialist. His frock coat was orthodox enough but he wore it with a shirt of startling hue, adorning the front of which was a 'diamond' as a big as a marble; and the jaunty butterfly tie vied in hue with the shirt. His patent leather shoes were a trifle cracked, and his face a warning to all observant beholders. The flabby gills, the shifty eyes, and the man's appearance generally, would effectually have prevented me from being taken in.[76]

Albeit some twenty-five years on from the early photograph portrait of Crippen reproduced earlier in this chapter, this description likewise presents a more ostentatious and self-possessed character than the Crippen who would be described by the Metropolitan Police in their 'wanted' bill of four years later as having a 'slovenly appearance'.[77] For all the challenges and business failures outlined above, here apparently was a Crippen still hustling and keeping up appearances. Indeed, the subsequent statement of his Drouet colleague William Long (who would later follow Crippen to the Yale Tooth specialists as his dental mechanic) reveals that, characteristically, Crippen was busy pursuing other money-making ventures while working at the institute, such as producing miniature paintings for sale, ascribed to the hand of 'Belle Elmore, Miniature Artist' (while in fact produced by colleagues from Drouet's and the defunct Sovereign Remedies company), and marketing a nerve tonic called 'Amorette'.[78] If Crippen and the Drouet Institute failed to command the confidence of Yellon and his readers, that pattern was repeated on sufficient scale for the enterprise to struggle, and the decisive blow was dealt by the adverse publicity arising from the death of a Staffordshire locksmith who died after self-administering a Drouet remedy.

In 1908, just as the Drouet Institute was folding, Crippen managed to recover

---

76   Evan Yellon, *Surdus in Search of His Hearing: An Exposure of Aural Quacks and a Guide to Genuine Treatments and Remedies, Electrical Aids, Lip-reading and Employments for the Deaf Etc Etc* (London: The Celtic Press, 1906), as cited in Cullen, *The Mild Murderer*, p. 49.

77   MEPO 3/198.

78   Statement of William Long, DPP 1/13. A search of the London newspapers from 1906 down to 1910 has not turned up a reference to 'Amorette', although competitors 'Nervaline', Coleman's 'Nervelettes' and Vend's 'Seaweed Tonic' appear. Perhaps Crippen's marketing method in respect of this product was principally word of mouth.

some favour with his old employer James Monroe Munyon and was re-engaged for one last stint with the company as London manager. The Munyon's offices had relocated since Crippen last worked for the company. No longer based in its opulent premises opposite the Palace Theatre on Shaftesbury Avenue, Munyon's had moved a short distance away to a busy office block, Albion House in New Oxford Street.

Albion House

A curious unity of setting distinguishes the Crippen case. Just as the vivid locations of 39 Hilldrop Crescent and the small steamship SS *Montrose* focus so many of the key scenes of the story, so, rather in the manner of a stage set, the setting of Albion House, New Oxford Street provides a distinct and compact backdrop for the crucial scenes in the last year of Cora Crippen's life. Both husband and wife converged on Albion House between 1908 and 1909: Crippen to establish his Yale Tooth Specialists and to finish up at Munyon's Remedies, and Belle to attend the weekly meetings of the charitable organisation with which she had become involved, the Music Hall Ladies' Guild.

The Crippens' path to Albion House had been forged by their respective professional disappointments. At much the same time as Crippen's fortunes waned with the decline of the Drouet Institute, Belle Elmore's uncertain music hall career also faltered. The unflattering portrait later painted by Filson Young in his edition of Crippen's trial proceedings is perhaps exaggerated, but it indicates the general trend of Belle's career as the decade wore on: 'From star appearances in a first-rate London music hall her ambitions dwindled down to appearances of any kind at any music hall...Mrs. Crippen's talents were so inadequate, and the failure was so obvious, that even these attempts (for which, of course, Dr. Crippen had to pay) were abandoned.'[79] The nadir of Belle's declining fortunes seems to have occurred in January 1907 when a dispute between music hall proprietors and performers was temporarily closing houses across the capital. The fading soubrette appears to have exploited the openings left by her striking colleagues, breaking the strike with appearances at the Bedford Music Hall and the Euston Palace of Varieties. At the latter venue, distressed by the audience's 'whistles, shrieks and catcalls', a

---

79   Filson Young, *Trial of Hawley Harvey Crippen*, p. xiii.

distressed Belle fled from the stage, to be comforted in the wings by popular actor Weldon Atherstone.[80] A possibly apocryphal story suggests she fared little better at the Bedford – it being suggested that music hall star and strike supporter Marie Lloyd had actively encouraged Belle to cross the theatre's picket line on the expectation that her appearance would inadvertently serve the strikers' cause: 'Let her in, and she'll empty the house!'[81] These experiences seem to have curtailed Belle's London stage appearances once and for all but, fortunately enough, a new avenue now presented itself in which she could continue to strive for some of the trappings of music hall celebrity by virtue of the company she kept. For in 1908, Belle became Honorary Treasurer of the Music Hall Ladies' Guild, a benevolent society established in autumn 1906 by stage veterans Lily Burnand and Lil Hawthorne. Modelled on the Theatrical Ladies' Guild which had been founded by Kitty Carson in 1891, the Music Hall Ladies' Guild garnered the support of retired music hall artistes Mrs Fred Ginnett, Mrs Fred Karno, and Mrs Kate Butler; its profile being elevated considerably by the election of the great Marie Lloyd as president. The guild aimed to provide 'assistance for the wives of artists who are in need of help through various causes', both in terms of financial assistance and also by means of access to resources, supplying baby clothes, toys, and books and even granting occasional shelter in a flat owned by Mrs Fred Karno and furnished by Lily Burnand.[82] Perhaps George R. Sims's assessment was correct that 'the theatrical profession is the most generous in the world. When it hears of a sad case, the more fortunate comrades of one who has fallen by

---

80 *Music Hall and Theatre Review*, 11 August 1910. In a curious twist of history, Atherstone would be murdered in July 1910 by an unknown assailant in Battersea. See further Richard Whittington-Egan, *Mr Atherstone Leaves the Stage: The Battersea Murder Mystery* (Stroud: Amberley, 2015), p. 134.

81 Cullen, *The Mild Murderer*, p. 56. Probably the story conflates more than one episode and was subsequently associated with Belle due to the infamy of Crippen and the proximity of Hilldrop Crescent. *The Era* confirms that the musicians and artists at the Bedford had been called out on strike in the last week of January ('The Music Hall Strike', Saturday 2 February 1907), while *The Daily Telegraph and Courier*'s report of a vociferous striker outside the Bedford summons a scene that might well have been enfolded into the Belle story: 'I happen to be on strike with my brother and sister artistes', said the striker. 'We don't all get the same salary as Miss Marie Lloyd.' ('Scene in Camden Town', 1 February 1907).

82 *The Era*, 20 October 1906 and 3 November 1906.

the wayside come to the rescue. A private subscription is made; a benefit is organised; the sympathy shown is whole-hearted, generous and practical.'[83] In support of such charitable endeavours guild members paid 2s and 6d annually, while the stricter requirements for committee members required that they be 'members of the music hall profession only' and must pay an annual subscription of £1 1s. In a stipulation that must have been attractive to Cora, members' clear affiliation with music hall was firmly preferred, though some flexibility was allowable at a cost: 'Ladies not connected with the music hall profession can be elected as honorary members of the Guild on payment of a donation of not less than 2s. 6d. and may attend the weekly sewing bee, the annual general meeting, and all social functions, but have no voting powers whatever.'[84] Engagement with the guild seems to have absorbed Cora and to have provided a new outlet for her energies and enthusiasms: 'It is quite four years since she ever went out to sing at halls,' said Crippen in 1910.[85]

It was in February 1909 that the office of Guild Secretary Melinda May relocated from an address in Covent Garden to Room 63 of Albion House, New Oxford Street – the very same premises from where Crippen's Yale Tooth Specialists and Munyon's Remedies operated.[86] This setting forms an important backdrop to the Crippen case for it is here that key episodes of the case played out between the protagonists. It was from Albion House that Crippen and mistress Ethel le Neve would walk out for long lunches, theatre trips, and other assignations. It was here that concerned friends of Cora Crippen would confront the doctor over their dissatisfaction at his account of her disappearance. It was here that Chief Inspector Dew would come calling to question Crippen and take his statement. And it was here that Ethel le Neve, her hair cut short, would assume her disguise in boy's clothes on the day the lovers absconded, William Long finding the pair's discarded clothes in an office cupboard on the following Monday morning. More immediately, it was here, on the very same floor of the building, that the Music Hall Ladies' Guild weekly Wednesday meetings were held – with the result that the two ladies

83   George R. Sims, *The Mysteries of London* (London: C. Arthur Pearson Ltd, 1906), p. 59.
84   *The Era*, 27 October 1906.
85   CRIM 1/117, indictment file, ex.39.
86   Guild Secretary Melinda May's recent change of address is notified in a call for charitable donations of clothing in the *Music Hall and Theatre Review* of 19 February 1909.

in Crippen's life, wife and mistress, were now brought into weekly proximity to one another. It lends a further theatrical aspect to an already curiously histrionic case that Belle and Ethel might now be brushing shoulders with one another in the stairwells and third-floor corridors of Albion House.

Perhaps, given the number of enterprises operating out of the New Oxford Street premises, they need not have bumped into each other too often. From suites 47 and 48, general investment brokers McKinley, Alexander and Sons practised; photographic equipment was sold from another suite; and yet another housed the London offices of the American Ted Snyder Music Publishing Company, publisher of 'American ditties' familiar from the London music hall stage.[87] Some of the more creative trading activities going on at Albion House suggest that Crippen must have found congenial company there. Press advertisements from 1909 encouraged, for example, Scottish readers to send a postal order for five shillings to Albion House should they wish to receive a correspondence course of instruction to have their accent 'Absolutely Corrected in a Few Weeks by a Method elaborated by a Scottish Gentleman'; balding readers were encouraged to apply to the same address to the private secretary of 'Spanish don' Jose Acuña, who would dispatch to them allegedly *gratis* bottles of 'a wonderful Hair Restorer, renowned in his family for years';[88] while ageing readers of *The Bystander* were advised of opportunities to learn the secrets of 'Madame Harriett Meta's Beauty Treatment' which purported to reduce facial wrinkles and improve skin tone within a mere eight hours: 'Her methods she will not reveal save only to her patrons, to whom it is imparted under a bond of secrecy. Write for an interview to Albion House, 61 New Oxford Street, W.C.'[89] The backers of these dubious, and in at least one case culturally affronting, enterprises must have been well known to Crippen and one wonders whether Aural Remedies proprietor Eddie Marr or even Crippen himself were behind them.

Crippen's own office in Albion House, room number 91, was staffed by his partner in the Yale Tooth Specialists, Gilbert Rylance, and long-term companion William Long. Ethel would work there until March 1910, when she would give up her role to become full-time housekeeper of an address that was shortly to become internationally famous.

87 *Referee*, 12 December 1909.
88 *Dundee Evening Telegraph*, 15 June 1909.
89 *The Bystander*, 23 June 1909.

39 Hilldrop Crescent

The four-storey Victorian house where Crippen spent his last years, where Cora's body would be found, and where doctor and mistress would live placidly over the remains for several months forms another of those elements of the case history that has passed into legend.[90] It was during Crippen's Drouet years that he and Cora moved from their flat in Store Street, Bloomsbury a short distance to North London. Crippen must have felt sufficiently secure in his position at Drouet's to sign a three-year contract on Hilldrop Crescent. He leased the property from landlord Frederick Lown on 21 September 1905 for £52 10s per year.

While the presence of nearby Holloway Gaol and the Caledonian Cattle Market served as reminders of a wider social composition, the recessed villas of the tree-lined Hilldrop Crescent enabled a certain measure of suburban retreat and comfort, even if Charles Booth's 1899 assessment of the area concluded that 'the district is going down'.[91] Writers on the case have speculated that this may well have dismayed Cora, as it would have dismayed another, albeit fictional, Holloway resident, familiar to Crippen's contemporaries since first appearing in the pages of *Punch* in 1888–9. Resemblances between Crippen and Charles Pooter, protagonist of George and Weedon Grossmith's *Diary of a Nobody* (1892), have been remarked by a number of writers on the case; Tom Cullen comments, for example, on the striking similarities between Pooter's Holloway residence 'The Laurels', with its 'little front garden and flight of ten steps up to the front door', and Crippen's comparable townhouse in Hilldrop Crescent,[92] both potential targets of H.G. Wells's 1909 description of 'endless streets of undistinguished houses, undistinguished industries, shabby families, inexplicable people'.[93] If the district had indeed declined since Pooter's day, this at least brought its rents within the means of London's theatricals, a number of whom settled in the area in the years preceding the case; indeed 37 Hilldrop

---

90 Demolished in the 1950s, the house has been described by Richard Whittington-Egan as existing 'like some Holmesian locus – Pondicherry Lodge or the Copper Beeches – only in the imagination, cosseting its secrets'. Foreword to Nicholas Connell's *Dr Crippen*, p. 9.

91 Larson, *Thunderstruck*, p. 189.

92 Cullen, *The Mild Murderer*, p. 14.

93 H.G. Wells, *Tono-Bungay* [1909] (London: Pan, 1972), p. 82. Appropriately enough, the subject of Wells's novel is the marketing of a patent medicine promising to promote health, beauty, and strength.

Crescent, the neighbouring house to the Crippens', was consistently advertising for tenants in the theatrical weekly *The Stage* between 1905 and 1906 – a congenial setting for 'Belle' and husband 'Peter' (the alternative name, useful to Crippen as a business alias, was likely suggested by Belle as his domestic soubriquet – certainly that is how most of the couple's friends referred to him).[94]

The layout of 39 Hilldrop Crescent, crucial to an understanding of the events that would unfold there, is carefully described by Erik Larson:

> Like all the others on the crescent, the Crippen's house had four storeys, including a basement level that, per custom, was used both for living space and for storage, with a coal cellar under the front steps and a kitchen and breakfast room toward the rear. The breakfast room was sunny and opened onto a long back garden surrounded by a brick wall.
>
> At the front of the house a flight of steps led to a large door fitted with a knocker of substantial heft and a knob mounted at the door's center, behind which lay sitting rooms and a dining room. […] The next floor up had another sitting room and two bedrooms; the fourth and final level had a bathroom and three more bedrooms, one at the front, two at the back.[95]

If the imposing Victorian frontage of the house and its dark, cramped coal cellar sit well with our now established associations of urban gothic, less conforming to type is the detail that most of the interior of the house had been decorated by Cora Crippen in a garish pink. This was not to the taste of Crippen chronicler Adeline Harrison, when she wrote about the house (and implicitly censured Belle's poor housekeeping) in *John Bull* in December 1910:

> They lived practically in the kitchen, which was always in a state of dirt and disorder. On the dresser was a heterogenous mass, consisting of dirty crockery, edibles, collars of the Doctor's, false curls of her own, hair-pins, brushes, letters, a gold-jewelled purse and other articles. The kitchener and gas stove were brown with rust and cooking stains. The table was littered with packages, saucepans, dirty knives, plates, flat-irons, a washing basin and a coffee pot. Thrown carelessly across a chair was a lovely white chiffon gown, embroidered with silk flowers and mounted over white glace.[96]

---

94 See for example *The Stage*, 27 September 1906, which advertises a well-furnished apartment in Number 37 and stresses proximity to the Holloway Empire.

95 Larson, *Thunderstruck*, p. 187.

96 *John Bull*, 10 December 1910.

There was briefly a servant or 'charwoman' in this disordered house, Rhoda Ray, who would attend the house from morning until early evening unless the Crippens were entertaining, in which case she would stay later.[97] Ray's tenure appears to have been short-lived, and none of the witness accounts of the couple's domestic life refer to their having kept a servant.

At least two lodgers are known to have stayed with the Crippens at Hilldrop Crescent, with their tenure at the house forming the subject of a good deal of poetic licence and elaborations in subsequent case histories. German student Karl Reinisch appears to have been the first to take lodgings at Hilldrop Crescent, being ensconced in the ménage in time for Christmas 1905, when Crippen made his wife a gift of a gramophone. Reinisch described Belle as somewhat childlike, still nursing her theatrical ambitions, competitive at card games, and responsive to flattery. He described the husband as gentlemanly, solicitous, and attentive to Belle's every need: 'He idolised his wife, and sensed her every wish which he struggled to fulfil.'[98] It was hardly a picture of a couple at loggerheads. Despite this comfortable sojourn with the Crippens, Reinisch was obliged to quit his billet in June 1906 to make way for a visit from Belle's half-sister, Louise Mills.[99] He was to be replaced in December 1906 by another German student, Richard Ehrlich, whose tenure coincided with two other lodgers of whom few details are known. Ehrlich, who remained with the Crippens until April 1907, paying a weekly rent of 24s, would subsequently report having detected a decidedly tense atmosphere between husband and wife in the North London townhouse:

> He declares that Mrs Crippen was extremely desirous of returning to the stage, which she had abandoned as a condition precedent to her marriage.... This gentleman further says she frequently gave way to ill-temper, which led to painful discussions. Her husband, however, rarely lost his temper. Even when he was the subject of unjust remarks, he minimized the troubles, spoke gently, and allowed the storm to pass. He appeared to be exerting great self-control. His lips would go white and his hands involuntarily clench but he never raised them.[100]

97   Statement of Rhoda Ray, DPP 1/13.
98   MEPO 2/10996.
99   David James Smith, *Supper with the Crippens*, p. 82.
100 'The Crippens' Domestic Life', *Western Morning News*, 6 August 1910.

Tom Cullen's 1977 case history posits a liaison between young Ehrlich and the increasingly frustrated Belle. With no known historical source or external support, the episode is depicted as taking place in late 1906 and involves Crippen walking in upon the illicit scene when he pops home unexpectedly to retrieve some copies of *The Otological Gazette*. The dramatic scene is narrated by Cullen in the historic present: 'Crippen returns home unexpectedly, and lets himself in by the side door as is his habit…Then he starts up the stairs, but noiselessly, avoiding the steps that creak…Just as noiselessly he turns the handle on the bedroom door. Does he not know what awaits him on the other side? Belle in bed with the German lodger.'[101] Perhaps Cullen's change of tense in presenting the episode is designed to signal a piece of poetic licence, for there is no historical verification of the bawdy scene Crippen encounters on this unexpected return home. Not that this has prevented its entering the Crippen legend: it has featured in all fictional retellings since the 1960s, including the recent novelisations by John Boyne and Martin Edwards, and the episode even found its way into Crippen's entry in the *Dictionary of National Biography*.[102]

Aside from a small number of reports of sharp words and tense moods between husband and wife, the household appears to have been an open and accommodating one: in addition to taking in lodgers for a spell in 1905–6, the odd couple hosted sufficient gatherings for house-guests to comment in later memoirs on the furnishings of the house, the household pets (two cats and later a bull terrier), and even Belle's taste for attaching pink ribbons to ornaments and picture frames. They equally remarked on the attentiveness of the husband, his quiet submission to her, and his ongoing willingness to support and bankroll her theatrical activities.

Indeed, at least one vignette of life at Hilldrop Crescent, relayed at Crippen's trial, very much paints a picture of merriment and good cheer. Melinda May

---

101 Cullen, *The Mild Murderer*, p. 79.
102 Cullen's suggestion of Belle's intrigue with the lodger has no verifiable source, though in 1938 Harold Eaton offered speculation on Belle's infidelity: 'Though one hesitates to make the imputation, it seems likely that she was not faithful to her husband' – Harold Eaton, 'The Crime of the Century: Crippen and the Belle Elmore', in *The Fifty Most Amazing Cases of the Last 100 Years* (London: Odhams Press, 1936), p. 103. This has been relayed as fact in subsequent accounts, including Pauline Chapman, *Madame Tussaud's Chamber of Horrors* (London: Constable, 1984), case summaries in crime compendia, and even as reputable a source as the *Dictionary of National Biography*.

was later to recount how she and fellow guild members Lil Hawthorne and
her husband, theatrical manager John Nash, spent New Year's Eve 1909 with
the Crippens, where they were served American cocktails made by Belle and
where the small party assembled on the steps of Hilldrop Crescent to see in
the new year:

> At midnight the street door was opened, and there, at the top of the flight
> of steps which led up to the entrance from the garden path, we stood – the
> doctor, his wife, Miss Hawthorne and her husband, and myself – to listen to
> the hooting of sirens, the ringing of church bells, the hammering of trays,
> and the rest of the strangely moving noises that are made by the watchers
> who hail the New Year.[103]

Such was the *modus vivendi* of the Crippens in January 1910, but three portents
occurring at the turn of that year suggested that life at Hilldrop Crescent would
not continue long in this established pattern. First, according to a statement
deposed by Melinda May at the inquest on Cora Crippen, though not at
Crippen's trial, Belle had told her that at Christmas 'she woke up in the middle
of the night with a curious strangling sensation, and said to Dr. Crippen, "Fetch
a priest; I am going to die."'[104] The curiously proleptic episode might have
been premonition or might even betray a first murder attempt. If, as some
writers have speculated, Belle's alarming symptoms were produced by the
administration of hyoscine, it must have been a different consignment from
that which killed her since Crippen is known to have purchased the latter dose
in mid-January 1910.

The second portent, another nocturnal episode, was related by Ethel's
landlady, Emily Jackson of 80 Constantine Road, Hampstead, at the inquest
and at Ethel's own brief trial as accessory to murder. Jackson recounted how,
late in January, Ethel appeared to be depressed: her lodger was quiet, lacked
appetite, and kept to her room. When one evening Jackson followed her to
her room to press her as to the cause, Ethel's agitation increased to fever
pitch: she trembled, clawed at her hair, and stared fixedly at a corner of her
bedroom before exclaiming: 'It is Miss Elmore!… She is his wife you know.
When I see them go away together it makes me realise what my position is…

---

103 *Survivors' Tales of Famous Crimes*, ed. Walter Wood (London: Cassell, 1916), p. 263.
104 'The Crippen Case: Inquest Resumed', *Nottingham Evening Post*, 12 September 1910.

She has been threatening to go away with another man and that is all we are waiting for.'[105] Some case histories have speculated that Ethel, who had been wearing an engagement ring since December, was party to a sinister secret, others that her nerves were so highly wrought at the prospect of a long-awaited change being finally at hand. Either way, it seems clear that Ethel anticipated an imminent dramatic development that winter.

The last of these indications of a dynamic or unfolding situation was the notice given by Cora Crippen on 15 December 1909 of her intention to withdraw the total balance of £600 from the deposit account she and Crippen had jointly held with the Charing Cross Bank since March 1906. The assistant manager of the bank would later testify at Crippen's trial that while the account was in both names, the bank would have paid over the amount without the signature of her husband. A one-year notice period applied: in December 1910 the funds would become available. Whether this withdrawal notice represented contingency planning by Belle alone or by the couple working in tandem will never be known. Either way, it indicated that a change was soon to come.

---

105 *Trial of Hawley Harvey Crippen*, p. 198.

CHAPTER FOUR

'ONLY A LITTLE SCANDAL': AN OUTLINE OF THE CRIPPEN CASE

The story as the Edwardian reading public would come to know it began in the late afternoon of 31 January 1910. Between 4 and 5pm that Monday, Crippen called at the address of friends Paul and Clara Martinetti on Shaftesbury Avenue to extend an invitation to dinner at Hilldrop Crescent. Mutual friends of the Crippens for some eighteen months, the American expatriate couple were retired music hall artistes. Paul was a veteran of the music stage whose own troupe of artistes included wife Clara, and who had been billed as 'the Prince of Pantomime Artists' as recently as 1905.[1] Clara was active alongside Cora in the Music Hall Ladies' Guild. When Crippen called to invite the couple to an impromptu 'pot-luck dinner' on that January afternoon, Paul was out attending a doctor's appointment and Clara demurred, not knowing how her husband might be feeling on his return. Crippen was insistent, suggesting an evening assembled at Hilldrop Crescent amongst company would prove just the tonic he needed: 'we'll cheer him up after dinner and have a game of whist.' Clara agreed that she would ask Paul on his return from the doctor's around six o'clock and Crippen, with rather curious persistence, said he would come back at the same time to see Paul for himself (the possibility that Crippen was pressing the invitation in order to enlist witnesses or alibis to some predetermined scheme will be explored below). In the event, the couple were prevailed upon to brave the cold January air for the prospect of a convivial evening in

---

1   *London and Provincial Entr'acte*, 22 April 1905.

Camden; they took a motor bus and then a tram to Hilldrop Crescent, finding Belle and Crippen at the door when they arrived at about eight in the evening.

'There were just four of us there', recalled Clara Martinetti at the trial. The small party had dinner in the breakfast room next to the kitchen before repairing upstairs to the parlour. 'We spent the evening playing cards… It was quite a nice evening.'[2] Clara's rather anodyne account is surprising given how most literary adaptations of the story have depicted the small gathering as the dinner party from hell, the hosting couple playing out deep-seated domestic grievances and tensions before their embarrassed guests (see Chapter Six). Yet there does seem to have been at least one sour note struck during the evening, when the already below-par Paul Martinetti returned from an unchaperoned trip to the top floor lavatory having caught a chill: 'he went into a certain room where there was a window open.' If, as has been speculated, Belle publicly upbraided Crippen for not playing the host more attentively, the reproach does not seem to have abbreviated the evening's proceedings too severely: it was half past one before the Martinettis left in a cab which Crippen had procured for them. Clara bade Belle farewell at the top of the house steps and urged her not to follow her down lest she catch a cold in the January night air. It was the last time Cora Crippen, or Belle Elmore, or Kunigunde Mackamotzki, was seen alive.

According to Crippen's trial testimony, Belle immediately became angry on the departure of their guests: 'my wife got into a very great rage with me, and blamed me for not having gone upstairs with Mr. Martinetti. She said a great many things – I do not recollect them all – she abused me, and said some pretty strong words to me.'[3] The upshot of the diatribe, according to Crippen, was Belle's declared intention to leave him the next day. But with the departure of the Martinettis and with them any source of verification of this claim, already we have crossed the threshold into Crippen's potential fictions and elaborations; just how fertile this speculative terrain has proven for crime novelists will be the subject of later chapters. What appears certain is that Crippen murdered Cora in the early hours of the morning, most likely by oral administration of the hyoscine he had purchased on 19 January from Lewis and Burrows' chemists. Possibly this had been administered during

2   Filson Young (ed.), *The Trial of Hawley Harvey Crippen* (Edinburgh and London: William Hodge, 1920), p. 13.
3   Ibid., p. 90.

the dinner party with the expectation that Cora would fall ill and die from apparent heart failure or apoplexy while in company with the Martinettis, or even while Crippen was absent procuring a cab to take the guests home. It is possible, from later reports from neighbours of hearing gunfire, and from Walter Dew's subsequent discovery of a revolver in a bedroom wardrobe at Hilldrop Crescent, that Crippen shot his wife when the hyoscine failed to work as predicted, perhaps causing Belle to become delirious. The exact details will remain forever a mystery: 'precisely what happened next was Crippen's secret', Martin Fido has observed, 'and he took it to the grave with him.'[4]

Witnesses would subsequently concur that Crippen was all self-possession and calm, his usual demeanour, the next morning. On 1 February 1910 he went to work as usual at Albion House, though today to focus solely on Yale Tooth Specialists business, his role with Munyon's having ceased. He seems to have spoken with new Munyon's manageress Marion Curnow, however, who noted nothing unusual about his behaviour or bearing that morning.[5] Later in the day, Crippen called again on the Martinettis in Shaftesbury Avenue to enquire after Paul's health. Clara reported that her husband was still in bed and asked in turn after Belle – 'Oh, she is all right', came the terse reply.

It was now Tuesday. Belle, as Honorary Treasurer of the Music Hall Ladies' Guild, would be expected at Albion House the following afternoon for the weekly Wednesday meeting. When the meeting convened as usual in Albion House, Guild Secretary Melinda May was thus surprised to find the Treasurer absent. The committee meeting was already underway when shortly before 1pm Ethel le Neve appeared at the door of the guild's meeting room with a pass book, deposit book, cheque book, and two letters signed in the name of Belle but not in her hand. The first was addressed to May as Secretary:

39 Hilldrop Crescent, February 2nd

Dear Miss May,
    Illness of a near relative has called me to America on only a few hours' notice, so I must ask you to bring my resignation as treasurer before the meeting to-day, so that a new treasurer can be elected at once. You will appreciate my haste when I tell you that I have not been to bed all night packing, and getting ready to go. I shall hope to see you again in a few

4   Martin Fido, *A Passion for Killing* [Audiobook] (Watford: MCI Spoken Word, 1998).
5   *Trial of Hawley Harvey Crippen*, p. 29.

months later, but cannot spare a moment to call on you before I go. I wish you everything nice till I return to London again.

Now, good-bye, with love hastily,
Yours, Belle Elmore, p.p. H.H.C.

The second letter was addressed to the full committee of the Music Hall Ladies' Guild. It included scant further detail to account for this sudden departure overseas:

39 Hilldrop Crescent, London, N.

To the Committee of the Music Hall Ladies' Guild

Dear Friends,

Please forgive me a hasty letter and any inconvenience I may cause you, but I have just had news of the illness of a near relative and at only a few hours' notice I am obliged to go to America. Under the circumstances I cannot return for several months, and therefore beg you to accept this as a formal letter resigning from this date my hon. Treasurership of the M.H.L.G. I am enclosing the cheque book and deposit book for the immediate use of my successor, and to save any delay I beg to suggest that you vote to suspend the usual rules of election and elect to-day a new honorary treasurer. I hope some months later to be with you again, and in the meantime wish the Guild every success and ask my good friends and pals to accept my sincere and loving wishes for their own personal welfare.

Believe me, yours faithfully,
Belle Elmore.[6]

'We were at once suspicious that something was wrong,' guild Vice-President Louise Smythson later recollected,[7] but no further information was to be had by quizzing Crippen, who had made himself absent from Albion House that afternoon (Ethel's memoir suggests he may have been attending his Aural Remedies business in Kingsway instead). The committee members' disquiet only deepened over the following weeks, while Belle's friends waited fruitlessly for any further communication from her. Dr John Burroughs, the honorary physician to the guild, and his wife Maud 'were daily expecting a letter or card from her. Maud could not understand it, as Belle always wrote her on

6   CRIM 1/117, Indictment, Exhibit 34.
7   *Daily Mail*, 18 July 1910.

such important occasions, so could only think Belle wanted to cut all her old friends.'[8]

According to Ethel's reminiscences, Crippen returned to Albion House about 4pm that day – by which time it appears the guild's meeting had safely broken up – and astonished his secretary by producing from his pocket a handful of jewels and asking her to pick a selection for her own keeping: 'I should like to know you had some good jewellery. They will be useful when we are dining out.'[9] Rather less sentimentally, those jewels Ethel passed up were carted by Crippen that same afternoon to Attenborough's pawnbrokers at 142 Oxford Street, where he secured an £80 loan against a diamond ring and set of diamond earrings.

If these actions implied Crippen's confidence that his absent wife would not be returning, her friends were increasingly agitated at her lack of contact with them. A week after Belle's apparent departure, Clara Martinetti took the opportunity to quiz Crippen for further details:

> I said, 'Did she take all her clothes with her?' He said, 'No, only one basket.' I said, 'Only one basket! She won't have enough.' He said, 'Oh, she can buy herself some more over there. I said, 'They are rather more expensive over there.' He shrugged his shoulders and did not say anything. I said, 'Oh, she is sure to send me a postcard from the ship.' He nodded his head and then he left.[10]

When Clara had still not received her expected postcard a week later, she asked for further details of her itinerary and suggested she might hear when she landed in New York: 'Oh, she does not touch New York, she is going straight on to California.'[11]

It is clear from subsequent accounts and memoirs that during these early weeks of February rumour and innuendo were building regarding Belle's mysterious disappearance, her lack of communication only heightening the atmosphere of speculation. Had guild members been aware that Ethel le Neve had stayed at Hilldrop Crescent on the night of 2 February and that Crippen

8   Connell, *Doctor Crippen*, p. 20.
9   *Ethel Le Neve: Her Life Story with the True Account of their Flight and her Friendship for Dr. Crippen* (London: Publishing Office, 1910), pp. 17–18.
10 CRIM 1/117 Brief for the prosecution.
11 Ibid.

had pawned more of Belle's jewellery on 9 February, there would have been still more matter to stimulate wagging tongues. Something of a field day for the swelling tide of gossip would be provided towards the end of the month when Crippen and Le Neve appeared together at the Music Hall Ladies' Benevolent Fund's Ball, held at the Criterion Restaurant, Piccadilly Circus. Clara Martinetti related that Crippen had initially been reluctant to attend the event scheduled for 20 February 1910 but warmed to her suggestion that Paul Martinetti could organise tickets for him: 'All right, I will take two.'[12] The event was much heralded in the theatrical press with chair of the event Eugene Stratton writing in *The Stage* to encourage attendance at the dinner and dance at the Criterion: 'I shall take it as a personal favour if you will strain a point to rally round me on that night and make it a record in the annals of music-hall history.'[13]

That the evening rather qualified for inclusion in the annals of criminal history was largely due to Crippen's continued evasiveness concerning Belle and the sartorial choices of Ethel le Neve that night. While Crippen continued to prevaricate under the questions of Guild Vice-President Louise Smythson concerning Belle's address in America ('he said she was right up in the wilds of the mountains of California'),[14] Ethel drew attention by sporting a 'rising sun' brooch which had belonged to Belle and while Clara Martinetti was tentative in identifying it at the trial ('I only thought that Mrs Crippen wore it but I am not sure') others were more certain of the identification.[15]

Approaching a month after Belle's disappearance, Ethel appeared to have usurped both her place at Crippen's side and her wardrobe. Her memoirs are defensive about the night at the Criterion ('Some people have said that I went to the ball in one of Belle Elmore's frocks. Nothing of the kind!')[16] but the episode would later be taken in conjunction with other reported sightings of Ethel in Belle's clothes – in the street, at the theatre, and in the front room of Hilldrop Crescent under the somewhat prying gaze of a neighbour: 'she noticed Miss Le Neve in an upper room trying on costumes which she had previously seen on Mrs. Crippen. They were being handed to her by Crippen from a large luggage

---

12 *Trial of Hawley Harvey Crippen*, p. 14.
13 'Mr. Eugene Stratton's Appeal', *The Stage*, 17 February 1910.
14 *Trial of Hawley Harvey Crippen*, p. 17.
15 Ibid., p. 14.
16 *Ethel Le Neve*, p. 24.

7.   The Criterion, Piccadilly Circus, where Crippen and Ethel attended
        the Music Hall Benevolent Fund Ball on 20 February 1910.

basket such as is used by theatrical people on tour.'[17] The neighbour's recollection might date from as early as March 1910 as from the 12th of that month,
Ethel gave up her post at the Yale Tooth Specialists and moved into Hilldrop
Crescent, quitting the Hampstead lodgings she had occupied since 1908 with
landlady Emily Jackson. With Ethel now installed as the new mistress of the
house, and as the year moved on towards Easter, Crippen took the story of
Belle's disappearance into a new phase. On Sunday 20 March, he wrote to the
last people who had seen Belle Elmore alive, Paul and Clara Martinetti:

39, Hilldrop Crescent, N.

Sunday, Mar. 20/10

Dear Clara and Paul,
      Please forgive me not running in during the week, but I have been so
upset by very bad news from Belle that I did not feel equal to talking about
anything, and now I have had a cable saying she is so dangerously ill with

17   *Daily Mail*, 16 July 1910.

double pleuro-pneumonia that I am considering if I had not better go over at once. I do not want to worry you with my troubles, but I felt I must explain why I have not been to see you. I will try and run in during the week and have a chat. Hope both of you are well. With love and best wishes.

Yours sincerely

Peter.[18]

Crippen had still not 'run in' on the couple by the time of the regular Wednesday meeting of the Music Hall Ladies' Guild and thus, following the meeting on 23 March, Clara Martinetti and fellow guild member Annie Stratton crossed the corridor of Albion House to quiz Crippen further in his office. He reiterated the story of the telegram and suggested that so grim was the prognosis, he expected at any moment to receive another with still graver news. If this were to happen, he told them, he was minded to travel to France for a week 'to have a change of air'.[19]

The next day, Clara herself received a telegram dispatched by Crippen from Victoria station: 'Belle died yesterday at six o'clock. Please 'phone to Annie [Stratton]. Shall be away a week. Peter.'[20] While Crippen and Le Neve were making their Easter sojourn in Dieppe, word of Belle's passing quickly spread within the guild and it was formalised by a short death notice appearing in *The Era* on 26 March: 'Elmore – March 23 in California, U.S.A., Miss Belle Elmore (Mrs H.H. Crippen)'.[21] Their well wishes and attempts to pay their respects to the deceased were to put further pressure on Crippen on his return from the continent. On 5 April guild physician Dr John Burroughs wrote to Crippen offering his condolences and requesting the address of Belle's sister in New York so that he might send her a letter of condolence. Crippen's evasive reply, written on black-edged mourning paper, was as follows:

My dear Doctor,

I feel sure you will forgive me for my apparent neglect, but really I have been nearly out of my mind with poor Belle's death so far away. She was not with her sister, but out in California on business for me, and, quite like her disposition, would keep up when she should have been in bed, with the

18   CRIM 1/117 Indictment file, ex.32.
19   CRIM 1/117 Brief for the prosecution.
20   CRIM 1/117 Indictment file, ex.32.
21   CRIM 1/117, Indictment file, ex.50.

consequence that pleuro-pneumonia terminated fatally. Almost to the last she refused to let me know there was any danger. So that the cable that she had gone came as a most awful shock to me. I fear I have sadly neglected my friends, but pray forgive, and believe me to be most truly appreciative of your sympathy. Even now I am not fit to talk to my friends, but as soon as I feel I can control myself I will run in on you and Maud one evening. I am, of course, giving up the house, and every night packing things away. With love, to both, and again thanking you for your kindness, I am, as ever, yours.
    Peter[22]

It seems likely that Burroughs's letter prompted Crippen's realisation that he had better inform Belle's family of the version of events he was now broadcasting. Accordingly, he wrote to Belle's step-sister Louise Mills and husband Robert in New York with his fullest written account of her death:

My Dear Louise and Robert,
    I hardly know how to write to you of my dreadful loss. The shock to me has been so dreadful that I am hardly able to control myself. My poor Cora is gone, and, to make the shock to me more dreadful, I did not even see her at the last. A few weeks ago we had news that an old relative of mine in California was dying, and, to secure important property for ourselves, it was necessary for one of us to go and put the matter into a lawyer's hands at once. As I was very busy, Cora proposed she should go, and as it was necessary for some one to be there at once, she would go straight through from here to California without stopping at all and then return by way of Brooklyn, and she would be able to pay all of you a long visit. Unfortunately, on the way my poor Cora caught a severe cold, and not having while travelling taken proper care of herself, it has settled on her lungs, later to develop into pleuro-pneumonia. She wished not to frighten me, so kept writing not to worry about her and it was only a slight matter, and the next I heard by cable was that she was dangerously ill, and two days later after I cabled to know should I go to her I had the dreadful news that she had passed away. Imagine if you can the dreadful shock to me – never more to see my Cora alive nor hear her voice again. She is being sent back to me, and I shall soon have what is left of her here. Of course, I am giving up the house; in fact, it drives me mad to be in it alone, and I will sell out everything in a few days. I do not know what I shall do, but probably find some business to take me travelling for a few months

22   CRIM 1/117 Indictment file ex.31.

until I recover from the shock a little, but as soon as I have a settled address again I will write again to you. As it is so terrible to me to have to write this dreadful news, will you please tell all the others of our loss. Love to all. Write soon again, and give you my address probably next in France.

From Doctor.

Maintaining a consistent version of events in both oral and written modes proved challenging for Crippen, especially when pressed for further details of Belle's last movements; the place and time of her death; and the fate of her mortal remains. When Clara Martinetti enquired after the name of the steamer on which Belle had sailed, Crippen prevaricated, finally suggesting 'a French ship with a name like La Tourenne'.[23] Likewise, when Clara and Louise Smythson on behalf of the ladies of the guild pressed him for a family address to which they might send a wreath, he was similarly evasive, suggesting that Belle's association with the guild would not be known to her American relatives, but at last reluctantly giving the address of his son Otto in California. Their subsequent letter of condolence brought a baffled response from Otto, whose letter of 9 May replied: 'The death of my stepmother was as great a surprise to me as to anyone. She died in San Francisco and the first I heard of it was through my father who wrote to me immediately afterward. He said he had through a mistake given out my name and address as my Stepmother's death place.'[24]

Crippen's efforts to enlist his son in the smokescreen around Cora's disappearance only delayed the inevitable. It was clear that his cover story was slowly unravelling and that the suspicions of Belle's theatrical friends were coming to a head. Accordingly, a confrontation awaited Crippen upon his return from another brief sojourn to the continent with Ethel, this time to procure the services of a French housemaid (another sign of Ethel's domestic pretensions as new mistress of Hilldrop Crescent). At Albion House, the doctor received a particularly uncomfortable visit from theatrical manager John Nash and his wife, Music Hall Ladies' Guild committee member Lillian Nash (known on the music hall stage as Lil Hawthorne). The Nashes had been good friends of the Crippens and had last seen Belle when the four had dined together at the Nashes' house on 19 January. After learning of Belle's resignation from

23   Young, *Trial*, p. 15.
24   CRIM 1/117.

the guild on 2 February, but apparently not grasping the suggestion that she had already left for America, the couple even went round to Hilldrop Crescent on the night of Saturday 6 February to try to dissuade her from resigning, but found the place dark and shut up.[25] Early in May, following Lil's run of appearances at the Tottenham Empire, the couple had travelled to New York, where they received a letter from Clara Martinetti with news of Belle's death. Their dissatisfied response resonated with that of Music Hall Ladies' Guild former president Mrs. Fred Ginnett, now living in New Jersey. Ginnett's enquiries that spring secured police confirmation 'that no such person as Belle Elmore or Mrs. Crippen had died at Los Angeles'.[26] Departing from New York, the Nashes had left Ginnett on the quayside with a promise to pursue the matter with Crippen on their return, and thus their appearance at Albion House on 28 June to offer condolences but also to press firmly for the precise details of Belle's funeral and cremation. Nash's description of the meeting captures his incredulity at Crippen's not knowing the particulars of his wife's death. That she had been cremated was difficult to reconcile with her Catholic denomination; that Crippen could produce no certificate from the crematorium was even more troubling:

> NASH: Peter, do you mean to say you don't know where your wife has died?
>
> CRIPPEN: I can't remember, I think it was Alamaio.
>
> NASH: I hear you have received her ashes?
>
> CRIPPEN: Yes, they're at home in my safe, as we had decided to be cremated.
>
> NASH: Where was she cremated?
>
> CRIPPEN: There are about four cemeteries about San Francisco and it was one of these but I cannot tell you which one.
>
> NASH: Surely, you received a certificate?[27]

The lack of any documentary verification for Crippen's version of events was increasingly troubling Cora's friends. A private detective employed by the guild could find no record of her departure by steamship from an English port. No

25   'Miss Belle Elmore's Death', *Era*, 23 July 1910.
26   'North London Crime – Inquest Opened', *Daily Telegraph and Courier*, 19 July 1910.
27   DPP 1/13.

one within her circle had received any correspondence from her transatlantic passage or arrival in the States. There was no sign of the telegrams Crippen claimed to have received notifying his wife's illness and subsequent death. There was no certification of her decease and the disposal of her remains. Small wonder that the Nashes went straight from their unsatisfactory interview with Crippen to Scotland Yard, where they made an appointment two days hence with their friend Chief Superintendent Frank Froest. Their visit had in fact been anticipated on 31 March by guild Vice-President Louise Smythson, who had attended the Yard's premises on the Embankment to report her suspicions, telling an unnamed officer 'the whole story of the different tales Crippen had told us, also of the incident at the ball with his typist and the brooch she wore'.[28] Apparently advised that nothing could be done unless she preferred a specific charge, Smythson had departed dissatisfied.

The Nashes' interview on 30 June with Superintendent Frank Froest was more productive of results. Froest called Chief Inspector Walter Dew into his office to hear the Nashes' lengthy tale of the missing variety performer, the evasive husband and his mistress. Rather curiously, Dew's memoirs suggested 'it is quite certain that neither of them dreamt for a moment that there was anything very sinister behind the affair'.[29] Perhaps this rather reflected his own first impressions, for a further week would elapse before he followed up on their visit by calling at Hilldrop Crescent to question Crippen.

According to Ethel le Neve, now firmly established in residence, it was approximately half-past nine on Friday 8 July when the Detective Inspector and Sgt Arthur Mitchell arrived on the doorstep of 39 Hilldrop Crescent. They were greeted by recently appointed housemaid Valentine LeCoq, who spoke little English and who led the officers to believe that Dr Crippen was at home, even though he had in fact left for the office soon after 8am. Admitted to the hall, Dew and Mitchell then met Ethel le Neve, who was sporting, Dew noticed, the same rising sun brooch that had formed such a talking point at the Criterion ball back in the winter. Dew and Ethel's respective accounts of the meeting make an interesting study in contrasts. According to Dew, Ethel described

28   *The Performer*, 21 July 1910. David James Smith notes: 'There is no coherent version of precisely why [Smythson] went and whom she saw.' *Supper with the Crippens*, p. 133.

29   Walter Dew, *I Caught Crippen* (London and Glasgow: Blackie and Son, 1938). Perhaps Dew was seeking the biggest possible contrast in mood between the tenor of the story pre and post the discovery in the Hilldrop Crescent coal cellar.

8.   Scotland Yard, where Inspector Dew was set on Crippen's
trail by concerned friends of Belle, John and Lillian Nash.

herself defensively as the housekeeper and a 'faint flush' rose to her cheeks
when the Inspector immediately identified her and insisted that she escort
them to Albion House to meet Crippen, forbidding her to phone ahead. In
Ethel's self-presentation she was much more self-possessed in the presence of
the policemen and 'had no compunction in making them wait a good long time'
while she dressed properly to escort them to Albion House.[30]

Rather oddly, given Dew's insistence that Ethel should not telephone ahead,
upon arrival at Albion House, he allowed Ethel to go up to the third floor alone
so that she might bring Crippen down to meet him on the stairwell. Crippen,
Mitchell, and Dew then went upstairs together where, as Dew later relayed at
the trial, a crucial turning point was reached in Crippen's account of his wife's
disappearance:

'I am Chief Inspector Dew, of Scotland Yard, and this is Sergeant Mitchell.
Some of your wife's friends have been to us concerning the stories you have

30   *Ethel Le Neve*, p. 30.

told them about her death, with which they are not satisfied. I have made exhaustive enquiries and I am not satisfied, so I have come to see you to ask if you care to offer any explanation.' He said, 'I suppose I had better tell the truth... The stories I have told them about her death are untrue. As far as I know, she is still alive.'[31]

In the lengthy statement that Crippen, 'in a quiet and confident voice',[32] went on to produce on that Friday afternoon in July, he painted a new picture of Belle having left him for another man – Bruce Miller, he believed. Unable to face the scandal, the cuckolded husband had confected the story of Belle's departure to tend an ailing relative before falling ill and dying herself. With Dew posing the questions and Mitchell taking down Crippen's answers, the composition of the statement proved to be a lengthy affair. Indeed, only the introduction had been set down by lunchtime and thus, in a bizarre episode much favoured by later novelists, policemen and suspect repaired together to a nearby Italian restaurant to take lunch, neglecting to invite Ethel, who reports, 'I became very hungry.'[33] Dew noted that Crippen 'ordered beefsteak and ate it with the relish of a man who hadn't a care in the world'.[34]

Whatever bonhomie was cultivated over lunch, serious business resumed in the afternoon and evening of that Friday. Having finished compiling Crippen's statement, Dew, Mitchell, Crippen, and Le Neve drove in a taxi-cab to Hilldrop Crescent so that the detectives could make a search of the property. Ethel reports how she sat in the sitting-room until dusk while the long search was conducted: 'What were these men doing? Would they never go?'[35] Dew, in contrast, reports that both Crippen and Le Neve escorted them on their search of the majority of the house, though they left them to venture alone into the coal cellar:

Both had followed Mitchell and me down the passage, and as I struck matches, poked around and sounded the flooring with my feet, they stood side by side in the doorway.

31   *Trial*, p. 34.
32   *I Caught Crippen*, p. 13.
33   *Ethel Le Neve*, p. 35.
34   *I Caught Crippen*, p. 15.
35   *Ethel Le Neve*, p. 36.

What were Crippen's thoughts at that moment? Only he among us knew that Mitchell and I were actually standing on what remained of Mrs. Crippen.

I am not at all sure that I should now be alive to tell the tale had I at that moment discovered the cellar's grim secret.

I believe that as Crippen watched us with such apparent unconcern he had a loaded revolver in his pocket, and that revolver would have been used upon Mitchell and myself had we made the find which Crippen feared.[36]

Finding nothing in the cellar (for now) or anywhere else in the house, Dew and Mitchell made ready to leave, but the Chief Inspector warned the doctor that he would have to find Mrs. Crippen in order to clear the matter up. The ever-resourceful Crippen suggested he might place a press advertisement calling for Belle to come forward and resolve the situation. Dew watched the doctor draft the text, which ran as follows:

Mackamotzki
Will Belle Elmore communicate with H.H.C. or Authorities at once.
Serious trouble through your absence. £25 reward.
Anyone communicating whereabouts to …[37]

The draft advert was on the mantlepiece of Hilldrop Crescent when Dew and Mitchell departed around 8pm, almost twelve hours after their arrival. It was to be Crippen and Ethel's last night at the property. Ethel's account of that night and the following morning relates a frosty supper between the lovers (claiming that the revelation that Belle was still alive was as much news to her as it had been to Dew), and a momentous conversation the following morning. Now that it was known that Crippen had lied there would be 'a tremendous scandal', its fervour stoked by the venerable ladies of the guild. The Albion House office would be a place of constant trial; the only solution was to go away and 'leave all these prying people' until the whole affair had blown over.[38]

Dependable Crippen associate William Long was enlisted in the couple's

---

36 *I Caught Crippen*, p. 22.
37 CRIM 1/117, indictment: Ex.41.
38 *Ethel Le Neve*, p. 39. While Dew's visit to Crippen clearly occasioned his flight, there are signs that he had originally intended to quit Hilldrop Crescent earlier in the year, having given notice to landlord Frederick Lown back in March. When the three-month notice period elapsed in June, Crippen had asked Lown if he might remain until September.

escape plan when he arrived at Albion House between 9 and 9.15am on Saturday 9 July, though it appears Long was told little about the exact circumstances and Crippen downplayed the trouble he was in as 'only a little scandal'.[39] Long was tasked with buying a brown tweed suit, a brown felt hat, two shirts, two collars, a tie, and a pair of boots. He reports seeing Ethel at Albion House at around 11.30am and he last saw Crippen around 1pm, unaware that it was the last time he would set eyes on him until he stood in the Old Bailey dock the following November.[40]

Munyon's manageress Marion Curnow was also approached by Crippen with a request that busy Saturday morning. Crippen asked her to lodge two envelopes in the shared office safe, asking her to disavow knowledge of them 'if anyone should ask you' and to pass them to Ethel Le Neve 'if anything should happen to me'.[41] Opened by Curnow the following Monday after Crippen's flight became apparent, one envelope contained nine deposit notes with the Charing Cross Bank for £600 and some insurance receipts; the other contained a watch and brooch.

Meanwhile, as Ethel paid a brief farewell visit to her sister Nina, Crippen busied himself in his office writing letters to Long and others in an attempt to put his affairs in some kind of order. Reunited at Albion House in the late morning, the couple effected Ethel's gender transformation as she donned the brown suit and Crippen cut her hair: 'You will do famously! No one will recognise you. You are a perfect boy!'[42] Taking little luggage with them, the couple had long since left London by the time Long received a letter from Crippen that evening on Yale Tooth Specialists paper requesting that 'you do me the great favour of winding up as best you can my household affairs', including two quarters' rental payments on Hilldrop Crescent, return of the housekeys to landlord Frederick Lown, and instructions to housemaid Valentine LeCoq to return to France. Long and his wife went to Hilldrop Crescent that same evening and found the unsent 'Mackamotzki' advertisement still standing on the mantlepiece.

Meanwhile, Dew had circulated a missing person's description of Cora Crippen to all London police offices and returned to Albion House for a further

39 *Trial*, p. 30.
40 Statement of William Long, DPP 1/13.
41 *Trial*, p. 27.
42 *Ethel Le Neve*, p. 44.

interview with Crippen on Monday 11 July. It was Gilbert Rylance who revealed that Crippen had fled, producing his own letter from his business partner, received that morning:

> Dear Dr. Rylance,
>   I now find that in order to escape trouble I shall be obliged to absent myself for a time. I believe with the business as it is now going you will run on alright so far as money matters go… Long knows pretty much all of the business, and can take over the book-keeping… I shall write you later on more fully. With kind wishes for your success.
>   Yours sincerely,
>   H.H. Crippen

'My quarry had gone, but the manner of his going pointed to guilt,' related Dew in his memoirs.[43] This conviction prompted Dew and Mitchell to make extensive enquiries in Camden Town and to undertake a renewed, more meticulous search of Hilldrop Crescent which began on the following day. Dew and Mitchell supplemented this new search of the house with excavations in the garden. These yielded nothing, but a quantity of clay in one corner suggested earthworks had taken place somewhere on the property in the recent past. Perhaps mindful of historic cellar murders, Dew's thoughts turned once again to the cellar which he had visited on the previous Friday: 'that cellar stuck in my mind. Even in bed, what little of it I got during those hectic days, I couldn't keep my mind from wandering back to the cellar.'[44] On the Wednesday following Crippen's disappearance, the pair made another visit to the house and made their most detailed inspection yet of the cellar. Probing with a poker between the bricks in the floor, Dew and Mitchell located an area of loose brickwork. Dew's memoirs relate a Doylean 'thrill of excitement' as a number of bricks came loose and the clay beneath showed signs of recent disturbance. Dew dug away two or three spadesful of the clay and uncovered what appeared to be human remains, a foul putrefactive stench giving confirmation of what the pair had found.

The gruesome exhumation task that followed was completed with the help of additional men. Daniel Gooch, PC 501 of Y Division, joined in the digging

43   *I Caught Crippen*, p. 25.
44   Ibid., p. 27.

between 4 and 5pm that day, leaving the remains *in situ* until the following morning when he and PC Martin helped to remove them, using their hands. Gooch noted that 'the remains were in a number of pieces' and that 'the smell was very bad'.[45]

In the photograph that survives in the National Archives of the excavation party, standing in the back garden of 39 Hilldrop Crescent with spades at the ready, a bravado face is put on what must have been a very difficult exhumation. Trying enough to recover an intact body from the grave; more traumatising still to uncover the muddled mass of filleted flesh that was buried in the cellar of Hilldrop Crescent: there was no head or limbs, the bones had been removed, the organs were missing. A quantity of quicklime had been poured over the remains apparently in an attempt to speed their decomposition. Dr Augustus Joseph Pepper, consulting surgeon at St Mary's Hospital and a friend of Metropolitan Chief Commissioner Sir Melville Macnaghten, attended the scene and dictated the measurements of the cellar and the disposition of the remains to Mitchell, who noted them down.[46] Pepper further distinguished a tuft of dark brown hair in a Hinde's curler and a portion of a pyjama jacket whose intact label would later be discovered to read 'Shirtmakers, Jones Brothers, Holloway'.[47]

From that Thursday 14 July and on into the weekend, the exclamatory headlines began: 'Variety Artist Murdered' (*The Globe*); 'Holloway Horror – Mutilated Remains under Cellar Floor – Husband and Boy-Girl Typist' (*Islington Gazette*); 'Cellar Mystery' (*London Daily News*); Revolver and Poison – Police Discoveries in the House of Mystery' (*Daily Express*). With so much rumour and innuendo already associated with the case, and with the weekend exhumation at Hilldrop Crescent attracting a crowd of onlookers as police officials, forensic pathologists, and mortuary attendants came and went, speculation was rife. The *Islington Gazette* of Monday 18 July carried claims of a neighbour in Brecknock Road recalling hearing gunshots and a woman's screams of 'Oh, don't!' coming from the adjoining Hilldrop Crescent in early January.[48] The witness is described as a Mrs. Clackner by the *Daily*

---

45 CRIM 1/117, Bow Street depositions, 16 September 1910.
46 'Measurements of remains and cellar at 39 Hilldrop Crescent', DPP 1/13.
47 *Trial*, p. 48.
48 'A Woman's Cry', *Islington Gazette*, 18 July 1910. An element of uncertain rumour seems to have found its way into the article, including the suggestion that 'the dead woman

Telegraph and Courier and as Mrs. Blackner by the *Islington Gazette*, though the only attestation to hearing gunshots in the police files is a deposition by Mrs. May Pole, latterly of 46 Brecknock Road, who recalled hearing the shots and discussing them with her landlady Lena Lyons.[49]

If these statements gave some clues as to how and when Belle met her death, others helped to account for some of the missing remains. Elizabeth Cox of 52 Brecknock Road, in amongst some poignant recollections of seeing Crippen and Belle in the garden and hearing Belle singing, attested to a rather more sinister fire in Crippen's dustbin in early June.[50] The statement of Frederick Evans of 54 Brecknock Road was perhaps the most evocative in showing how the Crippen drama so neatly fitted the established script of crime sensations in the London of George R. Sims and Lord Northcliffe. Evans reported having heard 'a terrible screech which terminated with a long dragging whine' emanating from Hilldrop Crescent back in January. 'It startled me and I at once thought of the Ripper murders, and knowing the locality, and that Parmetes Row, a turning out of Hilldrop Crescent, is frequented by prostitutes I thought it was one of those poor creatures in trouble.'[51] Though Evans's statement is somewhat muddled (Parmetes Row must be a transcription error in his statement for there is no such address, and the dates of his recollection do not match the night of Cora's disappearance), his invocation of the Ripper murders was more apposite than he knew. For in attendance at Hilldrop Crescent on that crucial weekend was not only Walter Dew, the man who had hunted Jack the Ripper on the mean streets of the East End, but also Sir Melville Macnaghten, the man who had effectively closed the Ripper file in 1892. Macnaghten's memoirs relate how he brought a handful of cigars to relieve the nauseated men undertaking the exhumation and contributed some wry comments on the selection of wines and spirits at Hilldrop Crescent, and the proximity of the dining room to the horrors of the cellar: 'From the doctor's chair at the head of the dining-room table to the cellar where the remains had been found was a distance of only some fifteen or twenty feet. How, for five long

---

was seen on several occasions with a young child in her arms', though this may reflect witnesses confusing Belle with Ethel, who hosted sister Nina and her young child at Hilldrop Crescent.

49   Statement of Mrs. May Pole, MEPO 3/198.
50   Statement of Mrs. Elizabeth Cox, MEPO 3/198.
51   Statement of Frederick Evans, MEPO 3/198.

months, good digestion could have waited upon appetite in such circumstances has always been a marvel to me!'[52]

It is possible to imagine the two veterans of the Ripper enquiry noting a number of parallels between the cases that weekend as they unearthed the grisly evidence of an equally nightmarish crime in the midst of leafy North London suburbia. The arrest warrant of Crippen and Le Neve, issued on 16 July 1910, was accompanied by an exclamatory 'Wanted!' police bill, circulated widely in both the national and continental press, its banner headline of 'MURDER AND MUTILATION!' raising ghosts of the Ripper:

> Wanted for murder and mutilation of a woman Hawley Harvey Crippen alias Peter Crippen alias Franckel, an American age fifty, 5 feet three or four, complexion fresh, hair light brown inclined sandy, thin bald on top, scanty straggling moustache, eyes grey, bridge of nose flat, false teeth, wears gold rim spectacles, may be wearing brown jacket marked Baker and Grey, found flat hat, Horne Bros. inside, wears hat back of head, rather slovenly appearance, throws his feet out when walking, slight American accent, very plausible and quiet spoken, speaks French and shows his teeth when speaking; and Ethel Clara Leneve travelling as his wife, age 27, height five feet five, complexion pale, hair light brown, large grey eyes, good teeth, good looking, medium build, pleasing appearance, quiet subdued manner, looks interested when in conversation, is reticent, walks slowly, probably dressed blue serge skirt, ditto three quarter jacket suit, large hat or may be dressed in boys dark brown jacket suit, grey hard felt hat, native of London, shorthand writer and typist.[53]

Phantom sightings of the fugitives by citizens keen to claim the advertised £250 reward were widespread in that first weekend. Macnaghten noted that 'the public favoured us with more correspondence than at any former time in the history of the Yard, with the possible exception of the period of Jack the Ripper's reign of terror.'[54] There were reports of sightings of Crippen in Kingsway, removing his nameplate from the Aural Remedies office door (this in fact turned out to have been Crippen's associate Eddie Marr);[55] in

---

52   Sir Melville Macnaghten, *Days of My Years* (London: Edward Arnold, 1914), p. 195.
53   CRIM 1/117.
54   *Days of My Years*, pp. 196–7.
55   *London Daily News*, 21 October 1910.

Chesterfield;[56] in Waltham Abbey, where the witness said Crippen carried a Ripper-like Gladstone bag;[57] and on the border between France and Spain sporting a straw hat.[58] Samuel Woolgar, labourer of Renda Road, West Ham went so far as to accost and restrain a man he took for the fugitive: 'You are Dr. Crippen, and I want that £250.'[59] Woolgar had clearly not been keeping up with the latest on the story in the papers: by the time he was charged with being disorderly on 6 August 1910 Crippen and Le Neve had been long since identified and arrested on the other side of the world.

For the fugitives had in fact crossed to Brussels on that first weekend of their flight from London. A train from Liverpool Street had conveyed them to Harwich where, according to Ethel's memoirs, they took a night boat to Holland at nine o'clock. Travelling on to Rotterdam the next day, the couple visited 'the quiet old canals' and 'quaint houses' before Crippen escorted Ethel to a barber to improve on the hair cut he had given her at Albion House: 'When I came out with a poll as closely cropped as Jack Sheppard we both burst out laughing.'[60]

This move to enhance Ethel's gender transition was a preliminary precaution in the next phase of the escape. Crippen had established that the steamship *Montrose* was due to sail for Quebec from Antwerp on 20 July. He planned that he and Ethel should be on board as Mr. and Master Robinson of Detroit, Michigan. It was in these personae that the pair checked into the Hotel des Ardennes, where Crippen presented Ethel to his hosts as his sick son and further told them he had been recently widowed. The police statement filed on 25 July 1910 quotes the hotelier who received the two mysterious guests: 'The younger of the two spoke only in whispers, Robinson senior stating that his companion was deaf and also suffering from an affection of the throat.'[61]

When they boarded the 5,000-tonne steamship *Montrose* between 8.30 and 10am on 20 July 1910, Crippen signed the ship's manifest as John Philo Robinson, Merchant, aged 55 and John George Robinson, Student, aged 16. The pair had little with them by way of luggage, Ethel's memoirs noting that

56   'A Chesterfield Scent', *The Globe*, 18 July 1910.
57   *Lancashire Evening Post*, 15 July 1910.
58   'Is Crippen in Spain?', *Islington Gazette*, 21 July 1910.
59   'Dr. Crippen', *Illustrated Police News*, 6 August 1910.
60   *Ethel Le Neve*, pp. 47–8.
61   Statement of PC Workman & Acting Supt J. McCarthy, DPP 1/13.

9. Ethel le Neve's disguise as a boy, recreated after the event for a publicity photo.

they carried only the one handbag they had brought from Hilldrop Crescent. Crippen hoped to offset some of the suspicion this might provoke by omitting to wear his glasses, by this point aware, by virtue of a continental newspaper, that the secret of the cellar had been discovered and that he was at the centre of an international manhunt. There was limited scope for the couple to blend in on board the relatively small steamship. While there were 246 passengers in steerage, there were only twenty travelling in the second-class cabins for which Crippen and Le Neve had opted, and a crew complement of only 107.

Given this relatively confined backdrop, it is perhaps unsurprising that the suspicions of vigilant ship's captain Henry Kendall should have been aroused within hours of the ship's departure from Antwerp. The immediate trigger for Kendall was seeing the young boy squeeze the older man's hand, a gesture which the Captain deemed 'strange and unnatural' behaviour.[62] Whether it was the taboo of potential incest or of homosexuality that weighed most heavily in his unease Kendall never made clear; the context was regardless one of transgression. In the same summer that 'Mr and Master Robinson' squeezed hands aboard the *Montrose*, Portsmouth mariner Herbert Powell, 30, and shop assistant William Pratt, 39, had been in court defending themselves against a charge of gross indecency;[63] and Alfred Dunwell had appeared before York Assizes 'for an unnatural offence'.[64] At the Essex Assize, Joseph Gray Broadhurst, 35, received three years' penal servitude for his 'unnatural offence', having already served twelve months' hard labour in 1902 for a similar perceived transgression. The newspaper report of his sentencing seemed as baffled as the judge that despite being 'smartly attired' and having 'very respectable parents', Broadhurst should have repeated his behaviour: 'His Lordship said it was obvious that it was half-madness which led persons to commit these offences.'[65] This handful of examples, drawn from a whole host of 1910 instances, gives an immediate sense of how Kendall's coded reference to 'unnatural' behaviour would have resonated with readers back home.

Already suspecting that these transgressive passengers might be Crippen and Le Neve, Kendall enlisted the assistance of Chief Officer Alfred Henry Sergeant in removing any copies of English newspapers which alluded to the

---

62   Connell, *Doctor Crippen*, p. 54.
63   *Hampshire Telegraph*, 25 June 1910.
64   *Hull Daily Mail*, 5 July 1910.
65   *Essex News*, 18 June 1910.

murder. On 22 July Kendall was employing further corroborative methods, such as engaging Robinson in a discussion on seasickness in the hope he would use tell-tale medical terms; making jokes with him in the hope his suspect's laughter would expose the tell-tale dentures mentioned in the police description; and calling out Robinson's name on deck to see if he would instinctively respond – he didn't but blamed his deafness. These sub-Holmesian methods even ran to Kendall experimenting with a home-made identikit in which he doctored the press portraits of Crippen and Le Neve to evaluate the resemblance to his passenger-suspects.

Convinced by these various sources of corroboration, Kendall resolved to make use of the ship's Marconi wireless before the *Montrose* passed beyond range of the last wireless station before the Atlantic, based at Poldhu in Cornwall. The resulting terse telegram despatched to Scotland Yard surely represents one of the most famous texts in criminal history:

> *Montrose.* 130 miles West of Lizard.
>
> Have strong suspicion that Crippen London Cellar Murderer and accomplice are amongst saloon passengers. Moustache shaved off, growing beard. Accomplice dressed as a boy. Voice, manner and build undoubtedly a girl. Kendall.

When Walter Dew was handed a relay of this telegram from the Liverpool police at 8pm on Friday 22 July 1910 'a wave of optimism' swept over him and he immediately jumped into a cab and went to consult Macnaghten.[66] Dew put to his superior the suggestion that he should board the faster steamship, *The Laurentic*, scheduled to leave the next day from Liverpool rather than Antwerp, overtake the fugitives, and arrest them before they made port in Quebec. Macnaghten gave his support to the audacious plan and Dew set off from Liverpool the next day. Courtesy of a Scotland Yard leak, the press were already alert to Dew's plan but cannot have known the finer details, such as his booking onto the ship under the alias Mr. Dewhurst and his attempts to contact Captain Kendall from the radio room once on board.

Meanwhile, on board the *Montrose* Crippen and Le Neve were oblivious to the suspicions of Captain Kendall, who had even gone so far as to inspect the

---

66 *I Caught Crippen*, p. 37.

pair's luggage and clothing in their cabin.[67] Unaware of this intrusion, Ethel regarded their second-class cabin as 'quite cosy, and to me the whole ship was wonderful'.[68] Kendall supplied both Crippen and Le Neve with plenty of reading material from the ship's library. Ethel's selection included novels, magazines, and detective stories, while an ironic choice for Crippen was Edgar Wallace's *The Four Just Men*, a 'locked room mystery' involving an international manhunt, disguises, and aliases. As the voyage approached its end Crippen spoke to Le Neve about the possibility they might be separated on arrival in Canada and that her best course might be to travel on to Toronto to seek employment via her typewriting skills. Possibly Crippen was contemplating suicide: a note found on his person at his arrest a few days later certainly implied as much:

> I cannot stand the horrors I go through every night any longer and as I see nothing bright ahead, and money has come to an end, I have made up my mind to jump overboard to-night. I know I have spoil [sic] our life but I hope someday you can learn to forgive me with last word of love. Your, H[69]

If the note suggests Crippen felt events were closing in on him, he is unlikely to have anticipated the precise form the denouement of this transatlantic chase would take. On 31 July 1910, *The Laurentic* having now overtaken the *Montrose* as planned, Inspector Dew arranged to be rowed down the St Lawrence river to Father Point, where he would meet the smaller ship, masquerading as the pilot who would navigate the *Montrose* down the river, and board her in midstream. Dew's discreet arrival was hardly made easier by the international press who had amassed in Quebec and whose intrepid photographers even planned to float down the St Lawrence river on a raft so that they might capture the moment of arrest on deck for posterity. Dew and the Canadian police ultimately persuaded them to stay put on the quayside at Quebec and await the photo opportunity of the prisoners' disembarkation instead.

Dew relates his 'thrill of excitement' as his small boat proceeded down the St Lawrence at Father Point and the *Montrose* hove into view shortly

---

67   The onboard surveillance extended to the pair being unwittingly photographed. J.P. Eddy later recollected seeing a picture of the couple in Scotland Yard's crime museum: *Scarlet and Ermine: Famous Trials as I Saw Them from Crippen to Podola* (London: William Kimber, 1960), p. 55.

68   *Ethel Le Neve*, p. 53.

69   CRIM 1/117.

before 8.30am on Sunday 31 July.[70] A ladder was thrown over the side of the steamship; the genuine pilot scaled it first, followed by Dew and then by Chief Inspector McCarthy and Inspector Dennis of the Canadian Provincial Police. Dew proceeded straight to Captain Kendall's cabin while McCarthy and Dennis fetched Crippen. The climactic moment of the arrest that followed, already evocative of a Doyle detective adventure novella, had already been somewhat mythologised in 1914 when Sir Melville Macnaghten reflected on it: 'Since Mr. H.M. Stanley discovered the missing missionary with the remark, "Dr. Livingstone, I presume," no meeting has ever been equal to that of Chief Inspector Walter Dew with the murderous doctor on the deck of s.s. *Montrose*. "Dr. Crippen, I believe," is as historically interesting a salutation as the one I have just quoted out of Central Africa.'[71] In fact, according to his statement at the trial, Dew's first words to Crippen were the less rhetorical: 'Good morning, Dr. Crippen; I am Chief Inspector Dew.'[72] Crippen bade Dew good morning in return but remained silent when Dew cautioned him that he would be charged with the murder and mutilation of his wife. Items of Cora's jewellery were recovered from Crippen's under-vest, along with the ostensible suicide note and a second mysterious communication, also written on the back of a 'Robinson' business card, which read: 'Shall we wait until tonight, about ten or eleven o'clock?'[73] The cards were claimed by Crippen at his trial to represent yet another twist in the audacious Crippen escape plan. Expecting the ship to be searched upon arrival in Quebec (Crippen having seen from the continental papers that the ports were being watched), he would stow away in the cargo hold, leaving his 'suicide note' to be discovered. This plan required the collusion of an on-board accomplice who would vouch to a cargo-hold free of stowaways and who would smuggle Crippen safely ashore, concealed inside a container.

Giving testimony at his trial, Crippen elaborated on this story of a quartermaster accomplice: 'I entered into an arrangement with the quartermaster to hide me... He told me that the captain knew who I was and also who Miss Le Neve was, and that I was to be arrested by the police at Quebec. He also told me that

---

70 *I Caught Crippen*, p. 33. Dew here gives his time of boarding the *Montrose* as nearer 9am but his trial statement recorded an 8.30am boarding.
71 *Days of My Years*, pp. 189–90.
72 *Trial*, p. 42.
73 Ibid., p. 85.

I must leave a note behind me saying that I had jumped overboard, and that in the middle of the night he would make a splash in the water and tell the captain that I had gone.'[74] Whether there really was such a *Montrose* crew member ready to risk reputation and a charge of abetting a felon has never been established and no such quartermaster was produced at the trial to corroborate the story. While Crippen's story helps to explain the otherwise mysterious second note, the notion that his first expresses genuinely suicidal ideation cannot be ruled out. Indeed, as Dew escorted Crippen to a different cabin after charging him, he professed: 'I am not sorry – the anxiety has been too much' and Dew's memoirs later recorded 'my belief is that Crippen really did intend to take his life and would have done so before the *Montrose* reached Quebec'.[75]

Ethel's memoirs likewise recount the moment Inspector Dew appeared at her cabin door. She claims to have penetrated his disguise immediately, but presents a less self-possessed picture of her reaction upon seeing him: 'That this inspector should have chased us all the way from England filled me with horrible forebodings. I gave a cry and then fell into a swoon.'[76] A less charitable line of comment in the case histories has stressed how this 'fugue state' in which Ethel appears to have spent much of the time in Quebec and during the voyage home enabled her to project uncertainty and inexactness as to exactly what she was being charged with and how much she knew about the events at Hilldrop Crescent. For his part, Crippen's comment to Dew that 'It is only fair to say she knew nothing about it; I never told her anything' was later to prove influential in persuading their respective trial juries of her innocence and of his guilt.[77]

When the fugitives were disembarked from the *Montrose* at Quebec in the small hours of 1 August 1910, and then detained in the city during the fifteen-day extradition proceedings, the international press continued to devote extensive coverage to the international crime sensation. The court proceedings that

---

74   Ibid., pp. 91–2.
75   *I Caught Crippen*, p. 47. In a curiously mirror-image case of the previous year, 21-year-old William Bedfort had used much the same phrase when he turned himself in at a London police station for a murder he claimed he committed the previous year in Canada: 'I have come to give myself up. I cannot stand the worry of it any longer.' *Daily Telegraph and Courier*, Wednesday 13 October 1909. In the event, Bedfort's account of the crime differed sufficiently from the evidence at the scene that the Canadian police declined to extradite him and he was discharged in November 1909.
76   *Ethel Le Neve*, p. 56.
77   *Trial*, p. 43.

commenced the extradition supplied little extra copy, Crippen simply confirming his name, his American citizenship and his Catholicism. These scant pickings, together with the ensuing period of inaction after the high drama of the transatlantic chase, prompted the international press to recycle self-generated speculations. These included reports of an attempted double suicide, 'the man with a revolver and the woman by poison',[78] bogus quotations from 'Inspector Drew' [sic],[79] and from the prisoner: 'When I am back to England I shall tell my story, and then you will understand that I am not guilty of murder, and that I told the truth when I pleaded that I was not a fugitive from justice.'[80] Other coverage suggested that Crippen had provided Dew with a detailed confession – the first of what proved to be many attempts to impose a traditional form of closure onto the story (see Chapter Five). A report in *The Times* of 5 August carried vehement denials of any such confession from both Dew and the Provincial Premier of Quebec, who was quoted as averring: 'Neither a confession nor an incriminating statement has been reported to me as coming from Crippen. You can deny all such stories emphatically. They are a tissue of lies.'[81] Probably the most reliable coverage in this period was that which confined itself to reporting Crippen's reading matter: the prisoner continued with his apposite and ironic choices, including John Graham's *Letters of a Self-made Merchant to His Son*.

When extradition procedures were completed, Dew set about organising the return voyage for his prisoners, while himself seeking to avoid the constant pursuit and questioning of the sensation-hungry press. Led by Dew, an augmented party now booked passage on the White Star liner SS *Megantic* for the return voyage across the Atlantic. The prisoners were now escorted by Dew, Sgt Mitchell (who had travelled over with the extradition papers) and two wardresses from Holloway prison, who were to take charge of Ethel during the voyage. Continuing the theme of masquerade and impersonation, there were press reports that at least four of the party travelled under pseudonyms – Dew as Silas P. Doyle, Crippen as Cyrus Field, Ethel as Miss J. Byrne, and Mitchell as F.M. Johnson, though Nicholas Connell has since

78 'Crippen in Court at Quebec', *Daily Telegraph and Courier*, 2 August 1910.
79 The *Vancouver Daily Province* of Tuesday 2 August 1910 quoted 'Drew' as declaring Ethel 'innocent of any share in the murder of Belle Elmore'. The same article reported 'Quebec Women Send Flowers to Crippen in his Prison Cell.'
80 *Dundee Courier*, 4 August 1910.
81 'The Crippen Case: The Reported Confession', *Times*, 5 August 1910.

confirmed from the *Megantic*'s passenger list that all in fact travelled in *propria persona*.[82] According to a number of press reports, a prophetic accident befell Crippen as he crossed the gangplank to embark: 'Dr. Crippen neglected to stoop while passing a taut guy rope above the gangway. The rope caught him beneath the chin, and jerked his head back painfully.' 'Had Inspector Dew not caught him he would have fallen into the water.'[83] The prisoners were kept apart during the return voyage on the SS *Megantic*. Sgt Mitchell was with Crippen for the majority of the voyage and was later to recall: 'He chatted with me from time to time on various matters, and seemed quite bright and jolly.'[84] Crippen reportedly remained immune to the seasickness which beset many of the passengers, Ethel among them, as the *Megantic* navigated the coast of Ireland. Dew's memoirs relate how Crippen showed deep concern for Ethel when he learned of her seasickness. He was equally effusive in his gratitude when he learned that Dew had acted on his suggestion of offering the patient a small amount of champagne to alleviate the symptoms.

As the voyage neared its end, Crippen asked Dew for a last meeting with Le Neve before arrival back in England since it was unclear 'how things would go for him' on his return. An on-deck reunion of the lovers seems not to have been granted (though it would feature in certain of the novelised accounts). Nevertheless, it appears that a compassionate Dew would later allow the couple a last parting glance on the train that would carry them from Liverpool to Euston and the rigors of the Edwardian criminal justice system.

The *Megantic* arrived in Liverpool eight days after departure from Quebec. When the prisoners disembarked on the arms of their Scotland Yard chaperones, the press men got their long-coveted photo of Crippen on the gangplank, albeit the fugitive was so dwarfed by Inspector Dew's loaned trenchcoat and so occluded by his hat pulled down over his eyes, he more resembled Wells's invisible man than the Edwardian homeopath of the press portraits. *Lloyd's Weekly News* proclaimed this attire a mistake on Dew's part since it made the prisoner rather obvious to the 'tall young fellow [who] dashed at Crippen with uplifted cane'. While the would-be assailant was kept back along with the rest of the crowds, the *Lloyd's* reporter memorably caught sight

---

82   Connell, *Doctor Crippen*, p. 69.
83   'Dr. Crippen Sails for England', *Lake's Falmouth Packet and Cornwall Advertiser*, 26 August 1910; 'Crippen and Miss Le Neve Returning', *Guardian*, 22 August 1910.
84   CRIM 1/117.

10. Crippen is escorted down the gangplank of the *Megantic*
at Liverpool by Inspector Dew, 28 August 1910.

of the prisoner's frightened eyes which 'revealed a terror-stricken gaze. His eyes seemed to stand out with fear.'[85] Ethel likewise was shrouded in a blue veil and closely chaperoned by two matrons from Holloway gaol. Huge crowds assembled both at Liverpool and at Euston, setting the pattern that would persist until Crippen's execution and sustaining the sense that everything and everyone connected with this case was a subject of spectacle.

Press reports suggest that once back in London, the criminal proceedings against Crippen and Le Neve began first at Bow Street Magistrates' Court, where they were indicted on 29 August. The charge levelled against Crippen inveighed that 'on or about the 1st day of February 1910 did feloniously wilfully and of his malice aforethought kill and murder one Cora Crippen otherwise called Belle Elmore'. That against Ethel alleged that 'well knowing the said Hawley Harvey Crippen to have done and committed the felony above mentioned did afterwards feloniously receive harbour comfort assist and maintain him'.[86] As they stood in the Bow Street dock where they were

85 *Lloyd's Weekly News*, 28 August 1910.
86 CRIM 1/117.

committed for trial on 2 September, the couple were surreptitiously photo-graphed by John Tussaud, grandson of the waxworks impresario, who had secreted a camera into a hat. As we shall see, like many of the influential attendees at Crippen's trial (Conan Doyle, H.B. Irving, W.S. Gilbert among them), Tussaud's concern to secure visual records and *realia* associated with the case was later to play an important role in the curation of a particular image of Crippen in the public imagination and, indeed, the sustaining of a resonant imaginative repertory for remembering and representing 'classic' crime.

The indictment and committal proceedings at Bow Street had been preceded by the inquest on Cora Crippen's remains, with the result that by the time of Crippen's five-day trial in October, the press had reported on no fewer than three sets of legal proceedings and certain witnesses such as John Burroughs, Melinda May, and Clara Martinetti had become household names by virtue of their substantive appearance in all three settings. These proceedings did their part to keep Crippen in the news throughout September, as did the auctioning of the contents of 39 Hilldrop Crescent, which drew a considerable number of bidders and spectators 'who examined the bedsteads, sideboards, and other articles of furniture with morbid interest'.[87] A letter from Crippen to Ethel from the Pentonville condemned cell poignantly records that the sale yielded £114.[88]

When the Old Bailey trial finally opened on 18 October 1910, the Lord Chief Justice Lord Alverstone was presiding. Crippen's hopes were not to be realised that Sir Edward Marshall Hall, who had secured the acquittal of Robert Wood for the Camden Town Murder three years before, would lead his defence, which would instead be conducted by Alfred Tobin, assisted by Huntly Jenkins and Henry Delacombe Roome. Crippen was allegedly discouraged when he learned that prosecuting counsel was to be the indomitable Richard Muir: 'I wish it had been anyone else but him. I fear the worst,' Crippen is reputed to have said.[89]

---

87 'Crippen's Furniture', *London Daily News*, 21 September 1910. The article notes that a representative from Madame Tussaud's purchased three articles: 'an old armchair, a shawl which was worn by Mrs. Crippen, and an oak dinner waiter.'

88 J.C. Ellis, *Black Fame: Stories of Crime and Criminals* (London: Hutchinson and Co., 1930), p. 311.

89 Douglas G. Browne and E.V. Tullett, *Bernard Spilsbury: His Life and Cases* (London: George G. Harrap and Co., 1951), p. 48. Travers Humphreys and future Westminster Coroner Samuel Ingleby Oddie, assisted by Cecil Mercer, completed the prosecuting team.

Muir and his team would call a formidable roster of witnesses to make the case for the prosecution. From among their circle of friends and acquaintances, Dr John Burroughs, Clara Martinetti, Louise Smythson, and Cora's half-sister Theresa Hunn would supply details of the Crippens' home life and of Belle's last known movements. Hilldrop Crescent landlord Frederick Lown would confirm Crippen's five-year residency of his property, while medical experts A.J. Pepper and Thomas Marshall would aver that the mutilated remains found in the cellar could have been *in situ* for no longer than a year. Damning forensic testimony would be deposed by Dr Herbert Wilcox, who would attest to the presence of hyoscine in the remains, while rising star of the field, Dr Bernard Spilsbury, would attest that, headless, boneless and limbless as the remains may have been, they nevertheless bore the identifying mark of an ovariectomy scar that linked them definitively to Cora Crippen. Ethel's landlady Emily Jackson, while at pains to assert the good character of her former tenant and her lover, nonetheless confirmed the indecent haste with which Ethel had been installed at Hilldrop Crescent and her adoption of Cora's jewellery (Jackson herself had inherited some of her clothes). Manager of *The Era* Frederick Pedgrift confirmed Crippen's placing of the bogus death notice in his paper, and William Long and Marion Curnow the details of Crippen's hasty wrapping up of his affairs and flight on 9 July. The most damning prosecution testimony was received late in the proceedings, after the defence case had already been presented, when one William James Chilvers, buyer to Messrs Jones Brothers of Holloway, fatally confirmed that a fragment of pyjama jacket found alongside the buried remains at Hilldrop Crescent was of a unique design produced only since 1908, and that a purchase of pyjamas of this very pattern had been made by Cora Crippen in early 1909.[90] This additional forensic evidence had come to light only when Muir and the prosecution team had themselves caused enquiries to be made, Dew showing a degree of reticence after the climax of the maritime arrest. As his biographer would later write, Muir was 'not only a great prosecuting counsel but also a man who possessed in high degree the instincts of a great detective'.[91] His close engagement in every detail of the

---

90 The evidence of the pyjama jacket was the most secure forensic evidence in the prosecution's case: the presence of hyoscine in the body had been sought only *after* the police learned of Crippen's purchase of the drug; the identification of the alleged ovariectomy scar was made only after Dew's suggestion that the pathologists look for it.

91 Sidney Theodore Felstead, *Sir Richard Muir* (London: Bodley Head, 1927), p. 83.

evidence against Crippen gave him a masterful command of his brief, patent in the very opening lines of his cross-examination of Crippen in the witness box:

> On the early morning of the 1st February you were left alone in your house with your wife? – Yes.
>
> She was alive? – She was.
>
> And well? – She was.
>
> Do you know of any person in the world who has seen her alive since? – I do not.
>
> Do you know of any person in the world who has ever had a letter from her since? – I do not.
>
> Do you know of any person in the world who can prove any fact showing that she ever left that house alive? – Absolutely not; I have told Mr. Dew exactly all the facts.[92]

As barrister Cecil Mercer would later comment, 'Crippen made a very poor witness. He put up no fight... We never even called the man who delivered the lime. It was a dead case.'[93] Journalist J.P. Eddy likewise viewed 'the result of Crippen's trial as a foregone conclusion'.[94]

Against the weight of this circumstantial evidence, defence counsel Alfred Tobin could do little more than marshal statements of good character from witnesses; press Bruce Miller unsuccessfully for an admission of an affair with Belle; attempt to cast doubt on the identity of the Hilldrop Crescent remains; and unsettle the jury with the suggestion that they might condemn the prisoner to death only to see Belle reappear hale and hearty some time later. There was thus scant surprise when, at the end of a relatively short trial of only five days, the jury took less than half an hour over their deliberations, and returned the unanimous verdict that Crippen was guilty of wilful murder. Chief Justice Alverstone's sentence, later echoed in many a literary rendering of the case, was likewise concise:

---

92 *Trial*, p. 94.
93 Cecil Mercer writing as Dornford Yates, *As Berry and I Were Saying* (London: Ward Lock, 1952), p. 258.
94 J.P. Eddy, *Scarlet and Ermine: Famous Trials As I Saw Them* (London: William Kimber, 1960), p. 55.

Pentonville Prison from Caledonian Road, N.

11.   Pentonville Prison where Crippen was incarcerated
and executed on 23 November 1910.

Hawley Harvey Crippen, you have been convicted, upon evidence which
could leave no doubt on the mind of any reasonable man, that you cruelly
poisoned your wife, that you concealed your crime, you mutilated her body,
and disposed piece-meal of her remains; you possessed yourself of her
property, and used it for your own purposes. It was further established that as
soon as suspicion was aroused you fled from justice and took every measure
to conceal your flight. On the ghastly and wicked nature of the crime I shall
not dwell. I only tell you that you must entertain no expectation or hope that
you will escape the consequences of your crime, and I implore you to make
your peace with Almighty God.[95]

With Crippen still protesting his innocence he was led from the dock and
so to Pentonville. He would lodge an appeal, but this would be dismissed on
5 November; a petition for commutation of sentence would be lodged, but this
would be refused by Home Secretary Winston Churchill.

Crippen's last weeks in Pentonville as prisoner 9146 were to prove crucial

95   *Trial*, p. 183.

in the posterity of the case. During this time, he seems to have garnered the respect of the majority of the prison officials and warders charged with the death watch, inspired by his devotion to Ethel: 'his one thought throughout was for the future welfare of the woman who had temporarily linked her fate with his.'[96] To Crippen's great relief, Ethel's own trial on 25 October 1910, on the charge of being an accessory after the fact, lasted only one day and resulted in her prompt acquittal. Le Neve was defended by Frederick Edwin ('F.E.') Smith, whose exculpatory line presented her as a young innocent, entranced and dominated by the magnetic personality of the older American doctor. Smith asked the all-male jurors to look on the 'young and inexperienced woman' as if she were one of their own kin: 'I am content you will judge her in her hour of agony with that consideration that you would wish shown to a daughter of your own if she were placed in the same position.'[97] The jury's deliberations in the trial of Ethel were as curtailed as they had been in the case of Crippen the previous week, though with the opposite outcome: 'Miss Le Neve was acquitted by the unhesitating verdict of the jury.'[98]

While elated at Ethel's acquittal, some cruel blows would befall Crippen in these last weeks. The Charing Cross Bank failed, taking with it the £600 deposit account which he had hoped would have funded a period of relatively comfortable seclusion for Ethel after his death. Crippen's father Myron died on 18 November, five days before his only son, the *London Daily News* poignantly reporting how the old man 'had haunted the news stands and newspaper offices seeking the latest news as to the progress of the case against Dr. Crippen. His plight became most pitiable, and the physicians declare that the worry and

---

96   Ellis, *Black Fame*, p. 308. Ten years after the execution, Prison Governor Major Owen Mytton-Davies wrote that Crippen's 'one redeeming feature was his devotion to Ethel le Neve': *Sunday Express*, 27 February 1921.

97   *Trial*, p. 205. In his later memoir of the trial, Smith (later Lord Chancellor of England and First Earl of Birkenhead) was unapologetic at taking this more emotive than evidence-based stance: 'It is an elementary rule of English law that the prisoner has to be proved guilty. It is only when the evidence for the prosecution has established a case that the defence is forced to give an explanation. In my opinion, the Crown did not prove their charge and I took my stand accordingly. My attitude was abundantly justified by the summing up and the verdict.' Earl of Birkenhead, *Famous Trials* (London: Hutchinson, 1933), p. 283.

98   *Famous Trials*, p. 285.

strain brought about his death.'[99] Finally, Crippen learned that both his appeal, and a petition raised on his behalf by Arthur Newton, had failed to secure commutation of the death sentence. His heartfelt letter to Ethel in the light of this news shows a renewed depth of emotion:

Monday, 21 November 1910

How can I find the strength and heart to struggle through this last letter? God, indeed, must hear our cry to Him for Divine help in this last farewell. How to control myself to write I hardly know, but pray God help us to be brave to face the end now so near.

The thoughts rush to my mind quicker than I can put them down. Time is so short now, and there is so much that I would say. There are less than two days left to us, only one more letter after this can I write you, and only two more visits, one tonight before you read this letter and one tomorrow.

When I wrote to you on Saturday, I had not heard any news of the petition, and though I never at any time dared hope, yet deep down in my heart was just a glimmer of trust that God might give us yet a chance to put me right before the world and let me have the passionate longing of my soul.

Your letter written early Saturday came to me late Saturday evening and soon after the Governor brought me the dreadful news about ten o'clock. He was so kind and considerate in telling me, in breaking the shock as gently as he could. He was most kind and left me at last with 'God bless you; good night', that I know you will ever remember him kindly for his goodness.

When he had gone I first kissed your face in the photo, my faithful devoted companion in all this sorrow. Oh! How glad I was I had the photo. It was some consolation, although, in spite of all my greatest efforts, it was impossible to keep down a great sob and my heart's agonised cry.

How am I to endure to take my last look at your face; what agony must I go through at the last when you disappear forever from my eyes! God help us to be brave then.

Crippen was hanged on 23 November 1910 at 9am by executioner John Ellis, who recalled the morning as being dark and foggy, in contrast to the expression on his prisoner's face: 'the smile never left his face up to the moment when I threw the white cap over it and blotted out God's light from his eyes forever.'[100]

---

99 'Crippen's Father Dies', *London Daily News*, 19 November 1910.
100 John Ellis, *Diary of a Hangman* (London: Forum, 1996), p. 65.

Such are the facts of the North London Cellar Murder of 1910, as far as it is possible to reassemble them. Already it will be clear how so much of the story is indivisible from the self-fashioning of the principal players themselves: from Crippen's peripatetic early years and his later recourse to the aliases and shadow enterprises, through Cora's romanticised lineage and creation of the stage persona Belle, to Ethel Neave's reinvention of herself as 'Miss Le Neve', the typist turned secretary turned mistress of Hilldrop Crescent, turned boy. Other key players would also contest the official narrative; Louise Smythson and John Nash would play out a spat in the papers over which of them had been responsible for alerting Scotland Yard to Belle's disappearance in the first place. Walter Dew would tell history it was he who dug the fateful poker between the bricks of that dark coal cellar in Hilldrop Crescent while, as David James Smith has shown, the evidence held in the National Archives rather suggests it was the loyal Sgt Mitchell who sounded the cellar floor.[101]

But much more than these isolated elaborations and embellishments, the Crippen drama was subject to a form of construction and curation for the Edwardian reading public and their descendants. The London press editors, the purveyors of street literature and murder ballads, and even a popular waxworks emporium in the Marylebone Road were busy constructing a textual and representation formation of 'classic' Crippen that was to endure for the best part of a century.

---

101 David James Smith, *Supper with the Crippens*, p. 144. As we shall see, other distortions and exaggerations can perhaps be more charitably attributed to faulty memory, Dew's main account of the case being drafted nearly thirty years after the event.

PART TWO

RECEPTION
AND ADAPTATION

CHAPTER FIVE

THE MAKING OF CLASSIC CRIPPEN

When Crippen's legal team contested his conviction in November 1910, five grounds for the appeal were set out. These included discontinuity in jury scrutiny (one of the jurors had briefly been taken ill at an early stage of the trial, thus missing a portion of the proceedings);[1] two substantive points regarding the forensic evidence and the disputed scar; and the suggestion that the identity of the remains at 39 Hilldrop Crescent remained unestablished.[2] The appeal was prefaced with an objection that bears closely on the current chapter: it held that Crippen's right to a fair trial had been jeopardised by sensational and speculative press coverage which had recklessly linked his name with known criminals of notorious memory. Even before the prisoner had returned to England to face trial, certain newspapers with mass circulation 'published false and misleading evidence about him, actually alleging in the most precise and detailed manner that he had confessed to having murdered his wife – one newspaper classing him with a number of well-known Murderers, who have long since been executed'.[3]

---

1   Juror George Craig of Acton fainted on day two of a trial which seems to have taken a considerable toll on him: 'Ever since the trial I have been confined to my house, and under the care of the doctor, who has ordered me to go away for some time to Eastbourne. I am suffering from dyspepsia and nervous prostration.' DPP 1/13.

2   It is surprising that the appellant did not cite the burial of the majority of the remains (some were retained as evidence at the trial) as Cora Crippen at St Pancras Cemetery in the week preceding the trial – an act that was surely prejudicial to the question of precisely whose remains they were.

3   HO144/1719 195492.

This chapter will detail just how sound was the basis for this claim. Crippen was indeed associated in that summer and autumn of 1910 with a lineage of criminal forebears. His case was effectively characterised as an Edwardian manifestation of an older criminological pattern. The appeal's claim that journalism was a central force in this process is surely true, but it is not the entirety of the picture. Police communications at the start of the manhunt summoned an atmosphere of sensation reminiscent of the Ripper crimes; press coverage of the fugitives' flight and capture saw frequent evocation of poisoners past; Crippen's own trial defence and certain of his actions and writings evoked gothic sensation and criminal romance; finally, the dedicated criminological section of a popular waxworks emporium enlisted Crippen amongst the ranks of notorious criminals of the past one hundred years, indelibly fixing Crippen in memory.

Murder, Mutilation and Mesmerism

The first classic crimes to be recalled were the Ripper murders. As we have seen, the association of the Crippen and Ripper crimes was forged from the outset by some curious coincidences of police personnel, with both Walter Dew and Melville Macnaghten closely involved in both investigations. The ghost of the Ripper had also been summoned to the public mind earlier in 1910 by the serialisation and then publication in book form of the memoirs of two other high-ranking police officials closely connected with the earlier case. Sir Robert Anderson had been Assistant Commissioner of the Metropolitan Police at the time of the Ripper murders and, while he had been out of the country on sick leave for much of that 'autumn of terror', he had sufficient involvement in the case for it to feature in his serialised memoirs in *Blackwood's Magazine* and subsequently in the volume *The Lighter Side of My Official Life*. In a prose style not unlike that of London chronicler George R. Sims, Anderson evoked the Victorian inheritance and atmosphere of the case with references to Sherlock Holmes, house-to-house searches, and a characterisation of the murderer as 'a sexual maniac of the virulent type'.[4] Anderson's writings were followed in October 1910 by the reminiscences of Sir Henry Smith, Acting Commissioner

---

4   Sir Robert Anderson, *The Lighter Side of My Official Life* (New York and London: Hodder and Stoughton, 1910), p. 137.

of the City of London Police at the time of the Ripper murders. Smith's *From Constable to Commissioner* included the brag, 'There is no man living who knows as much of those murders as I do' and the breathless suggestion that he was 'within five minutes of the perpetrator one night', luridly embellished with the claim that Smith happened upon the public sink at which the murderer had briefly stopped to wash his bloodstained hands.[5] Both claims were rightly treated with some scepticism by *The Observer*'s reviewer, who noted that Smith's book added 'little to the public knowledge and ignores recent statements as to the identity and fate of the criminal'.[6] Yet the appearance of both Anderson's and Smith's memoirs in 1910, the involvement of Dew and Macnaghten, and the simple homophony of the names Crippen and Ripper, remarked by Catharine Arnold, would have encouraged the linking of the two figures in the minds of the metropolitan reading public from the outset.[7]

More than this, when news broke of the gruesome discovery in the cellar of 39 Hilldrop Crescent, emphasis was firmly placed on the appalling mutilation of the corpse. Memories were evoked of the Whitechapel killer's fearful *modus operandi*; his victims suffered progressively worse mutilations as the sequence of murders unfolded. Walter Dew himself would later note how 'mutilation of the bodies was a feature of both crimes'[8] though he did not remark on the ostensibly very different motive in each case, the Ripper apparently deriving a deranged pleasure from his mutilatory activity while the killer of the Hilldrop Crescent corpse was clearly seeking to obliterate all signs of his victim's identity. This distinction was likewise overlooked by the early accounts of the murder in the press. The experience of the Ripper murders, more recent crimes such as the Camden Town Murder of 1907, and the increasing currency of Freudian understandings of sexually motivated murder, meant that mutilation was a particular trigger for readers of the sensationalist press. Its perpetration was widely read as a signature of 'lust murder',

---

5   Sir Henry Smith, *From Constable to Commissioner: The Story of Sixty Years, Most of them Misspent* (London: Chatto and Windus, 1910), as cited in Paul Begg, Martin Fido and Keith Skinner, *The Complete Jack the Ripper A to Z* (London: John Blake, 2010), p. 477.
6   'City Commissioner's Reminiscences', *The Observer*, 9 October 1910.
7   'The name itself seemed evil, with its nuances of criminal, ripper and cripes!' Catharine Arnold, *Underworld London: Crime and Punishment in the Capital City* (London: Simon and Schuster, 2012), p. 220.
8   *I Caught Crippen*, p. 82.

with the assumption that the mutilation had been undertaken as a means for the killer to achieve a depraved satisfaction or gratification compounding the horror of the murder itself.

Certainly, the mutilation of the Hilldrop Crescent corpse was given strong prominence in the Metropolitan Police handbill circulated during the Crippen manhunt. Illustrated with portraits of Crippen and Le Neve and samples of their handwriting, the poster announces 'Murder and Mutilation' – the latter word in smaller but still bold type and partially underlined. Barrister Cecil Mercer later averred in his memoirs that 'It was the handbill, I think, that gave [the case] a flying start... Who it was that drafted that bill I never knew: but I need hardly say that the crime of mutilation is quite unknown to the law.'[9] It is tempting to speculate that the unknown draftsman might have been mindful of the Ripper handbill of two decades before with its comparable banner headline 'GHASTLY MURDER ... DREADFUL MUTILATION.

Parallels between Crippen and the Ripper were further heightened when it became widely known that Crippen was a doctor (the dubious nature of his qualifications was not emphasised in the earlier press reports). This detail resonated with a firmly established trope in the Ripper legend, which cast the killer as a Jekyll and Hyde-like medic – respectably practising for the good of his patients by day; turning his talents and training to diabolical ends by night. This image of a 'gentleman Jack' with medical training was one of the earliest of the Ripper myths and was current even while the later murders were taking place. Its purchase on the public imagination was secured by the presentation in summer and autumn 1888 of a production of *Dr Jekyll and Mr Hyde* at Henry Irving's Lyceum Theatre. Starring American actor Richard Mansfield, the play boasted the endorsement of Robert Louis Stevenson and had transferred to London from a highly successful run in New York. So authentic and unsettling was Mansfield's portrayal of the respectable medical man harbouring a murderous alter ego that many a press column and letters page that autumn drew parallels between the play's protagonist and the unknown perpetrator of the Whitechapel crimes. A leader from the *Pall Mall Gazette* of early October 1888 is indicative, proposing a Ripper who was both: 'Jekyll and Hyde – Possibly the culprit is an army doctor suffering from sunstroke. He has seen the horrible play, lives in Bayswater or North London, in perhaps

9   Cecil Mercer writing as Dornford Yates, *As Berry and I Were Saying* (London: Ward Lock, 1952), p. 239.

12.   The police handbill for the Crippen case of 1910 was evocative of the Jack the Ripper 'Ghastly Murder' poster of two decades before.

a decent square or terrace. Dresses well. Goes out about 10 P.M. straight to Whitechapel. Commits deed. Home again to breakfast. Wash, brush-up, sleep. Himself again.'[10]

The curious coincidence of art and life in 1888 was to be repeated in 1910 when Henry Irving's son H.B. Irving, actor and true crime enthusiast, reprised Jekyll and Hyde in the West End, impressing the *Illustrated London News* with his portrayal: 'Mr H.B. Irving has scored a personal success in his extraordinary interpretation of Stevenson's ghastly tale, the adaptation of which was produced at the Queen's Theatre on Saturday January 29. Nothing more tense can be imagined than those moments when the pathetic Dr. Jekyll changes before the eyes of the audience into the repulsive, shrunken figure of Edward Hyde, the incarnation of all that is evil.'[11] Premiering a mere two days before Belle Elmore, wife of Dr Hawley Harvey Crippen, would disappear forever, the play was firmly back in the minds of metropolitan audiences in early 1910. Indeed, trading on this contemporaneity, Crippen's defence counsel at his trial would effectively dare the jury to picture Crippen as a Jekyll and Hyde, gathering from each witness in turn the assurance that Crippen was ever a gentle, polite, and mild-mannered man:

> From every witness who had known him came the same tale; these were the characteristics in the very words the witnesses had used – 'amiable', 'kind-hearted', 'good-hearted', 'good-tempered', 'one of the nicest men I ever met.' The people who gave him that character were people of different ages, of different interests, and of both sexes. Could the jury say that reputation was not deservedly earned? Yet it was openly suggested that a man with those characteristics suddenly became a fiend incarnate.[12]

As we shall see, this argument to the jury that Crippen made an unlikely Jekyll and Hyde was supported by Crippen's own downplaying of his medical knowledge. In his trial testimony Crippen emphasised his affiliation to homeopathic medicine and disavowed his surgical (and gynaecological) training and experience. In this way, he arguably managed to avoid the worst of parallels with 'the doctor gone wrong' as described by Sherlock Holmes in *The Speckled*

---

10   *Pall Mall Gazette*, 3 October 1888.
11   *Illustrated London News*, 5 February 1910.
12   *Trial*, p. 79.

Band: 'When a doctor does go wrong he is the first of criminals. He has nerve and he has knowledge.'[13] The wayward medic who prompts Holmes's reflection, Dr Grimesby Roylott, would also have been readily brought to mind for metropolitan audiences in the summer of 1910: a production of *The Speckled Band* opened at the Adelphi Theatre in June, just as Cora Crippen's friends were preparing to take their concerns to Scotland Yard: 'a nice example of the sensational play' remarked *The Bystander*, 'It is melodrama, of course, but of a quiet and impressive kind.'[14] In the Holmes drama, Dr Grimesby Roylott combines his knowledge of toxicology and exotic animals to murder one stepdaughter, and attempt the murder of the other, by means of a barely-detectable snake bite. When the story was first published in *The Strand Magazine* in February 1892 the case of true-life doctor-poisoner Thomas Neill Cream would shortly come to trial. In the autumn of that year, Cream would be charged with the murder of four women in Lambeth over the previous year, the attempted murder of a fifth, and the sending of blackmailing letters. Cream had dispensed poison to his victims in pills which he had presented to them as abortifacients. With the trappings of a stage villain, Cream even sported false whiskers and beard as a disguise.[15] One of the last prisoners to be executed at the medieval Newgate Prison in November 1892, Cream would have been one of the chief examples of the 'doctor gone wrong' in Edwardian memory at the time of Crippen, perpetuating a late Victorian mistrust of medical men which was only heightened by such notorious trials. One contributor to the *British Medical Journal* that summer was concerned to distance the 'quackery' of imposters like American-born Crippen and Cream from the licensed practice of reputable practitioners: 'Here, then, is a chief danger to the public. Crippens and Neill Creams may flood our metropolis; they may successfully compete with our duly qualified members of an overworked and underpaid profession; they may, without question or suspicion, obtain large amounts of poisons; they may commit murders, and their detection may be entirely due to some accidental circumstance.'[16]

---

13 Arthur Conan Doyle, 'The Speckled Band', *The Adventures of Sherlock Holmes* [1892] (Harmondsworth: Penguin, 1981), p. 185.
14 *Bystander*, 15 June 1910.
15 'Neill Cream Committed', *North London News*, 3 September 1892.
16 Seymour Taylor, 'Unqualified Practice and Crime', *British Medical Journal* 2:2604 (1910), pp. 1747–8. A third American-born 'quack' doctor, Francis Tumblety, has since 1995

Quack doctors might also be associated, even as late as 1910, with such pseudo-sciences as mesmerism. Even as the Crippen trial was taking place a series of articles in *Pearson's Weekly News* chronicled the curiously parallel career of one William Fletcher Hall, 'a remarkable quack doctor from America who has been touring the principal English cities and towns.' Hall claimed affiliation with the otherwise undocumented Alloway Medical Institute, under whose auspices he offered a 'special treatment' for a range of ailments. Straddling the spheres of medical practice and music hall, the efficacy of the doctor's cures would be advertised by means of his theatrical appearances accompanied by a 'Boy Phenomenon'. This young assistant would appear onstage swathed in a white blanket and subject to an entranced state while Hall, as operator of the trance, would channel a 'current of life' from the Boy Phenomenon to any sick or afflicted audience members who were prepared to pay extra for the privilege.[17]

Other examples from 1910 join with Hall's act in attesting to an abiding Edwardian interest in mesmerism. This curious pseudo-science provoked both fascination and, as Ruth Harris has observed, an element of alarm given 'the dramatic way in which it demonstrated the reality of unconscious mental activity, explored the recesses of memory, and showed the immense possibilities of manipulating subjects through the imposition of authority'.[18] The year 1910 saw the publication of London psychiatrist Bernard Hollander's *Hypnotism and Suggestion*, which explored the effectiveness of techniques of 'suggestion' in the spheres of education, 'daily life', and medicine, and of alienist L. Forbes Winslow's monograph *The Suggestive Power of Hypnotism*. The review of the latter in *The Tatler* sought to dispel the more sinister associations of mesmerism: 'Can anyone whilst in a state of hypnosis or otherwise be influenced by the operator to commit a crime? Impossible.'[19] Winslow was also propounding his ideas in public lectures. In February 1910, days

been under consideration as a Jack the Ripper suspect. See Stewart P. Evans and Paul Gainey (1995), *The Lodger: The Arrest and Escape of Jack the Ripper* (London: Century).
17 *Pearson's Weekly*, 27 October 1910.
18 Ruth Harris, *Murders and Madness: Medicine, Law, and Society in the fin de siècle* (Oxford: Oxford University Press, 1989), p. 157. In an interesting parallel, one of the case studies of mesmerists Harris gathers from a French context features an itinerant dentist using hypnotism to assault one of his patients.
19 *The Tatler*, Wednesday 6 July 1910, reviewing L. Forbes Winslow, *The Suggestive Power of Hypnotism* (London: Rebman Ltd, 1910).

after Crippen had been in Oxford Street pawning items of his missing wife's jewellery, Winslow, as Vice-President of the Psycho-Therapeutic Society, was addressing the society's members at the Caxton Hall, Westminster, making bold claims for the power of suggestion: 'The lecturer considered that more than half the ills to which flesh was heir could be cured by suggestion, whereas half the world could be laid low and protracted by the same power.'[20] Encouraged by his recent visit to Parisian exponent of hypnotism Dr Edgar Bérillon, Winslow's conclusion looked forward to a time when the naysayers would at last acknowledge 'the power of suggestion as a great factor in the treatment of disease'.

Popular interest was also reflected by the appearance of a cluster of early films on the theme, including *The Hypnotic Wife* (1909), *The Criminal Hypnotist* (1909), and *Hypnotism* (1910), in which a young girl commits robbery while under mesmeric influence.[21] And just as H.B. Irving would revive Jekyll and Hyde on the London stage in the year of Crippen, so Herbert Beerbohm Tree had been appearing at His Majesty's Theatre in the autumn of 1909 as Svengali in the stage adaptation of George du Maurier's *Trilby*. The plot, in which musical maestro Svengali transforms an unaccomplished young female singer into a *prima donna* by the power of hypnotism, again held out suggestive parallels with Crippen, making available a typology to which the quack doctor and theatrical manager, and his younger mistress, might easily be approximated. And Tree's production would summon the memory of Svengali beyond London and on into 1910, the year of Crippen. He led the Majesty's Theatre troupe on a successful national tour of the production, in repertory with a number of other plays, and gathering positive reviews: 'In very popular parts like Svengali… he has fascinated playgoers in their thousands in town and country;'[22] 'The effects of Svengali's uncanny mesmeric powers over the hapless girl were convincingly simulated.'[23] Tree would be back in London that autumn to sit in the public gallery during the Crippen trial, where it seemed he

20 *Daily Telegraph and Courier*, 15 February 1910.
21 Sharon Packer, *Movies and the Modern Psyche* (Westport, CT: Praeger, 2007), pp. 57–8. Cinema also offered more light-hearted takes on mesmerism: the cinema listings in *The Era* for 12 February 1910 include a billing for *Lessons in Hypnotism*, 'a most laughable film': *The Era*, 12 February 1910.
22 *Aberdeen Press and Journal*, 10 September 1910.
23 'Sir Herbert Tree at Harrogate', *Yorkshire Post and Leeds Intelligencer*, 27 May 1910.

would cultivate a sympathy for the mild-mannered prisoner; Hesketh Pearson later recalled a shared cab journey shortly after the death sentence was handed down where Tree repeatedly muttered the refrain, 'Poor Old Crippen'.[24]

Sure enough, tropes from this literary and theatrical tradition also found their way into the production and reception of Crippen. On 1 August 1910, the *Evening Telegraph and Post* ran an extensive front-page story on Crippen's arrest at Father Point. The coverage included an interview with Ethel le Neve's mother, Charlotte Neave, who, concerned to exculpate her daughter, introduced suggestions of mesmerism into the Crippen drama: 'I am convinced she was hypnotised by the man who took her away ... If this had not been so Ethel would never have dressed herself in boy's clothes.'[25] Mrs Neave's suggestion doubtless traded on the current high profile of mesmerism on the national stage; in addition to Tree's popular turn as Svengali, another mesmerism drama was making its London debut on the very same evening that her interview went to press. Edward Marris's *A Criminal's Bride* had previewed in Brighton during the previous week. The villain of the piece 'possesses hypnotic powers, which he exercises over women in particular' and which are deployed on several hapless victims during the course of the drama.[26]

Once seeded in this way, the hypnotism rumour persisted throughout the month while Crippen languished in a Quebec gaol. *The Daily Telegraph* of 17 August carried an advertisement reading: 'Crippen Case: Hypnotism talked of' and encouraged readers to consult Dr Albert Moll's treatise on the subject.[27] The same day's number of the *Newcastle Daily Journal* carried a more detailed claim connecting Crippen with mesmerism. One of many 'lucky escape' stories

---

24 Hesketh Pearson, *Modern Men and Mummers* (London: Allen and Unwin, 1921), p. 51. Tree was likely quoting one of the many contemporary street songs that grew up around the case (see further below).

25 *Evening Telegraph and Post*, 1 August 1910. The coverage in this paper contains some intriguing details not occurring elsewhere, including the suggestion that Crippen was carrying 'a bottle containing poison' and the claim that 'when Le Neve was being searched by a stewardess she threw something out of the cabin window.'

26 *The Stage*, 4 August 1910. The review deems the plot 'exciting and not too improbable' despite instances of hand-severing and a subsequent single-handed strangulation. In a curious twist, the Scotland Yard detective who serves as foil to the villain is named Mitchell, the namesake of Dew's right-hand man.

27 *Daily Telegraph*, 17 August 1910.

that featured in the wake of the Crippen case, the story related how a young woman from Peckham could offer confirmation of the theory that Crippen exercised hypnotic influence over Le Neve, having been mesmerised by the doctor himself during a visit to his dental surgery for a dental extraction: 'I had not up to then by any means consented to take gas, but immediately "Dr" Crippen began to look at me, I wavered, and after a few words, he won me over. His kindly and thoughtful countenance, and, above all – if I may say so – the sympathetic expression of his eyes, seemed to cast a spell over me. I felt almost hypnotised as he gently remarked to me: "Come, now; there is no danger."'[28] The patient remarks that Crippen was still holding her hand when she regained consciousness, the teeth having been successfully extracted. Compulsion to remain focused on Crippen overcomes the pain and side effects of the gas and 'on leaving, I inwardly remarked that he was one of the nicest men I had ever met. His calm, confident, and sympathetic manner has left a lasting impression on my mind, and his connection with the Hilldrop Crescent affair came as an awful shock to me.'[29]

Thus already we can observe the interplay of melodramatic and theatrical traditions in the cultural formation of Crippen. Overtones of murder, mutilation, and mesmerism in the reportage of the case evoked echoes of the Ripper and effected a cultural interchange between details of the Crippen drama and contemporary melodramatic renderings of the murderous Mr Hyde and the mesmeric Svengali. The vibrancy of this essentially Victorian melodramatic tradition at this late date is striking. A 1909 parliamentary committee on theatrical censorship by the Lord Chamberlain gathered insights on the 'gruesome plays' that were still to be seen on the national stage and the 'vicious sensationalism of the melodrama in the smaller towns'. One witness gave a detailed illustration of one such entertainment: 'It was in Halifax about a year ago. It was called "The Face at the Window". I don't know exactly what the plot was. It was unintelligible drivel. The whole raison d'être of the play appears to be the introduction of a creature entitled "Le Loup" – half-man, half-wolf. He had green lines upon him, and was wearing a hideous mask, and his entrance

28 *The Newcastle Daily Journal*, 17 August 1910.
29 The heightened profile of mesmerism in the Crippen case may have suggested the line of defence adopted by George Hackshaw of East Ham when charged with the murder of his brother in August 1910: 'I believe my brother hypnotises me ... I believe he had some influence over my wife as well.' *Daily Telegraph and Courier*, 16 August 1910.

was preceded by unearthly yells and groans. This gentleman went through the play stabbing various people and doing murder indiscriminately.'[30] The same year saw the West End staging of a new melodrama, *The Woman in the Case* by Clyde Fitch. 'Melodramatic in quality it may be,' said the *Telegraph*, 'but the proof of the pudding is in the eating, and the public, by its ready acceptance of *The Woman in the Case*, has given the best possible evidence that it is prepared to accept and to enjoy fare of a highly flavoured description.'[31]

By virtue of his status as doctor-poisoner and fugitive, Crippen intersected both with this melodramatic tradition and with an equally well-established Victorian ambivalence towards medical men. As Richard Altick has observed, the prominence of medics in notorious murder trials, 'either as protagonists or as conspicuously incompetent and/or discrepant "expert" witnesses,' left a deep impression on the public mind: 'Whereas most of the genuinely great Victorian medical men worked in relative obscurity, their achievements recognized in the main only by their colleagues […] those who proved morally or scientifically fallible won a notoriety wholly disproportionate to their number.'[32] Such notoriety was particularly acute in the case of doctor-poisoners, where the patient's trust in the hand that proffers a curative or restorative dram is cruelly betrayed by administration of a lethal dose. Two notorious doctor-poisoners of this kind were gathered up into the narrativising of Crippen by the press; Palmer and Pritchard.

The Doctor-Poisoners

In 1910 William Palmer still lingered in collective Edwardian memory as 'the Rugeley poisoner', his case having come to trial at the Old Bailey in 1856. Born in Rugeley, Staffordshire in 1824, the first twenty years of Palmer's life saw him gain the credentials for a promising medical career. He trained at St Bartholomew's Hospital Medical College, London, became a member of the Royal College of Surgeons, and returned in 1846 to his native Staffordshire to establish himself in practice. Marriage and a young family soon followed,

---

30   'Dramatic Censor', *Daily Telegraph and Courier*, 20 August 1909.
31   *Daily Telegraph and Courier*, 24 August 1909.
32   Richard Altick, *Victorian Studies in Scarlet: Murders and Manners in the Age of Victoria* (London: Dent and Sons, 1970), p. 147.

though only one of Palmer's five children was to survive infancy. The doctor's fortunes worsened further when a taste for keeping racehorses and speculating supplanted Palmer's interest in attending to his practice. Judith Flanders relates the concatenation of sudden Palmer family deaths which coincided with the doctor's accrual of mounting debts as a result of his racing:

> In 1854, overwhelmed by debt, he insured his wife's life for £13,000 (some said £30,000). Soon after the first premium was paid, she was dead. That same year, Palmer attempted to insure his brother Walter's life. Walter, an alcoholic, had been rejected by two companies. One finally agreed to insure him, and in August 1855 Palmer bought Prussic acid from a chemist; his brother died two days later.[33]

Alarmingly, it was not these family deaths, nor those of Palmer's many illegitimate children, which attracted suspicion but rather the very public death in 1855 of fellow racegoer and speculator John Parsons Cook. After Palmer and Cook attended Shrewsbury Races together, the former losing bets while Cook won, the pair returned to Rugeley where Cook took lodgings at the Talbot Arms Hotel opposite Palmer's house. Cook was already unwell, having been dosed by Palmer during a drinking session back at Shrewsbury on 13 November. Over the course of the following week Palmer repeatedly administered strychnine (and likely other poisons) to his companion until on 20 November Cook suffered extreme convulsions and finally died.

The death was not immediately thought suspicious, an aged Dr Bamford recording the cause of death as apoplexy. Yet of the seventeen death notices carried in *The Leicester Chronicle* of Saturday 24 November, Cook's stood out starkly: 'On Wednesday at Rugeley, suddenly after a few days illness, aged 29, John Parsons Cook Esq.' A week later *The Staffordshire Advertiser* reflected growing unease around the death, reporting on Cook's autopsy and inquest under the headline: 'Mysterious death of a sporting gentleman'.[34] The suspicions of Cook's stepfather had by now been aroused and were heightened by Palmer's obvious attempts to withhold from the family the dead man's betting papers and account books.

---

33 Judith Flanders, *The Invention of Murder: How the Victorians Revelled in Death and Detection and Created Modern Crime* (London: Harper Press, 2011), p. 259.

34 *The Leicester Chronicle*, Saturday 24 November 1855; *Staffordshire Advertiser*, 1 December 1855.

The family looked to the post-mortem to shed some light on the death and thus Palmer did his best to disrupt it, actually gaining admission to the autopsy as an 'interested professional' and even jostling the doctor who removed Cook's stomach, with the result that the contents spilled out onto the floor (he later attempted to bribe the attendant charged with conveying the mortician's jars to London). Yet Palmer's efforts to cover his tracks proved unavailing and in a milestone of forensic investigation in England, the analyst Dr Alfred Swaine Taylor deposed in his findings to the coroner that the body of James Parsons Cook had contained traces of antimony. The exhumed bodies of his wife and brother also indicated the hand of the poisoner had been at work in their deaths and thus by the time Palmer came to trial in May 1856 three separate inquests had already returned a verdict of murder against him. Flanders notes the abundance of sensational press coverage of the Palmer crimes long before the trial itself, further remarking that this was the first sensational murder case since the abolition of the newspaper tax first levied in the reign of Queen Anne. Accordingly, the reading public might now afford to follow the unfolding of a sensational murder case day by day, charting its progress through fresh editions of the papers.[35] Indeed, Altick observes that it is in these press accounts, rather than in the more clinical transcripts of the trial proceedings, that the imaginative power of the case is conveyed: 'the public, devouring columns upon columns of additional details, inadmissible as evidence, which were uncovered by the tireless employees of a press little inhibited by law, knew a great deal more about – and in particular against – Palmer than the jury was permitted to hear'.[36]

Palmer was executed in front of Stafford Gaol at 8am on Saturday 14 June 1856. A large body of police, including 130 special constables, kept order over the huge crowd that had assembled to witness the hanging: 'The populace, infuriated, tore the air with clamours – "Murderer!" "Poisoner!" "Blood!" were loudly shouted and screamed in hideous mockery.'[37] These cries, incited by the particular Victorian dread of the doctor who destroys life, clearly reverberated down to 1910.

---

35 Flanders, *The Invention of Murder*, p. 262. See also Martin Hewitt, *The Dawn of the Cheap Press in Victorian Britain: the End of the 'Taxes on Knowledge', 1849–1869* (London: Bloomsbury, 2013).
36 Altick, *Victorian Studies in Scarlet*, pp. 153–4.
37 'Execution of Palmer', *London Evening Standard*, 14 June 1856.

So too did the case of Dr Edward William Pritchard. This second doctor-poisoner enjoyed a maritime career as a naval surgeon in the 1840s, including a stint on board HMS *Victory*. After marriage in 1851, he established a general practice in Yorkshire, but by the end of the decade, having accrued debts and a dubious reputation, he relocated with wife and family to Glasgow. The doctor's unquiet household at 11 Berkley Terrace first hit the headlines in early May 1863 when a serious fire broke out in the dead of night, claiming the life of young house servant Elizabeth McGrain. In the press accounts of the fire, Pritchard claimed to have been awoken by McGrain's screams in the early hours of the morning, alerting him to the fire. He rushed his two infant sons to safety outside, aided by Police Constable Robert Hartley, who had spotted the fire from the street. Doctor and policeman then raced together to the attic of the house where, amidst the smoke and flames, they could dimly discern McGrain's body still in bed, 'a frightfully charred mass'.[38] Pritchard's account of McGrain's screams accorded ill with this disposition of the body, which rather suggested the maid had been drugged or otherwise incapacitated in her bed at the time of the fire. But if murder had been done (and there were suggestions of an affair between Pritchard and McGrain) it remained undiscovered and the family relocated to a new home at 131 Sauchiehall Street. Here, and in quick succession, Pritchard's mother-in-law Jane and wife Mary died in early 1865. Pritchard, who had attended both patients, claimed that apoplexy had claimed the life of his mother-in-law and gastric fever that of his wife. The other doctors in attendance were unconvinced and when the bodies were exhumed and examined, antinomy was found to be present in both. Press accounts of Pritchard's trial and execution again expressed the particular horror of the doctor-poisoner: 'when the dart of destruction is levelled by the hand which should cherish and protect … we may well shudder at a depravity which sinks human nature to a depth as inconceivable as it is revolting.'[39] Reminiscent as it was of the Palmer poisonings, the Pritchard case differed on the crucial question of motive. While the avaricious motives driving Palmer's crimes were patent, Pritchard's own motives were obscure. Possibly he was conducting an affair and viewed his wife as an inconvenient obstacle. Possibly there was pure malice and sadism in the murders of both wife and mother-in-law. This obscurity of motive has played a significant part in the posterity of the crime, as remarked by one

38 'Shocking Occurrence in Glasgow', *Northern Whig*, 7 May 1863.
39 'The Execution of Dr Pritchard', *Caledonian Mercury*, 29 July 1865.

early twentieth-century criminologist: 'The motive of his crime has baffled every psychologist who has attempted to review the case, and it would be impertinent after so long an interval, to suggest causes which can now neither be proved nor disproved ... Either there must have been some secret motive which escaped contemporary observers or [a] theory of homicidal mania must be upheld. If murder be one of the fine arts then this indeed was art for art's sake.'[40]

The names of Palmer and Pritchard were promptly linked with that of Crippen as it became clear that the body discovered at Hilldrop Crescent had been the victim of poisoning. National and regional papers of July 1910 suggested 'the details of the crime so far as known bear a resemblance to the Deeming [see below] and Pritchard murders',[41] and appealed to the memories of those readers 'who recall the trial of Palmer and Dr Pritchard', both of which involved poison.[42] *The Dundee Courier*'s front-page report of Crippen's arrest under the headline: 'Crippen I want you' on 1 August 1910 was accompanied by an immediately adjacent column on 'The Murderer's Fallacy' revisiting the cases of these two notorious doctor-poisoners. Meanwhile, *The Gloucestershire Chronicle* of 6 August 1910 noted 'it would be grossly improper to prejudge [Crippen's] case' yet went on in the same article to reflect on the character traits of historical poisoners from Pritchard to as far back as the Borgias.

It is striking that the press accounts of the Crippen case generally looked back to these Victorian murder sensations rather than to more recent, ostensibly more apposite, cases. There were few press comparisons drawn, for example, with the highly comparable Muller case of 1864 which had likewise involved the transatlantic pursuit by a Scotland Yard inspector of a man wanted for murder. German-born Franz Muller was wanted for the violent murder and robbery of banking clerk Thomas Briggs aboard a train on the North London railway on 9 July 1864. Pursued by the Yard's Inspector Tanner, Muller took flight aboard the sailing ship *Victoria*, bound for New York. In a curious anticipation of Dew's pursuit of Crippen fifty years later, Tanner set out two days later on the faster, steam-powered *City of Manchester*. In a denouement which, as *The New York Times* remarked, was 'much the same as the arrival of Crippen at Father Point',[43] the Yard's man overtook the unsuspecting

40   Harold Eaton, *Famous Poison Trials* (London: Collins and Sons, 1923), pp. 66–7.
41   *Ballymena Observer*, 22 July 1910.
42   *Stonehaven Journal*, 27 October 1910.
43   *New York Times*, 7 August 1910.

criminal and summarily arrested him upon arrival in New York. Extradition proceedings and a return to England aboard the *Etna* swiftly ensued.[44] Muller was convicted, despite the purely circumstantial nature of the evidence against him, and executed on 1 November 1864. A small number of papers remarked on the parallel between the Muller and Crippen cases, including *The Globe* (11 August 1910) and *The Referee*, which pointed out how many of the details of the Crippen case 'were quite along the old lines', going on to invoke the Muller case: 'those who are old enough to remember the capture of Muller, the author of another North London crime […] cannot help being struck with history's repetition of itself.'[45] *The East London Observer* also followed the promptings of 'Dagonet', the pen-name of the aforementioned George R. Sims, to note that 'many of the incidents of the hunt after Crippen across the Atlantic resemble those of the capture of Muller'.[46] Yet for the most part, the press tended not to emphasise these more immediate connections and parallels with the 'North London Railway Murder'. Instead, they moved swiftly to associate Crippen with a lineage of earlier more notorious killers – specifically poisoners – many of them multiple homicides and several of them doctors. This tracing of lineage started early. In mid-July 1910, *The Belfast Weekly News* and *The Norfolk News* respectively reported how the North London Cellar Murder involved 'circumstances which recall the notorious Deeming crime' which had 'so shocked London many years ago', an allusion to Frederick Bailey Deeming, who was executed in 1892 after murders in both England and Australia and who at one stage was suggested as a candidate for Jack the Ripper.[47]

The conflation of Crippen with these historical poisoners was in some cases the result of invention and speculation, especially during the period of the manhunt and during the extradition proceedings following Crippen's arrest. It was during this period that stories appeared regarding Crippen's first marriage, the untimely death of first wife Charlotte Bell, and the suspicions

---

44   The curious parallels between the two cases extend to similar reading habits on the voyage home; both prisoners took up a copy of Dickens's *Pickwick Papers* (*London Daily News*, 17 September 1864); Connell, *Doctor Crippen*, p. 56.

45   *Referee*, Sunday 7 August 1910.

46   'The Murder of Mr Briggs', *East London Observer*, 17 September 1910.

47   *Belfast Weekly News*, Thursday 21 July 1910; *Norfolk News*, 23 July 1910. Deeming's murder of Emily Mather is related by Gordon Honeycombe, *The Murders of the Black Museum* (London: Hutchinson, 1982), pp. 31–4.

of her brother. Likewise, witness testimony of dubious provenance began to flesh out the known details of the case, such as one paper's report of Crippen's accompanying of Dew and Mitchell during their search of Hilldrop Crescent. In an account that cannot have originated with either of the Scotland Yard men in question, we learn additional 'details' of their search of the cellar: 'after some moments of awkward search in the semi-darkness he called out, with a sinister laugh, "You will never find anything there," and then "It's not a nice place to stay in."' The report goes on to suggest that something was seen 'glinting' in the hand of Crippen as he stood on the cellar stairs – this being assumed to be the revolver with which he would have despatched the officers had they discovered the fearful secret of the cellar.[48] Such apocryphal details, legion in the press accounts of the Crippen case, took their derivation not only from the concordance of past crime histories but also from melodrama and sensation literature. Responsibility for the inter-penetration of these genres with the Crippen case lay not only with the press, but also rather closer to home with Crippen himself.

'I have been a reader of romances to a great extent'

While his appeal could hardly have adverted to the fact, Crippen's actions in 1910 played their own part to encourage a 'classic' view of the case, evocative of notorious crimes of criminal history and sensation literature. His choice of hyoscine as the poison for his task seemed exotic (antimony and arsenic were the more familiar toxins) and, as we shall see, in fact transpires to have been a fictional murderer's drug of choice in a sensation novel that Crippen may just have known.[49] His disposal of parts of the body in the coal cellar evoked a whole host of famous cases, some of which may even have inspired his actions. Bodies in cellars or under floors had been a feature of the 'Euston Square Mystery' of 1879, where a body had similarly been discovered in the coal cellar of an apparently respectable London townhouse, not far from

---

48 '"Something" glinted in Crippen's Hand', *The Courier*, 27 July 1910.
49 The Crippen case seems to have raised awareness of hyoscine on both sides of the Atlantic: at the very end of 1910 a New York banker arraigned in connection with the collapse of the Northern Bank collapsed in court having attempted suicide by taking a tenth of a grain of hyoscine: 'the poison brought into prominence by the Crippen case': *Guardian*, 31 December 1910.

Hilldrop Crescent, and 'the Bermondsey Horror' of 1849, where husband and wife Maria and Frederick Manning had concealed the corpse of Maria's lover Patrick O'Connor under the flagstones of their kitchen. The memory of both murders had been kept current in Edwardian memory – the Mannings by virtue of their central place in Madame Tussaud's Chamber of Horrors and the Euston Square murder in such contexts as Charles Peace's 1903 short story 'The Hidden Hand', where two women walking in the neighbourhood of the murder recollect the events of thirty years before: 'There was a murder committed in that house,' said the woman, dropping her voice and pointing across Angela. 'The body of a woman was found in the coal cellar and it was never discovered who murdered her. She was lying there about two years.'[50] The Hilldrop Crescent killer's attempt to speed the destruction of the buried remains by application of quicklime was also a feature of the previous crimes.[51]

These, and related details in the case, reveal Crippen's own imaginative participation in a Victorian and Gothic inheritance of criminal romance. A prime example is his line of defence at trial, the premise of which was that the remains interred in St Pancras Roman Catholic Cemetery in Finchley were not those of Belle Elmore, and that the missing woman was in fact still alive, poised to break cover and return to society as soon as the jury made the fatal mistake of sending Crippen to the scaffold. The prosecution's closing speech to the trial jury gave short shrift to this gothic image of a revenant Belle, associating it with a bygone age rather than this modern age of technology and progress:

> There were cases in the books, said his learned friend, which showed that men had been tried for murder, convicted, and hanged, and then their

---

50 As cited in Sinclair McKay, *The Lady in the Cellar: Murder, Scandal and Insanity in Victorian Bloomsbury* (London: White Lion, 2018), p. 292. McKay provides a detailed account of the Hacker case and of the perjury and libel actions that ensued, concluding with a reassertion of the case against original suspect housemaid Hannah Dobbs.

51 The Euston Square murder was also referenced in a January 1911 letter to *The Kilburn Times*. Commenting on the petition by Hilldrop Crescent residents to have their street renamed to escape its infamy, the correspondent writes: 'The only instance in London that I can recall where the name of a place was changed owing to its association with a murder was in the case of the Euston-square mystery in the seventies, where an eccentric old lady was murdered under extraordinary circumstances. Mr W.M. Rossetti, who lived in the square, headed a petition which resulted in the south side of Euston square becoming Endsleigh Gardens.' *Kilburn Times*, 6 January 1911.

supposed victims had turned up alive. There were such cases in books. Sir Matthew Hale, who died in 1676, mentioned two such cases, which were old cases in his time. The world had contracted since then for the purpose of finding absent persons. Steamships, railway trains, electric telegraphs, and newspapers had made a vast difference to the administration of justice since Sir Matthew Hale's time. But it was thought necessary to flutter before their eyes that ancient bogey, as if they were not grown men, and as if they would be afraid to go home in the dark because, according to their consciences, they had done their duty.[52]

Nor was this the only 'ancient bogey' to be summoned in the posterity of the Crippen case by the prisoner himself. Crippen's assertion 'I have been a reader of romances to a great extent' was likely part of a calculated attempt to project an unworldly and naïve demeanour, in line with the way in which he played down his medical knowledge and business acumen in favour of the persona of innocent abroad.[53] Yet whether by virtue of his early reading habits as peripatetic homeopath or through his long immersion in the milieu of music hall, Crippen's own imaginative investment in the fictions betrays theatrical and literary influences which again serve to affiliate his story with established tropes and traditions.

The starkest example is Crippen's ruse to disguise Ethel in boy's clothes during their escape to Antwerp and on to Quebec. The police thought it possible that the absconding couple would resort to disguise – but the general assumption was that it was Crippen who would do the dissimulation, perhaps as a priest, perhaps even, according to *The Globe* newspaper, as an old woman.[54] Cross-gendered masquerade on the part of his young mistress was firmly not anticipated. In fact, when this boy playing is considered in the music hall milieu in which Crippen had spent so much of his time, it appears less outlandish. Cross-dressed female performers had been a familiar element of both the American

52   *Trial*, p. 153.
53   Ibid., p. 128.
54   'Dr Crippen still at large: Masquerading as an old woman', *Globe*, 18 July 1910. Ethel's father Walter Neave encouraged this suggestion: 'It will not surprise me to hear that he is masquerading as an old woman. His gait, his effeminate mannerisms, and his gentle manner all combine to make such a make-up easy for him. The peculiar marking of his features will, I am sure, impel him to effect some disguise of the sort. His heavy gold-rimmed spectacles will probably have been replaced by goggles.'

and British music hall stage for half a century in 1910. When Crippen and Cora worked the music hall circuit in the early 1900s, top of the bill was the highly successful Vesta Tilley, whose cross-dressed masquerade garnered the adulation and fan mail of both male and female audiences and provided her licence to pronounce on men's sartorial advice: 'Vesta Tilley's "Don'ts" in Men's Dress.'[55] Tilley led a field of male impersonators advertising in the theatrical press that year, including one Lizzie Round, Hetty King, Edna Latonne, Madge Hefton, and Winifred Ward. Ethel's masquerade would have seemed less audacious amongst the bohemian music hall set of London town, incongruous as she may have been, dressed in boy's clothes on the deck of the *Montrose*.[56] Or was she? Further literary and historical context in fact suggests a recognised tradition of cross-dressing in maritime settings may also have influenced Crippen. In the twenty years preceding Ethel's masquerade, numerous press accounts appear of cross-dressed female sailors. In September 1897 an American music hall male impersonator successfully masqueraded as a man aboard the *Templemore*, working as part of the ship's crew for the duration of the passage from New York: 'Her disguise was not discovered till near Liverpool, when she was injured lifting a bale.'[57] In January 1899 ordinary seaman David McKinley was revealed, after six months at sea, to be a woman whose identity and 'motive for so strange a freak are alike unknown'.[58] Apparently obscure in this instance, the motives driving the many female sailors appearing in the press in the century before Crippen were sometimes professional, sometimes romantic. This is the motive in an example from 1839, where Sarah Ann Sage adopted cross-dressed nautical disguise to accompany her lover abroad – a ruse which fell through when her lover embarked without her. The details of Sage's disguise are curiously anticipatory of Crippen and Le Neve's flight:

> I left Cheltenham with him in my own dress, and when we reached Gloucester he took me to a barber's shop and had all my hair cut off. He then took me to a tailor's shop, and said, 'I must rig you out in sailor's clothes,' and having

55 *Bournemouth Daily Echo*, 9 November 1903.
56 Intriguingly, Susannah Stapleton has recently discovered that cross-dressing 'lady detective' Maud West was not only working in London in 1910, but had an office in Albion House alongside Crippen and Belle: Susannah Stapleton, *The Adventures of Maud West, Lady Detective* (London: Pan Macmillan, 2019).
57 'A Female Sailor', *Hartlepool Northern Daily Mail*, 9 September 1897.
58 'A Female Sailor', *Sevenoaks Chronicle and Kentish Advertiser*, 6 January 1899.

purchased a suit, he made me throw off my own garments and put on the
suit that I have on now.[59]

The startling correspondences between this account and the events of the
Crippen masquerade are in fact connected by a literary thread, embodied in
a ballad tradition entitled 'The Wearing of the Blue' or 'The Lady's Trip to
Kennady'. Attested from 1839 in Bodleian MS Bod16715, the ballad relates
the attempts of 'a gallant lady / All in her tender years' to join her sailor lover
aboard his ship and to see the distant shores of 'Kennady-i-o' – a goal that
assumes paramount importance as the ballad progresses:

> She bargained with a sailor,
> All for a purse of gold.
> And soon they did convey the lady,
> Down into the hold;
> Then dressed she up in sailor's cloaths,
> The colours are true blue,
> 'You soon shall see the pretty place
> Call'd Kennady-i-o.'
>
> When her true-love he came to hear,
> It put him in a rage.
> And all the whole ship's company,
> His passion to engage!
> 'I'll tie you hand and foot my love,
> And overboard you'll go,
> You ne'er shall see the pretty place
> Call'd Kennady-i-o.'
>
> O then spake our captain bold,
> 'Such things shall never be,
> For if we drown this lady,
> Then hanged we shall be;
> We'll dress her up in sailor's cloathes,
> The colours are true blue.
> And she soon shall see the pretty place
> Call'd Kennady-i-o.'

59 *London Evening Standard*, 25 June 1839.

> She had not been in Kennady
> Scarcely half a year
> Till the captain he married her,
> And made her his dear;
> She dresses in silks and satins,
> And she cuts a gallant show,
> She's the grandest captain's lady
> That's in Kennady-i-o.
>
> Come all you pretty fair maids,
> A warning take by me,
> Be loyal to your husbands,
> In every degree;
> For if the mate deceiv'd me,
> The captain he's proved true,
> And the captain he's prolong'd my days,
> For wearing the true blue.

Coincident with this ballad tradition, cross-dressed sailors also sporadically appear in press accounts from at least the 1840s, reflecting the lively exchange of popular cultures, oral and written traditions in Victorian and Edwardian England. The endurance onto the Edwardian musical stage of this tradition, and of the trope of the cross-dressed female sailor, is indicated by the many sketches and programmes on nautical themes. Given Belle's repertoire and the couple's immersion in the music hall circuit, it is certainly possible to imagine that Crippen was familiar with the tradition and that it may even have prompted the notion of Ethel's disguise. The ballad's inclusion of a biddable crew-member willing to aid the impersonator might even account for the elusive quartermaster described by Crippen at his trial. There the direct parallels end, for the ship's captain in Crippen's real-life rendering of 'Kennady-i-o' delivers not the promise of a new land and a new life for the adventurers but instead hands them over to the judgement of the law.[60]

---

60 Familiarity with stories of the high seas might even account for Cora Crippen's stage name. Her adoption of the name 'Belle Elmore' in early 1900 follows a decade after the death of female pirate 'Spanish Belle', who according to *The Evening World* of 9 September 1889 was a 'notorious woman, known all over the Pacific coast' and who 'died at Elmore, Idaho, last Sunday, aged eighty-seven years … It is said Spanish Belle boasted of having murdered four men herself alone for money.'. Crippen's link with the

One further literary source, this time a novel, offers further curious anticipation of elements of the Crippen case. Indeed, so close are some of the
correspondences in this instance that it is again tempting to speculate literary
influence on some of the very details of the crime. While this source has gone
unremarked in the context of Crippen for 110 years, it was in fact spotted at the
time by one highly perceptive reader of *The Referee*. Published in the paper's
letters page on 9 October 1910, the correspondent notes the startling coincidences between the Crippen case and an 1875 work of sensation fiction by
Joyce Emmerson Preston-Muddock (1843–1934), a prolific writer of detective
stories between the 1880s and the 1920s, many of them appearing initially in
serialised form in *The Strand Magazine* under the pseudonym Dick Donovan.
Julian Symons has noted how much of Muddock's work spans the intersection
between early detective fiction and the more incident-based and episodic penny
dreadfuls; it is just such hybrid territory that Muddock's sensation novel *A
Wingless Angel* occupies.[61] Published in 1875 as a one-volume novel and also
serialised between May and December that year in *The Dundee Courier*, the
novel had been relatively well received on publication: 'There is plenty of plot
and incident and interest here', wrote *Lloyd's Weekly Newspaper*[62] while *The
Sunday Times* traced the novel's influences in averring it 'has not a few of
the merits and some of the defects of the novels of Mr. Wilkie Collins'. *The
Field* considered the book an ideal *vade mecum* for holiday reading: 'We can
commend "A Wingless Angel" for the moors, the Rhine, and the seaside.'[63]
The sharp-eyed reader of the novel who wrote in to *The Referee* in the autumn
of Crippen had either recently re-read the novel or had an excellent memory.
The correspondent writer draws attention to the remarkable correspondences
between the novel and the Crippen case now coming to trial:

Pacific coast is established and we know the name was current in New York in 1900
from the appearance in the fourth race of the October Manhattan Handicap of a horse
called 'Elmore's Belle': *New York Tribune*, 3 October 1900.

61   Julian Symons, *Bloody Murder: From the Detective Story to the Crime Novel*
(Harmondsworth: Penguin, 1972), p. 92.

62   *Lloyd's Weekly Newspaper*, 26 September 1875; *Sunday Times* review as cited in *The
Dundee Courier*, 8 March 1877.

63   '"A Wingless Angel" by J.E. Muddock', *The Field: The Country Gentleman's Newspaper*,
11 September 1875.

A mysterious lady, the Belle Belmore, was accused of poisoning a young woman with hyoscyamine, an alkaloid extracted from henbane … The poisoning in the story is eventually discovered to be the work of an Indian prince of effeminate appearance, who is married to the Belle Belmore, and disguised as an Indian ayah, has accompanied her everywhere. He is arrested on board a ship while endeavouring to escape from England disguised in the clothes of the opposite sex.[64]

Closer examination of the novel reveals it to be curiously anticipatory of many aspects of the Crippen case. At least four points of striking similarity can be observed between novel and true-life drama of fifty years later.

In *A Wingless Angel*, hyoscyamine, an extract of henbane, is the cause of the victim's poisoning; in the Crippen case, hyoscine, an extract of henbane, is found in the human remains at Hilldrop Crescent. The case was the first known use of hyoscine as a means of murder.

In the novel, the post-mortem examination of the victim detects the presence of hyoscyamine 'by way of experiment to a cat'; in the Crippen case, pathologist William Henry Wilcox confirmed the presence of hyoscine in the victim's remains by a pupil-dilation test on the eye of a cat.[65]

The novel's killer engages in cross-dressed masquerade for the greater part of the story: 'He was peculiarly feminine in appearance, and when dressed in female costume, detection by a stranger was almost impossible.'[66] Ethel le Neve's rather less successful attempt at cross-dressed disguise forms a point of contrast.

The wanted suspects in both novel and true crime case attempt escape aboard ship. However, *The Referee*'s correspondent is in fact mistaken that the novel's killer is cross-dressed when boarding the ship; the masquerade by this point is instead as a medical student: 'When he first started nobody on board imagined that the well-dressed young Indian gentleman, dressed in the height of European fashion, was a guilt and crime-stained wretch for whose capture a large reward was offered.'[67]

Taken alongside the curious coincidence of name – Mrs Belmore being a

64   *Referee*, 9 October 1910.
65   *A Wingless Angel*, p. 121.
66   Ibid., pp. 260–1.
67   Ibid., pp. 261–2.

key protagonist of the novel and Belle Elmore being the unfortunate victim in the Crippen case – these strange correspondences and parallels certainly give pause for thought. The novel's uncanny foreshadowing of the Crippen case is a curiosity of literary history, sitting alongside the 1898 novel *Futility* which tells how modern steamship the *Titan* races across the Atlantic in an attempt to set a record until she 'plunges into a huge iceberg and founders'.[68] It is of course impossible to say whether the outlandish plot of *A Wingless Angel* might have impinged on Crippen's crime as some dimly remembered literary influence. The novel was described as 'long forgotten' by *The Observer* when it ran its own story on the curious parallels between novel and the case in December 1910.[69] Yet irrespective of any specific connection, *A Wingless Angel* supplies further evidence of the centrality of literary texts and melodramatic traditions in the cultural production of the Crippen drama. Those very elements of the case which, as Catharine Arnold has noted, 'would have been discarded as outrageous by any crime novelist' in fact turn out to have been already established in the Edwardian readership's horizon of expectations by virtue of previous literary and criminological treatments.[70] What was remarkable in the Crippen case was the combination and concatenation of such incidents, as if the force of these established traditions were being channelled into the one case.

Street Songs and Murder Ballads

If these literary and theatrical influences and interpenetrations suggest that the Crippen case was in part played out against an established melodramatic script, the impression is further heightened when we consider the vestigial currents of street literature and murder ballads still circulating in 1910. Here

68 *New York Times*, 11 June 1898. Morgan Robertson's *Futility* (New York, 1898) predated the *Titanic* disaster by fourteen years, though parallels between fiction and fact did not extend to Robertson's imagined battle on the iceberg between a survivor and a polar bear.
69 'Literary Notes', *Observer*, Sunday 4 December 1910. The article details the sporadic publication history of the novel and announced that a timely new edition would be forthcoming from the press of Messrs Digby, Long and Co. under the title *Whose Was the Hand?*
70 Catharine Arnold, *Underworld London: Crime and Punishment in the Capital City* (London: Simon and Schuster, 2012).

was another long-established and archaic tradition persisting into the early twentieth century and summoned into one last demonstrative flourish by the international sensation of the Crippen case. Since the early nineteenth century, murder had been marked by the mass publication of cheap broadsheets carrying the lurid details of the crime. Transported to all regions of the country, these broadsheets were vociferously marketed by street-sellers or 'patterers' who would retail headlines and key details from this 'gallows literature' to attract sales. These verbal accounts were often accompanied by illustrative street-hawkers' pictorial boards which, as Henry Mayhew described first-hand, would be 'glowing with a highly-coloured exaggeration of the interesting terrors of the pamphlet he has for sale' such as lurid scenes of the murder in question or 'faithful' depictions of criminal and victim.[71] Sales of these murder broadsides seem to have been reliably high, with records suggesting that such notorious Victorian murder cases as the Mannings' murder of O'Connell and Rush's murder of Thurtell garnered sales of 2,500,000 each.[72]

The broadsheet format gave scope for serialisation. Details of a crime and arrest might make up the contents of one publication; an account of the trial might occupy another; while details of the murderer's confession, penitence, and execution would supply material for a third. This last phase of each murder story provided a powerful rhetorical close to the drama. Often cast as a farewell letter to a loved one, the last words of the condemned criminal, uttered within shadow of the scaffold, would reverberate beyond the confines of the prison cell. There is some evidence that these histrionic death speeches and confessions were among the most popular of the murder broadsides and that the absence of such a closing chapter in a murder case was resented, prompting printers to source apocryphal envoies where no authentic text had been supplied.

Vestiges of this tradition of street literature, overlapping somewhat with music hall songs, were still current in 1910 and enjoyed a last resurgence with the advent of the Crippen case. Perhaps bolstered by Crippen's own associations with music hall, a number of patter songs arose during the manhunt, remaining current through the trial (after which one particularly persistent street singer in Barkingside was considered a nuisance by police and hauled

---

71 Henry Mayhew, *Mayhew's London – Being Selections from 'London Labour and the London Poor'*, ed. Peter Quennell (London: The Pilot Press, 1949), p. 138.
72 Altick, *Victorian Studies in Scarlet*, pp. 46–7.

away for his vociferous rendering of 'the new Crippen song')[73] and on into the aftermath of the execution.

Four of these songs were collected and published in a traditional-style murder broadside: *London Murder Mystery: Trial and Sentence of Doctor H.H. Crippen for the Murder of Belle Elmore (Mrs. Crippen) whose Mutilated Body Found in a Cellar in London – The Naughty Doctor*. A second edition including two further songs was issued immediately after the execution entitled *Execution of Dr. Crippen – The Naughty Doctor*. The *London Murder Mystery* pamphlet's bold type mirrored the placards of the street hawkers and the aforementioned 'Murder and Mutilation' bill that had been circulated by the Metropolitan Police and reprinted in the papers.

Three of the broadside's four songs were attributed to James Lauri and one to H. Poulson. Established tunes were indicated for their performance: 'The Naughty Doctor' should be set to the tune of 'Yip-i-addy-i-ay'; 'He Left You for Another', a song addressed to Cora Crippen, was set to the air of 'Nelly Dean'; 'Sentence on Dr. Crippen' should be performed to the tune of 'Please Mr Conductor'; and 'Crippen Adieu' to that of 'Top of the Morning'. As these titles indicate, the four songs chart key dramatic episodes of the crime sensation and exploit the sentimental potential of apostrophes to the deceased Belle and the condemned Crippen. The songs' style reflects what Peter Bailey has described as the 'knowingness' of music hall culture, appealing to 'the continuing force of custom and … strong sense of community'[74] with an arch and mischievous tone.

THE NAUGHTY DOCTOR

Tune: Yip-i-addy-i-ay.

We all know a man who done all he can
To cause a sensation all round,
With fright we was filled, for they fancy he killed
His dear wife and put her underground.
Then he hooked it away from us all one fine day,
With his dear little typewriter too,
And they had a nice chase to find his sweet face,

73 *Tower Hamlets Independent and East End Local Advertiser*, 12 November 1910.
74 Peter Bailey, 'Conspiracies of Meaning: Music-Hall and the Knowingness of Popular Culture', *Past and Present* 144 (1994), 138–70: 167.

Soon right over the ocean he flew.
Chorus:

The second verse abounds with euphemistic allusions to Crippen's likely fate
with metaphors drawn both from the prisoner's profession and from the very
music hall milieu that Belle had so long courted:

Crippen, my laddie, they'll make you pay,
Whatever made you run away,
And pop off with your love right over the sea,
Dressed as a boy, and so smart was she?
Soon the piper you'll have to pay, hooray,
They'll give you some physic one day,
At a end of a string, some day you might sing,
Yip-i-addy-i-ay.

The urban gothic locale of the Hilldrop Crescent coal cellar features in the
third verse, as do hints of the melodramatic characterisation of Crippen as
stage villain, traced above from the London stage:

Now this artful gay feller he had a coal cellar.
And we hear it was covered with bricks,
'Twas the scene of the crime if they'd [held] him in time
'Twould have put a stop to his tricks.
He smiled it appears, when he took 'em upstairs,
And show'd 'em all over the house,
He bid 'em good-bye. Then next day done a guy
With his donah as quiet as a mouse.

Interestingly, the final verse reflects some of the uncertain intelligence and
conflicting news reports concerning Crippen's movements on the continent
and letter on the *Montrose*. The alleged sighting of Crippen on the border
of France and Spain is referenced and the climax presents Crippen being
betrayed, presumably by a fellow passenger, to Captain Kendall, rather than
being identified by the mariner-turned-detective himself:

His escape, wild it made 'em, he tried to evade 'em,
And bunked off from France into Spain,
In and out they both trott'd, his scheme was well plott'd,

> Too wide to come back again.
> Then him and his Ethel, they boarded a vessel
> To bunk off to Canada's shore,
> But somebody sold him, the captain he [holds] him,
> To send him to England once more.

The second song in the sequence, 'He Left You for Another', takes the sentimental stance of an extended address to Cora Crippen. Centred on a refrain of 'Cora dear' and on a chorus that summons betrayed love, the song employs a more sombre tone:

> He left you for another, Cora dear,
> He took your life for her, Cora dear,
> In your grave now as you lay low,
> He'll be punished as we know,
> For the harm he did to you, my Cora dear.

The song is unambiguous as to motive, viewing the murder as prompted solely by the displacement of wife by mistress in the husband's affections.

The third song in the sequence relates key details of the trial, blending archaisms, slang, and music-hall-style quippery in its tale of a crowded court, 'a sensational case', and the blood of the audience in the public gallery running cold. With uncertain scansion, the chorus refrain rehearses the outcome of the trial:

> But guilty was the verdict, Crippen he had been doomed
> He must die on the scaffold and lie in a murderer's tomb,
> Short is the time for Repentance, let him forgiveness implore,
> For sentenced has been Dr. Crippen for the murder of poor Belle
>   Elmore.

The title page of the *Execution* pamphlet is illustrated with a crude representation of Pentonville, a cut-away section revealing the hanging shed and the executed criminal dangling from the scaffold. The woodcut illustration is evocative of the execution broadsides of old and is likely adapted from such a source: the depiction of the execution appears to be modelled on a public execution and anachronistic figures are shown, including what appear to be three soldier-like guards holding pikestaffs.

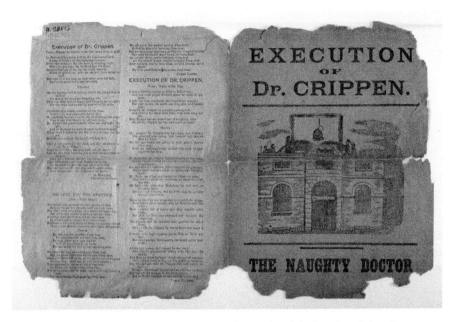

13.   The murder broadsides which circulated during the trial and execution of Crippen represented the last flourishing of a tradition of 'gallows literature' that stretched back 150 years.

This *Execution* edition of 'The Naughty Doctor' includes two ballads on the execution of Crippen. The first, by H. Poulson of Newcastle-on-Tyne, and set to the tune of 'Where the Sunset Turns the Ocean Blue to Gold', depicts Crippen in the condemned cell at Pentonville, pondering his crime and reproaching himself: 'Why did I kill the old love for the new?' In contrast to the depiction of Belle in most case histories, from Filson Young's edition of the trial proceedings onwards, Crippen's wife is depicted in all of the murder ballads as devoted and trusting of her poisoner husband: 'he killed the wife he should have loved so well.'

The second *Execution* ballad, set to the tune of 'Topics of the Day', is striking for speculating a different or additional motive for the murder: 'gold and lustful gains.' Ascribed to Frank Garrett, this is the most detailed of the Crippen ballads while also achieving relatively more fluency and metrical regularity than the other examples:

It was a London murder as filled us full of woe
And how some people do these deeds we really do not know;

> A lady has been murdered, they buried her remains,
> The only motive we could see was gold and lustful gains.
> Naughty doctor Crippen he married a young wife,
> And tired of her he must have been so he took away her life;
> Belle Elmore was an actress one of wondrous fame.
> Sly old Dr. Crippen he was very much to blame.[75]

Such comedic stereotyping of older lover Crippen and younger wife Belle, exaggerating the age difference between them of seventeen years, contributes to the jocular tone and further reflects the inter-penetration of this street literature with music hall patter songs.

The remainder of the ballad contains a surprising level of specificity, mentioning John Nash's visit to Scotland Yard, Dew's sea voyage to intercept the *Montrose* and, in line with the rollicking tone, details of Ethel le Neve's easily penetrated transvestism: 'The Captain and the Steward soon guessed she was a Miss, / And sly old Dr. Crippen he would throw her many a kiss.' The concluding stanza retails the details of Crippen's execution but is also significant for attesting ongoing suspicion in the public mind regarding the possible involvement of Ethel in the commission of the crime:

> At the late Assizes, old Crippen he was tried,
> And that he poisoned his young wife, the jury did decide,
> And Miss Le Neve his typist though she got off scot free.
> Many people think to-day she was guilty as could be.
> She was charged with Dr. Crippen but they had to let her go,
> Because the learned counsel had no evidence to show.
> She was a lucky woman, it cannot be denied.
> But as for Dr. Crippen, on the scaffold he has died.

As the compilers of the 'Naughty Doctor' pamphlet would have been keenly aware, the most satisfying resolution to the tried and tested murder broadside formula was the inclusion of the killer's confession and penitence prior to the execution, allowing a sentimental and dramatic close to the narrative complete with moral admonitions. So popular was this confession motif that apocryphal confessions would often find their way into the murder broadsides when none

---

75   Wellcome Library A.28513/NN22902.

had been forthcoming from the condemned cell.[76] The force of this tradition was keenly felt in the lively expectation of a Crippen confession. Reports of a confession had started as early as the fugitive's capture aboard the *Montrose*: 'It is believed that Crippen has made some sort of confession or at least an acknowledgement of the crime' reported the 31 July edition of *Lloyd's Weekly News* immediately after Crippen's arrest.[77] The clamour for a confession increased after the trial and failed appeal. Days before his scheduled execution, the newspaper *John Bull* published an open letter to the prisoner (incorrectly addressing him as Harvey Hawley Crippen) and challenging him to share his story: 'The days are rapidly passing, and every sunrise brings you nearer to that grim morning when you will hear the solemn announcement that your time has come.' Given that Ethel le Neve had already been tried and acquitted as an accessory after the fact, the insinuations that follow in the letter are striking:

> Was it *your* hand which did the deed, and was it your hand *alone* which sought to destroy all traces of the tragedy? … Is there *no one* in the world who can tell us aught? I decline to believe that alone you did it. I decline to believe that day after day, and night after night, you worked, unaided, at the ghastly task of dissection, dismemberment and destruction. And, above all, I decline to believe that there is not an explanation of the tragedy itself, as yet untold. You see, I know much of your life – your "home life" I was going to say; but it hadn't been that for several years, had it? There were stormy scenes and angry altercations – and you were not always, or originally, the cause of them. That, at least, is due to you to say. And more than once she had threatened to poison herself, and more than once you had said you wished she would. *Did she?* Or did someone else administer the fatal drug? And in your fright, and horror, did you then lose your mental balance?
>
> You must remember it. Tell me, by what superhuman strength was the body of a heavy woman carried down below? Did you alone do that and, in addition, dig the floor, remove the clay, cover up, rebrick and make good – you, a little half-blind, elderly, weak and timid man? And including the butchery, all in twenty-four hours? I am assuming, you see, that no one else was concerned in the affair, and that when anyone called at your house after the period I have mentioned all was peaceful and orderly. Did you alone get

---

76   Altick, *Victorian Studies in Scarlet*, p. 48.
77   *Lloyd's Weekly News*, 31 July 1910.

rid of the head, the legs, the arms; powder up the bones, the skull? And all in twenty-four hours! ...

It is a great mystery. Won't you unravel it? Or may it be that, black as you are painted, you will go to the scaffold with lips sealed in loyalty? Verily; Truth is stranger than fiction!

JOHN BULL

The open letter reflects some of the popular criminological theories about the case that had taken root in that autumn and winter of 1910. While it would be some years before the suggestion would appear in print, it seems likely that Edward Marshall Hall, who had declined the opportunity to defend Crippen, had already propounded his theory that the hyoscine was only ever administered by Crippen as an anaphrodisiac to suppress Belle's demanding physical urges or, more sordidly, as a sedative to render her unconscious so that Ethel might be smuggled into Hilldrop Crescent by night. Both this theory and suggestions of Ethel's more active involvement in the planning and commission of the crime are gathered up in the letter's many insinuations and rhetorical questions.

Meanwhile, two days before Crippen's execution and with no response to the open letter from the condemned cell, *John Bull* published an apparent response from Crippen, relayed by his solicitor, Arthur Newton:

Pentonville Prison

Monday, Nov. 21st, 1910

To the Editor of JOHN BULL

DEAR SIR, – I am extremely grateful to you for the interest you have taken in me, and I am much touched by some of the passages in your letter. I am not, however, in a position to-day to say much more.

As to making any statement which could implicate anyone else in this terrible business, that is altogether out of the question. I have only just heard of the Home Secretary's decision, and to-morrow I am expecting to see an old friend – to whom I may possibly say more than I can now.

I wish, however, to say most emphatically that under no circumstances shall I say anything which would bring trouble to others. Mr Newton has not only been my solicitor, but, especially during these past few dreadful weeks, has been a sincere friend to me in my trouble. He has my fullest confidence, and I am leaving all my affairs in his hands.

If when it is all over, he cares to tell you more than I can say to-day, I am sure you will treat the matter in the same broad and sympathetic spirit in which you have written me – and that in any case you will not forget poor Miss Le Neve if in any way you can be of assistance to her.

Again thanking you for your kindly expressions,

H.H. CRIPPEN

The allusion to the Home Secretary's decision references Winston Churchill's refusal to commute the death sentence and grant Crippen a reprieve, something discussed at a meeting between Crippen and Newton on 21 November. When 'Crippen's letter' appeared in *John Bull*, Churchill caused inquiry to be made into its provenance and origin, something that swiftly led to the conclusion: 'The letter purportedly to be signed by Crippen is an entire fabrication.'[78] The Home Office files on this closing episode of the drama reveal the astonishing willingness of Arthur Newton (who would be permanently struck off and detained at His Majesty's pleasure himself by 1913) to fill the vacuum created by Crippen's refusal to confess and to meet the public appetite for this conventional conclusion to the murder-tragedy. The depositions of the prison warders who witnessed Crippen and Newton's last interview on 21 November establish that the prisoner had in fact not even seen the *John Bull* letter. Warder George Ball confirmed that the short visit took place at 12.30pm on that late November afternoon and lasted only five minutes:

On entering the room where prisoner was seated Mr Newton said 'Good Morning Doctor,' then sitting on the chair placed for him at about 15 feet from where prisoner was sitting said, 'Well I am sorry to say all our efforts have been in vain. I have received an unfavourable reply to the petition.' Prisoner replied, 'I have been informed there is no hope.'

Mr Newton then told prisoner the number of signatures obtained for his petition, prisoner replied that he felt all had been done that it was possible to do and thanked Mr Newton for all his efforts on his behalf and further said, 'You have acted through this terrible business more like a big brother in addition to being my solicitor.'

Mr Newton then told prisoner there was an open letter in *John Bull* asking prisoner to say something about the case. I told Mr Newton that wouldn't do, as I said those words prisoner had replied, 'I know nothing about that' meaning the article in *John Bull*. Nothing more was said about the matter.

78 HO144/1719/195492.

Mr Newton said, 'I must thank you for your kind words; there is no more I can say under these circumstances. I hope you will remain brave as you have been all through.'

Mr Newton then rose, passed out of the room with me saying, 'The rules won't allow me to shake hands.' I replied, 'No sir.' On leaving the room Mr Newton shook his hand to prisoner, said 'Good-bye. Good-bye.'

Ball further confirmed that no writing materials were present and no document was passed between Crippen and Newton. The mysterious letter had originated instead with the unscrupulous solicitor, determined to address the deficit in the conclusion of the Crippen case according to the established conventions foregrounded by the 'Naughty Doctor' murder broadsides. Churchill's own Home Office memo of 1 December 1910 confirmed the apocryphal origins of the response letter:

It is clear that Newton simply concocted the reply from Crippen and whether he did so with the knowledge of the 'Editor' or not does not matter so far as his character as Solicitor is concerned. In spite of his reassurance to the Governor (see note from Governor within) he has used the fact of his interview with the prisoner to manufacture lying copy for a newspaper. He should be reported to The Law Society.

Churchill's closing commentary on fabricated news stories remains highly resonant a century and a decade later and, indeed, includes a specific term for apocryphal news stories which is generally assumed to have originated in the age of digital social media rather than in the Home Office files of 1910: 'The publication of this sort of stuff should be stopped if possible and the best way of doing it is to show it up in the press and let the public know that *such "news" is faked*' [author's emphasis].[79]

79 A Law Society enquiry subsequently had Newton struck off as a solicitor for twelve months, finding 'that the respondent, having in his capacity as solicitor, in the months of October and November 1910, obtained access to his client one Hawley Harvey Crippen, when a convict detained in His Majesty's Prison, Pentonville, abused the privilege extended to him and willfully published through the medium of certain newspapers false statements relating to Crippen, well knowing them to be false, and further, aided and abetted the editor of one of the newspapers in question to disseminate false information purporting to emanate from Crippen, whereby the public might be deceived.' HO144/1719 19542.

Newton also had a hand in the appearance of another 'full confession' which appeared in the *London Evening Times* on the night of Crippen's execution. This more detailed text had been sourced by Newton and elaborated by mystery writer Edgar Wallace, whose 1905 novel *The Four Just Men* had been one of Crippen's reading choices aboard the *Montrose*. Proposing to tell 'a story which speaks for itself, and is, perhaps one of the most remarkable and thrilling narratives which the annals of crime can furnish', the 'confession', which Crippen had allegedly vouchsafed to 'a friend' outside the prison, suggested that the doctor had poisoned Belle by means of hyoscine concealed in Munyon's indigestion tablets. Her body had been cut up with a surgeon's knife (shades of the Ripper once more) which had been hidden by the killer in the garden of a vacant property in Hilldrop Crescent, while the bones had been burned. *Evening Times* posters went up across London announcing 'Crippen Confession!' while rival papers, who had established from Newton and, more reliably, from the governor and warders of Pentonville that no such confession had been proffered, produced equivalent bills announcing 'Crippen: No Confession.' In his later memoirs, executioner John Ellis would relay how he had been asked 'a hundred times' if Crippen confessed: 'as far as I know, he didn't confess … I think he was much too clever to say any such thing so long as there remained the slightest hope of escaping the supreme penalty.'[80]

Although no authentic confession was forthcoming, Crippen did offer a 'Farewell Letter to the World' which appeared in *Lloyd's Weekly News* on 20 November 1910 and which went some way to fulfil the traditional expectation of the prisoner's words from the condemned cell: 'This is my farewell letter to the world. After many days of anxious expectation that my innocence might be proved, after enduring the final agony of a long trial and the suspense of an appeal, and after the final endeavour of my friends to obtain a reprieve, I see that at last my doom is sealed and that in this life I have no more hope.'

Thus did the street songs and murder ballads of late 1910 play their own part in the making of 'classic Crippen', encouraging the adoption of a nostalgic and traditional mode in the public recognition and rehearsal of murder and heightening expectations, partially met by an unscrupulous solicitor and an obliging press, of confession and conclusion of the drama on the traditional model.

---

80   Ellis, *Diary of a Hangman*, p. 64.

The Chamber of Horrors

While the grafting of the Crippen case into the lineage of classic crime was led largely by these textual and theatrical traditions, one last mode of representation was to play a crucial part in imprinting Crippen in memory. Before the prisoner's fate had even been sealed, in the basement of a waxworks emporium in the Marylebone Road, a space was being prepared for a wax effigy of Crippen so that he might take his place in a long line of murderers, extending back to the early Victorian era. Within months of the effigy's installation there, Hawley Harvey Crippen was to become synonymous with Madame Tussaud's Chamber of Horrors and would remain so for a century.

By 1910 the Chamber of Horrors had long been a fixture of Tussaud's waxworks emporium and had been central to the establishment of a fixed central London premises for the previously itinerant exhibition. Marie Tussaud (1761–1850) had developed her collection under the mentorship of medical doctor turned wax-modeller Philippe Curtius, whose own late eighteenth-century waxworks exhibitions had been boosted in popularity by his inclusion of a *Caverne des Grands Voleurs* that was stocked first with the waxen effigies of executed thieves and latterly with representations of victims of the guillotine during the revolutionary Terror. The Curtius formula also traded on the inclusion of authentic historical artefacts interspersed among the wax effigies, rendering the *caverne* as a unique and macabre fusion of crime museum and sideshow. The result sorted well with a public appetite for framed encounters with criminal and state violence. As Tussaud's biographer has observed: 'The *caverne* let them linger over the details of murder and the legalised violence of the subsequent execution, which in the flesh might be over too soon for those who liked to savour it.'[81] Tussaud's own version of the *caverne*, initially styled mysteriously as 'the separate room', gathered in the effigies of revolutionary figureheads Jean-Paul Marat and Jacques Hébert and Maximilien Robespierre as well as the death heads of Louis XVI and Marie Antoinette.[82] The separate room proved one of the most popular attractions when Tussaud first brought her travelling exhibition to London's Lyceum Theatre in 1802.

81 Pamela Pilbeam, *Madame Tussaud and the History of Waxwork* (London and New York: Hambledon, 2003), p. 18.
82 Pauline Chapman, *Madame Tussaud's Chamber of Horrors: Two Hundred Years of Crime* (London: Constable, 1984), p. 21.

The choice of venue was reflective of Tussaud's 'keen social awareness', as remarked by Rosalind Crone; the continental waxworker's Parisian milieu and her pedigree as a serious student and practitioner of her art helped to mark out her exhibition, and even the separate room, as 'a respectable form of leisure to which the affluent classes would flock'.[83] This distinctive cachet was retained during the thirty years of touring that followed for Tussaud's exhibition, its itinerary ranging the length and breadth of England, crossing to Dublin and north to Scotland. That Tussaud should have been considered 'to have raised the art which she professes to a pitch which can hardly be expected to be surpassed'[84] was the more remarkable given the low status associated with the waxworks of travelling fairgrounds, whose combination of macabre spectacle and glib moralising were spoofed in Dickens's depiction of exhibition guide Mrs Jarley in *The Old Curiosity Shop*:

> 'That, ladies and gentlemen,' said Mrs. Jarley, 'is Jasper Packlemerton of atrocious memory, who courted and married fourteen wives, and destroyed them all, by tickling the soles of their feet when they were sleeping in the consciousness of their innocence and virtue. On being brought to the scaffold and asked if he was sorry for what he had done, he replied ye, he was sorry for having let 'em off so easy, and hoped all Christian husbands would pardon him the offence. Let this be a warning to all young ladies to be particular in the character of the gentlemen of their choice. Observe that his fingers are curled as if in the act of tickling, and that his face is represented with a wink, as he appeared when committing his barbarous murders.'[85]

There would be no risk of Tussaud being confounded with Mrs Jarley after March 1835, when she and sons Theodore and John established a permanent London base for the exhibition at the corner of Baker Street and Portman Square. Admittance to the collection cost one shilling, with an additional sixpence payable by those wishing to visit the separate room. Installed in the fashionable premises of the Baker Street 'bazaar', Tussaud was at last in a position to augment the collection, constantly adding likenesses of contemporary figures to renew the portfolio and ensure a steady stream of visitors.

83 Rosalind Crone, *Violent Victorians: Popular Entertainment in Nineteenth-Century London* (Manchester: Manchester University Press, 2012), pp. 86–7.
84 *Morning Chronicle*, 26 January 1835.
85 Charles Dickens, *The Old Curiosity Shop* [1841] (London: Vintage, 2010), p. 214.

The exhibition's status as a respectable and fashionable West End desti-
nation was quickly confirmed by visits from royalty and aristocracy. Likewise,
Tussaud's rolling programme of press advertisements announcing additions to
the collection flatteringly refer to the paying public as their 'numerous patrons'
and 'friends'. Here indeed was as genteel a context as might be found for a
Victorian taste for murder and the macabre to be indulged with impunity.

By the 1840s the subterranean separate room had been renamed 'The
Chamber of Horrors'. The origin of the new name is disputed, some historians
ascribing it to Tussaud and her sons while others suggest it was proffered by
Punch magazine, which in 1849 featured a cartoon depiction of the chamber by
Richard Doyle. Doyle's illustration showed a crowded chamber with top-hatted
and bonneted spectators thronging around the exhibits and especially around
the group of effigies labelled by Doyle 'Ye celebrated murderers', and including
Edward Oxford, failed assassin of Queen Victoria; James Greenacre, executed
in 1837 for the murder and dismemberment of his fiancé; and Victorian double-
murderer James Bloomfield Rush.

Doyle's illustration also depicted the chamber walls as bedecked with a
shotgun and other items of crime *realia* – a reflection of Tussaud's concern to
distinguish her waxworks exhibition from the macabre sideshows associated
with travelling fairs, and to elevate it to the status of quasi-museum. This
combination of representation and curation quickly became a signature of the
collection and is perhaps best emblematised by Joseph Tussaud's visit to Paris
in 1854 to acquire the actual guillotine blade of Charles-Henri Sanson, seasoned
executioner of the French Revolution.[86] Purchased alongside Sanson's detailed
drawings of his killing machine, all for the considerable sum of £220, the blade
was installed in a full-scale replica of the guillotine and thereafter the flow of
acquisitions of true crime *realia* only increased. In 1878, ten years after public
hangings in England were discontinued, the authentic gallows of Hertford Gaol
found its way into the chamber, the museum catalogue alerting spectators that
it was the very apparatus that had hanged notorious murderer John Thurtell
in 1824. The object's authenticity might have been attested by aforementioned
executioner William Marwood, who had many an opportunity to inspect the
gallows. John Theodore Tussaud later recalled how Marwood would regularly
visit the Chamber of Horrors, lingering to gaze on the effigies of the criminals

86   Chapman, *Madame Tussaud's Chamber of Horrors*, p. 68.

he had dispatched.[87] Marwood's common patronage of Scotland Yard's crime museum (see below) and the Chamber of Horrors alike illustrates the inter-penetration of the two spaces at a time when both were actively acquiring and curating the paraphernalia of the criminous.

By the Edwardian period, Tussaud's taste for acquiring such relics was unabated. When in 1903 the original Old Bailey and the adjacent Newgate Prison were closed for demolition, the Tussaud brothers hastened to the resulting auction with a priority list of purchases from among the lots. The list included the very bricks of the condemned cell from which eighteenth-century robber and highwayman Jack Sheppard had escaped in 1724, and the bell of Newgate Prison which had tolled across the city each time a criminal had been executed within the prison's walls. Successfully purchased, the transportation and installation of these items to Tussaud's Marylebone Road premises was a considerable expense and undertaking. Yet this investment in the *realia* of crime was deemed essential to the Tussaud's formula and paid dividends in the steady footfall to the exhibition in the years that followed.

While this emphasis on the *realia* of crime was part of Tussaud's inheritance from Curtius, it appears that, by the late nineteenth century, the appetite for collecting crime artefacts in the Chamber was increased by the rival presence in London of Scotland Yard's own Crime Museum, first named the 'Black Museum' on its inauguration in 1875. From the late 1860s, legal practice required that prisoners' property should be retained by the police until such time as they were free to reclaim it. By 1874 the Metropolitan Police was presiding over a burgeoning prisoners' property store where unclaimed items were placing a considerable demand on the available storage. In 1875 Chief Inspector Percy Neame lighted upon the notion that a selection of these objects might offer a learning resource for officers in training and began to assemble a collection principally for this purpose.[88] Before long however, admission to select members of other professions was granted on application and by 1885 Neame was boasting to a journalist for *The People* that the museum 'is our own chamber of horrors, and I think eclipses anything to be seen even at Madame Tussaud's'.[89]

Neame's comment points the way for the cross-fertilisation that would

87   Ibid., p. 70.
88   Jackie Keily and Julia Hoffbrand, *The Crime Museum Uncovered: Inside Scotland Yard's Special Collection* (London: Museum of London, 2015).
89   'Criminal London', *The People*, 8 February 1885.

increasingly exist between the two institutions, with distinguished visitors and criminologists regarding both locations as an obligatory part of their tourist itinerary. The guest book of the Met's crime museum would in time come to boast the names of royal visitors (HM George V, HRH Edward, Prince of Wales, the later Edward VIII), Stanley Baldwin, Sir Arthur Sullivan, W.S. Gilbert and, taking something of a busman's holiday, executioner William Marwood.[90] In 1892, while in mid-flow producing the serialised stories that would make up *The Adventures of Sherlock Holmes*, Arthur Conan Doyle visited the museum accompanied E.W. Hornung and Jerome K. Jerome. Doyle spent some time viewing the Jack the Ripper hoax letters among other exhibits.[91]

Both the Crime Museum and the Chamber of Horrors were well placed, then, to mould the perception and memory of crime in the minds of visitors. The presentation of key objects and artefacts, accompanied by the framing explanations of signage and museum catalogues, played a crucial role in shaping the visitor's encounter with the criminous. This was still more the case in the context of the Chamber of Horrors, where the inclusion of waxwork effigies enabled the rendering of entire vignettes and tableaux that captured, in the manner a three-dimensional *Illustrated Police News* portrait, compelling and dramatic scenes frozen in perpetuity.

The uncanny quality of waxworks, their occupation of 'the border country between people and things',[92] earned a central place in the late Victorian and Edwardian imaginative repertory of murder. In 1914, Metropolitan Police Commissioner Sir Melville Macnaghten's memoirs recalled the fascination the Chamber exerted on his boyhood imagination:

> I used to hurry over lunch, and almost invariably make my way to Madame Tussaud's (then situated at the Baker Street Bazaar) and revel in the Room of Horrors till hunger and tea-time called me home. The boy, seemingly, was to be father to the man – Crime and criminals had a weird fascination for me at a very early age. I used always to take away the sixpenny catalogues and study them deeply, with the result that I really remember the details of the murders committed by J. Blomfield, Rush, the Mannings, Courvoisier, Palmer, the Rugely poisoner, and their contemporaries, better than many

---

90 Honeycombe, *The Black Museum*, p. x.
91 Sir Arthur Conan Doyle, *Memories and Adventures* (Ware: Wordsworth, 2007), p. 225.
92 John Carey, *The Violent Effigy: A Study of Dickens' Imagination* (London: Faber and Faber, 1973), p. 101.

of the cases which came before me at the Yard in recent years. And what a gruesome Room of Horrors that old Madame Tussaud's exhibition boasted! Ill-lit by gas, one found oneself in an underground chamber.[93]

Macnaghten's stressing of the subterranean nature of the chamber highlights another of those features of the setting which contributed an uncanny and compelling quality. This was increasingly noted in mid-Victorian commentary and in literary representations of the Chamber of Horrors, particularly after Marie Belloc Lowndes set her denouement to her Ripper-inspired novel *The Lodger* in the chamber 'where waxen effigies of dead criminals stand grouped in wooden docks'.[94] The heightened interest in the Chamber at this time reflected the growing accessibility of the metropolis and its attractions for tourists travelling from the provinces by train, and a recognition that the Chamber continued to afford opportunities for macabre spectacle at a time when the cessation of public executions had reduced the opportunity for shared sanguinary spectacles on the streets.

When the Crippen waxwork was installed in the dock of the Chamber in November 1910, the full force of this tradition was gathered into the new waxen effigy. Crippen immediately became the figurehead of the Chamber, with subsequent press and literary evocations of the setting guaranteed to mention his dominant presence there.

There is also evidence of other Crippen effigies in circulation in travelling waxworks during the winter of 1910–11. In Redhill, effigies of Dew, Miss Le Neve, Crippen, and Belle were exhibited in November, alongside Ethel's typewriter and Crippen's portmanteau.[95] A month later, the *Fifeshire Advertiser* encouraged visitors to Edinburgh 'to visit the Historical Galleries' Waxwork and Museum at South Bridge. The latest effigies added are life-like presentations of Dr. H.H. Crippen; his wife, Belle Elmore; and his typist, Miss Le Neve.'[96] The Boxing Day edition of the *Belfast News* of 26 December 1910 advertised the 'ARRIVAL OF CRIPPEN, LE NEVE AND BELLE ELMORE'

93   Sir Melville Macnaghten, *Days of My Years* (London: Edward Arnold, 1914), p. 4.
94   Marie Belloc Lowndes, *The Lodger* [1913] (Oxford: Oxford University Press, 1996), p. 192.
95   'Madame Barton's Royal Waxworks', *Surrey Mirror*, 11 November 1910.
96   *Fifeshire Advertiser*, 10 December 1910.

Tussaud's big red building in the Marylebone Road drew me into the great waxwork show.' The journalist's encounter with the Crippen waxwork evokes the power of this newest addition to the Tussaud's collection and its affiliation with a tradition that reaches back at least to effigies of William Corder, the murderer of Maria Marten in the Red Barn in 1840:

> Then I went down into the Chamber of Horrors where I found H.H. Crippen in the post of honour, leaning over the bar of the dock, with his hands clasped, and with an expression of calm interest on his face. His big forehead and his protruding eyes, his scanty hair, and his spectacles are all there, and a policeman stands hard by apparently lost in admiration of the criminal. Crippen's easy chair and Belle Elmore's Paisley shawl, and a piece of mahogany furniture from Crippen's dining-room are placed near his wax effigy. The wax figure gives one quite a good idea of the bad man of whom we have all heard so much during the past few weeks.[100]

Further demonstration of Crippen's 'post of honour' in the Chamber is supplied by the accounts of the serious fire that destroyed much of the waxworks emporium in March 1925. The efforts of the firefighters to control the blaze left the Chamber of Horrors flooded. The huge crowd that assembled offered 'expressions of sympathy intermingled with occasional remarks of a humorous character regarding the safety of Charles Peace, Crippen and others of that notorious kind'.[101] After the fire, John Tussaud particularly mourned the 'destruction of so many historic mementoes which it was the pride of Madame Tussaud and her descendants to acquire and exhibit to the public'. Yet to the relief of the crowd, 'the representations of Crippen, Charles Peace, Edith Thompson, and Frederick Bywaters emerged from their ordeal unscathed to be propped against a neighbouring wall after they had been taken from the inferno of flames by the firemen.'[102] According to one eyewitness account, when the assembled crowd around the burning site learned that the Crippen effigy had been saved 'a lusty cheer went up'.[103]

---

100 'Madame Tussaud's', *Sporting Times*, 3 December 1910.
101 *Kensington Post*, 20 March 1925.
102 *Daily Herald*, 20 March 1925.
103 Nicholas Connell, *Doctor Crippen*, p. 170. Just as the Crippen effigy became a metonymy for the entire Chamber, so the Chamber and the whole Tussaud's institution came to be synonymous from this period until at least the 1960s. At the conclusion of Christie's

Finally, further illustration that Crippen and the Chamber of Horrors became effectively synonymous after 1910 is supplied by his absorption into a popular legend associated with the setting – the dare to the brave to pass a night in the Chamber. According to John Theodore Tussaud, this tradition was inaugurated by the ubiquitous George R. Sims, who as a friend of the Tussauds indulged his fascination for the Chamber on repeated visits until, in 1891, he apparently lighted upon the notion of challenging himself to sleep a night in the company of the criminals' effigies. If Sims's subsequent report, penned as 'Dagonet', is to be believed, the attempt was permitted and thus the journalist found himself locked in the bowels of the dimly-lit chamber, setting himself to stare out the effigies of William Corder and James Rush. 'Wandering around in the semi-darkness', the more contemporary figure of Marcy Pearcey began to unnerve Sims and soon he was pleading for release: 'I made one wild rush at the closed door and hammered on it till the kindly watchman came and let me out. *I never want to be shut up alone at night in the Chamber of Horrors as long as I live!*'[104]

Whether Sims did indeed inaugurate this tradition is uncertain. The premise of sleeping in a fearful or even haunted setting has a literary pedigree and appears to have been current at the time of Dagonet's letter; just a few years later H.G. Wells's short ghost story 'The Red Room' would present the night terrors experienced by a young man seeking to dispel the ghostly tradition of a room in a gothic castle. A year after Wells's story was first published, an uncredited short story in the *West Middlesex Herald* elaborates the tradition in full gothic style. The story's narrator falls asleep in the Chamber and finds himself locked in after hours. When he awakes, the Chamber is 'still as a tomb', though illuminated by moonlight which picks out the faces of the infamous criminals arrayed around him in effigy. As the moon clouds over and the narrator's nerves become over-wrought, he muses on the Chamber's uncanny conflation of authentic and representational: 'these mute statues were clothed in the very garments in which the crimes had been committed – garments from

---

Lord Edgware Dies (London: Collins Crime Club, 1933) the killer closes her letter to Poirot with the postscript: 'Do you think they will put me in Madame Tussaud's?' (p. 252) while in the 1960s British comedy-horror *What a Carve Up* (Dir. Pat Jackson, 1961), the presence of a lugubrious butler in a gothic mansion prompts one character to quip: 'Ring up Madame Tussaud's – see if anyone's missing.'

104 'Dagonet's Letter in *The Referee*', *Shields Daily Gazette*, 6 October 1891.

which the guilty stains had never been washed.' As his imagination runs riot, the narrator becomes increasingly terrorised by the 'awful mute mummery going on in the darkness of the night' as he turns to confront the effigies of Burke and Hare, James Rush, the Mannings, Palmer the poisoner, and others. Suggestively, he is transfixed by the stare of one figure in particular: 'Who he was I did not know, but I could not take my eyes from his face.' Fifteen years before Crippen's effigy would be installed in the Chamber, it appears the notion of a criminal's waxwork with a mesmeric stare already held currency and resonance. When the now hysterical narrator of the story hears jangling and creaking, he takes these sounds as emanating from the instruments of torture around him. His last rush to escape the enveloping blackness is distinctly evocative of Wells's 'Red Room': 'I sprang to my feet and rushed like a maniac in the darkness, striking wildly at everything in my way in search for the door … I was struggling madly for life with this terrible unseen something that held me by the throat and was strangling me in the dark.'[105] Fainting, the narrator awakes at home in his bed, tended by his sister, who explains the noise he heard was the jangling of the keys of the night-watchman who, on hearing his screams, had hastened to retrieve him.

While this tradition is principally evocative of Victorian Gothic, it passed alive and well into the Edwardian age and even intensified in the years preceding the Crippen case. Apparently fuelled by a combination of Tussaud's own marketing and word of mouth, the notion of a general challenge to the public to spend a night in the Chamber was even getting out of hand by early 1903. The *Dundee Evening Telegraph* of early March that year relayed:

CHAMBER OF HORRORS HOAX. An extraordinary report has got abroad touching the famous Chamber of Horrors at Madame Tussaud's, which is endless trouble to the management of the famous waxworks exhibition. From all parts of the country letters are pouring in – over 3000 have already been received – stating that the writers have heard there is a reward offered to any one who will pass the night in the Chamber of Horrors, and offering themselves as candidates. Some of the correspondents state they understand the reward is £50, others name £5 a week for life, while one gentleman places it at £20,000. I have seen some of these marvellous epistles. One of the writers is a widow of 61, evidently an educated woman; another a soldier;

---

105 'A Chamber of Horrors', *West Middlesex Herald*, 5 June 1895.

while a third describes himself a total abstainer, 35 years old, who 'wishes to try his luck.' A woman writes: – "I should not undertake this somewhat grim task with any idea of fun or levity. It is the money, and the money only, that attracts me," while a young man of 21 says he is a relation of the late P.O. Robinson, who caught Charles Peace … How the report got into circulation no one seems to know.[106]

Crippen's complete absorption into this tradition is also demonstrated by a Chamber of Horrors scene in Cecil Raleigh's highly popular stage melodrama *The Whip*, which opened in the autumn of 1909 at the Drury Lane Theatre. The eponymous 'whip' is an aristocrat's racehorse, bred in the stables of the Marquis of Beverley, whose participation in a climactic Newmarket race forms the climax of a story in which aristocratic fortunes are at stake and rivals' plots and attempts at sabotage unfold. The action-packed melodrama exhibits that signature Edwardian admixture of old and new that so characterises the era; a classic stage villain, Captain Greville Sartoris, and a pair of imperilled aristocratic lovers supply the continuities with Victorian melodrama while onstage depictions of horse-racing, motoring, and even a train crash reflect both Edwardian technological advances and the specific enthusiasms of Bertie himself. The production enjoyed an elaborate advertising campaign (handbills were distributed on opening night offering a reward of £100 to anyone who would spend the night in the Chamber of Horrors), and proved to be a winning formula with reviewers and theatre-goers alike, its enduring appeal noted by *The Sporting Times* on the eve of the production's first anniversary: 'So big is the business, even through what is generally known as the dull season, that there are to be Saturday matinées.'[107] Other reviewers relished the play's class commentary (suffragettes and class mobility are satirised) and knowing topical references – extending to the inclusion of cameos by real-life celebrity jockeys in the finale of the play's first anniversary performance.[108]

This topical focus is sustained in the play's Chamber of Horrors episode, where dated criminological traditions are satirised in a humorous scene centred on the Crippen waxwork. The scene's central intrigue involves The Whip's trainer, Tom Lambert, leading a household excursion to Madame

106 *Dundee Evening Telegraph*, 5 March 1903.
107 *Sporting Times*, 3 September 1910.
108 *Globe*, 12 September 1910.

Tussaud's and, while in the Chamber of Horrors, learning from a young female informant of a threat to The Whip from a rival. Lambert hears that the villainous Captain Sartoris plans to sabotage The Whip's journey by train to an upcoming race, derailing the horsebox, and thus leaving a clear field for the rival runner he has backed. Lambert is also involved in a comic-romantic subplot with the indomitable and easily jealous widow, Mrs Beamish. When the trainer realises that Mrs Beamish is about to find him alone in the Chamber of Horrors with his young female informant, he ushers her away and looks for a place to hide. He notes that among the effigies of Palmer and peers there is a vacant space left by the Crippen waxwork which, at the start of the scene, has been removed for repairs, having been damaged by the constant press of sightseers. Lambert dashes into the vacant space in the rogues' gallery left by the Crippen waxwork and stands as motionless as the effigies that surround him, just as Mrs Beamish enters the chamber followed by a young woman 'in the shabby weeds of a poor widow'.[109] Matching the effigies to the listings in the Tussaud's catalogue, Mrs Beamish, who apparently recognises her would-be-suitor and sparring partner, enjoys some jokes at his expense while also lampooning the tradition of Lombrosian positivist criminology which held that the criminal mentality and character was writ large in the features of the face:

> "No. 9 – Dr. Crippen. Just what I should have guessed. You can see the man is a monster of wickedness."
>
> "So you can, my lady," agreed the other.
>
> Lambert shook in his boots, but not with amusement.
>
> "Crime written large across his ugly face in every line of it," resumed Mrs. Beamish, who was having her revenge. "And there are a good many of them – a hardened old villain. I could believe anything of a man with that face."
>
> "So could I, my lady," agreed her companion readily.[110]

109 Richard Parker, *The Whip: Novelized from Cecil Raleigh's great Drury Lane Melodrama* (New York: The Macaulay Company, 1913), p. 233. A review of the play from September 1909 reveals that in the original version of the scene, Lambert took the place of roguish murderer Charles Peace (*Daily Telegraph and Courier*, 10 September 1909); the substitution of the Crippen waxwork is further reflection of the complete dominance of the case in 1910 and the rapid ascendancy of the Crippen waxwork in the chamber.
110 Ibid., pp. 236–7.

15.   Criminological critique in the popular melodrama, *The Whip* (1909–10).
When the Crippen waxwork is temporarily removed from the Chamber
of Horrors, horse trainer Tom Lambert hides in his place in the rogues'
gallery. His sparring partner and romantic interest Mrs Beamish issues
a sarcastic Lombrosian commentary on the physiognomy of criminals
– while she is robbed by her innocuous-looking companion.

The satirical force of the scene implies agreement with contemporary criminologist and actor H.B. Irving, that the 'comforting theory of the Lombroso
school has been exploded', and likewise with *The Times*'s 1909 obituary of
Lombroso, which held 'an increasing number of crimes are committed not
by professional or habitual criminals, but by those who, given other circumstances, and not exposed to temptations, would have lived lives no worse than
their neighbours.'[111] The point is brought home when Mrs Beamish, busily

---

111 H.B. Irving, *A Book of Remarkable Criminals* (London: Cassell and Co, 1918), p. 2;
'Professor Lombroso's Work', *The Times*, 21 October 1909. Some 1910 reports of the
Crippen case did however show pronounced Lombrosian influence: reporting on
Crippen's appearance, the 7 August 1910 edition of the *News of the World* suggested: 'It
is said that his physical conformation lends support to the belief that he is a degenerate.'

expounding on the visibly criminal features of 'Crippen' fails to spot the true criminal under her nose. Her companion in widow's weeds is a pickpocket who promptly makes off with her purse.

The scene concludes with a reprise of the chamber challenge theme. Mrs Beamish chases the thief out of the chamber, leaving the hapless Lambert alone at closing time, unaware he is about to become the latest participant in the challenge of passing a night in the Chamber of Horrors: 'the unseen attendant on another floor pulled a lever and the door closed with a hard bang. Lambert was locked within the Chamber of Horrors, with no way of escape until Monday morning.'[112]

The myth of the chamber challenge would endure well into the mid-twentieth century with references increasing during wartime (perhaps implying how stress and trauma might partially be relieved in the catharsis of encountering make-believe horrors in place of the realities of war). The *Berks and Oxon Observer* of Friday 11 October 1940 reported a spike in recent chamber challenge dares: 'there is probably no legend that has died harder than that relating to the reward offered to anyone who slept in the Chamber for one night ... It was even stated (on good authority, of course) that two young men had slept there, and had appeared in the morning raving mad and with snow white hair.' An early 1950s report relates how one daredevil who attempted the challenge was particularly perturbed by the Crippen effigy: 'Mr Johnston said that he was given a chair but it was next to Crippen and in the dimly-lit Chamber of Horrors some of the wax figures seemed "pretty life-like." He started to walk around but felt that all eyes were upon him, so he sat down again. "It was a very uncanny experience and at times I was extremely frightened."'[113]

Crippen's absorption into the chamber challenge reflects how complete was his alignment by the end of 1910 with the tradition of classic Victorian murder. Just as his story had been narrated against an established script of 'classic' crime and influenced by dramatic and textual traditions which perpetuated tropes from gothic romance and sensation fiction, so his effigy in the Chamber of Horrors seemed to gather into itself the full force of an older tradition of memorialising

---

112 *The Whip*, p. 251.
113 *Hampshire Telegraph*, 9 November 1951. Nearly twenty-five years later, an *Observer* business feature on the profitability of the Tussaud's franchise referenced 'Henry VIII, Horatio Nelson, Dr Crippen' as three of the pre-eminent attractions: 'Tussauds Still a Model Outfit', *The Observer*, 3 March 1974.

murder. Crippen had been textually inscribed and physically installed at the very heart of an imaginative repertory of murder – that same pantheon of classic crimes that George Orwell was to invoke in his famous essay on the decline of English murder. The effigies in the Chamber of Horrors gave physical manifestation to the notion of Crippen's lineage. The protagonist had become indelibly linked with a long line of murderers, particularly doctor-poisoners, and associated with long-established melodramatic and sensational traditions that eschewed nuanced criminological accounts in favour of gothic thrills.

These then were the textual and representational contexts that were central to the making of 'classic Crippen' in 1910. The formation of Crippen's story in these varied contexts was shaped by the force of a nostalgic tradition of murder as public spectacle, coloured by dramatic and literary traditions of melodrama, Gothicism and sensation. Against the grain of those elements of the case that signalled the advent of a contrastive modernity (the use of wireless telegraphy; a transatlantic steamship race; the forensic evidence of Crippen's trial), the cultural formation of the case looked instead to the Crippen story for one last great affirmation and flourishing of a culturally nostalgic paradigm.

Strong as this dominant rendering of the case was on sensation and melodrama, it was somewhat lighter on psychological and criminological insights. What did cultural preoccupation with the Crippen case say about Edwardian England and why should the British public's appetite for murder have been 'at a new high during the Edwardian age'.[114] What was driving the recourse to Old Bailey trials as public entertainments, where a rotation-ticket system enabled maximum throughput in the public gallery and where, as one letter-writer to *The Times* put it, opinion finds it 'seemly that actresses, fashionable ladies, and others should see a man tried for his life'.[115] These undercurrents arguing for a different view of the case, confined at first to trickles of dissenting lay comment in the press, would gather force after 1920 when Filson Young's edition of the trial proceedings appeared just as criminological and literary engagement with murder was embracing new forms of understanding and conceptualisation. This convergence would lead to nothing less than a 'second wave' version of Crippen, a rewriting of the story from multiple perspectives – the subject of the following chapter.

---

114 Diane Janes, *Edwardian Murder: Ightham and the Morpeth Train Robbery* (Stroud: Sutton Publishing, 2007), p. 257.
115 HO144/1719/1955492 543.

CHAPTER SIX

CRIPPEN REWRITTEN

The notion that alternative or fuller accounts of the Crippen case were possible first emerged from dissenting voices in the press and public discourse. Abolitionist commentators expressed deep anxieties at the circumstantial basis of Crippen's conviction and the prurient public interest in all stages of the trial and failed appeal.

A focus for these concerns was Arthur Newton's petition to Home Secretary Winston Churchill 'praying for a remission of the sentence on Dr. Crippen' in favour of a sentence of life imprisonment. Copies of the petition were distributed nationwide, the *London Globe* advising that the copy lodged in Newton's offices on the corner of Regent Street could be signed between the hours of 10am and 6pm.[1] The petition would garner over 15,000 signatures by the time it was submitted to Churchill[2] but it was to prove no more effective in saving Crippen than did the elderly man who presented himself at Cambridge Police Court in early November 1910 to offer himself as surrogate: 'He said he thought doctors do a lot of good in the world, and he himself had received benefits at the hands of medical men, and he felt that Dr. Crippen should not be allowed to suffer the extreme penalty.'[3]

In the week of Crippen's execution, socialist weekly *The Clarion* carried an article from a clergyman protesting at the prurience and morbidity of spectators at the trial: 'Lorgnettes and opera-glasses were freely used on the prisoner, and one gentleman was particularly intent on witnessing the effect

---

1   'Dr. Crippen's Case', *Globe*, 8 November 1910.
2   Nicholas Connell, *Doctor Crippen*, p. 130.
3   'Extraordinary Offer', *Cork Examiner*, 9 November 1910.

of the death sentence upon him.' Pronouncing such experimentalism fit for the laboratory rather than the court of law, the cleric went on to criticise the Tussaud's publicity campaign that had followed Crippen's trial: 'large posters appeared shortly after sentence was passed informing the public that his wax-work effigy has been added to the chamber of horrors, a show which is regarded by many as a national institution.'[4]

Such impassioned commentary, contesting the dominant, Northcliffe-led rendering of the Crippen case as melodrama and spectacle, continued into the following month. 'What is the duty of society towards the criminal?' asked Emily Lutyens, signatory of the Crippen reprieve petition and abolitionist correspondent to *The Times* in early December 1910. 'Surely not to pursue him with vindictive feelings of hatred and abhorrence, to gloat over the details of his crime and his punishment, and then to murder him deliberately and in cold blood in the name of justice and Christian charity.'[5] Lutyens's letter was one of a number of submissions prompted that week by a lengthy epistle from Cambridge academic Arthur C. Benson which had offered a sustained and stringent critique of the spectacle and 'hideous drama' that had attended the conviction and execution. Benson had protested in more secular terms that there was 'something frightfully cold-blooded, in the midst of our boasted humaneness and our ordered civilization, in allowing the perpetration of so sickening a drama to continue as the execution that has just taken place … I believe that the solemn barbarity of the whole proceeding has an entirely debasing and degrading effect on the public mind.'[6] Moreover, Benson cannily observed that the expanded press and new journalism had effectively 'recovered a good deal of the publicity which the suppression of public executions temporarily removed' – a suggestion that *Times* readers could hardly deny that December as the 'Naughty Doctor' murder broadsides were being hawked about the metropolis. 'Confirmed disbeliever in the efficacy of capital punishment', A. Chichele Plowden wrote to *The Times* in late December 1910, supplying an image of the notorious Crippen that ran quite counter to the dominant discourse: 'It is a popular fallacy to regard a murderer as the worst of criminals. The real truth is that in many cases it is hardly fair to describe him as a criminal at all. There is nothing inconsistent, human nature being what it is, in a man of blameless antecedents being driven in a moment

4   'You and the Murderer', *Clarion*, 25 November 1910.
5   'Executions', *The Times*, 9 December 1910.
6   'Executions', *The Times*, 5 December 1910.

of frenzy into committing an act of violence from which his whole soul would recoil in saner moments.' Plowden goes on to suggest that had Crippen only met Ethel before he had met Belle 'he would probably have lived a life not better nor worse than his neighbours, and enjoyed with the best of them the reputation of a contented, law-abiding citizen.'[7] Abolitionist commentary thus tended to eschew Lombrosian notions of criminal degeneracy; here was a Crippen with a subjectivity to be understood rather than reductively ascribed to an inherent criminality.

While largely confined to the letters pages of the daily press, the abolitionists' view of Crippen was more nuanced than the exculpatory narrative that would emerge from Ethel le Neve's 'life story', serialised in *Lloyd's Weekly News* shortly before Crippen's execution. While Ethel's primary concern was to remove any remaining doubt in the minds of the public 'as to my complete innocence', she also took the opportunity to proffer a different view of Crippen from that which the dominant discourse had promoted.[8] First among these was the suggestion of Crippen himself as victim; Ethel suggests that so unhappy was Crippen in his marriage that he had even attempted suicide in his office at the Drouet Institute back in the early days of their association: 'He was very ill, and I believed that he had taken poison. He told me that he could bear the ill-treatment of his wife no longer.'[9] Next she remarks on Crippen's apparently relaxed state and normal demeanour the night after the Hilldrop Crescent dinner party: 'If he had really just come from committing a dreadful crime … it is remarkable that outwardly at any rate, he was his own calm self.'[10]

Later in the text, Ethel lends support to Crippen's account of their flight, suggesting that this was prompted largely to escape scandal and the prying eyes of those who disapproved of their relationship. The most audacious element of the escape plan, the cross-dressed disguise, is played down as a romantic adventure. Suggesting there was in any case precedent for her disguise in the 'tomboy pranks' she used to engage in as a child, Ethel presents the episode in the most jocular of tones:

---

7   'Executions', *The Times*, Tuesday 20 December 1910.
8   *Ethel Le Neve: Her Life Story with the True Account of their Flight and her friendship for Dr Crippen, also startling particulars of her life at Hilldrop Crescent* (London: Publishing Office, 1910), p. 5.
9   Ibid., p. 9.
10   Ibid., p. 13.

When the new suit was presented by Dr Crippen he was very much amused.

'You will look a perfect boy in that,' he said. 'Especially when you have cut off your hair.'

'Have I got to cut my hair?' I cried.

'Why of course,' he said gaily. 'That is absolutely necessary.'

Honestly, I was more amused than anything. It seemed to me an adventure.[11]

This evocation of a romantic and adventurous context for the disguise displaces speculation on Crippen's true motives even as it seeks to mitigate any gender ambiguity implied by the cross-dressing. Ethel is at pains to dismiss her masquerade as continuous with the tomboy larks of her youth, disavowing any subtexts that might be deemed evocative of the 'New Woman' or of transgressive sexuality. Certainly, Ethel's depiction of the episode shares none of the ambivalence of exactly contemporary romance novel *Max*, published just weeks before the Crippen trial began, where a young cross-dressed Russian princess masquerades as a Bohemian artist, and in this male persona captures the affection of free spirit Ned Blake. Blake and Max play out a protracted, ambivalent, and lively courtship against the Parisian backdrop and whilst Max must ultimately transform into 'Maxine' for the pair to be formally united at the novel's end, the novel's readiness to countenance gender fluidity and ambiguity suggests such a formal resolution of the 'dilemma' facing Blake and Max is ultimately unnecessary (even if one contemporary reviewer took the novel's ultimate meaning to be: 'sex in the end must assert itself, no matter how effectual is its disguise').[12]

Whilst these writings from 1910 made initial moves to present a view of Crippen that differed from the culturally nostalgic and melodramatic view of the case that the dominant discourse had created, it was largely due to the efforts of the novelists who followed in the subsequent decade to offer a more sustained 'rewriting' of Crippen. The first tranche of Crippen-themed novels was born out of an intersection between crime fiction and expert criminology made possible since 1903 by the existence of a 'Crimes Club' – some of whose members had been constant visitors to the public gallery during Crippen's trial. Also more discreetly referred to as 'our society' by the *cognoscenti*, the Crimes

---

11 Ibid., p. 43.

12 *The Globe*'s review of Katherine Cecil Thurston's *Max* is quoted in the *Observer*, 16 October 1910.

PRICE THREEPENCE

ETHEL LE NEVE

HER LIFE STORY

With the True Account of Their Flight and Her Friendship for

DR. CRIPPEN

TOLD BY HERSELF

Ethel C. Le Neve

COPYRIGHT

16.   Ethel le Neve's memoirs of late 1910 which protested her innocence of any guilty knowledge and down-played the subversive undertones of her cross-dressed disguise.

Club had been founded by writer Arthur Lambton and Westminster Coroner Ingleby Oddie for a group of relatively leisured men with a professional interest in crime. Academic John Churton Collins, novelist Sir Arthur Conan Doyle, forensic pathologist Sir Bernard Spilsbury, barristers Edward Marshall Hall and Travers Humphreys, actor and criminologist H.B. Irving, journalist and novelist William le Queux, and the prolific George R. Sims were among the society's early members. In due course, as membership increased to forty, press baron Lord Northcliffe would join. The society's evening meetings, conducted in comfortable club settings and rounded off with convivial dinners, would involve debate and disputation on classic crime cases, strictly one per meeting. Papers would be presented revisiting notorious cases; points of interpretation would be debated and questionable circumstantial evidence revisited. A recent study of the origins and development of the club explores how 'Our Society' was established in a period when criminology was becoming recognised as a legitimate discipline and when the findings of forensic science were increasingly being admitted into murder trials and weighing more heavily in the deliberations of juries:

> Its purpose therefore reflected the growing concerns of an age in which both criminal justice and criminal activity were becoming more sophisticated. At the same time, the sensational press had begun to dominate the public's understanding of criminality and criminal investigation. Members of this private club included authors, actors, journalists, editors, and medical and legal professionals who all had varying levels of influence on the public's understanding of contemporary debates about crime.[13]

While the club's members were driven by a range of interests in their attendance and engagement with the Crimes Club, perhaps criminologist and actor H.B. Irving spoke for the majority in describing the particular fascination the criminal mind held for him:

> It is rarely indeed that a man lays bare his soul, and even when he does we can never quite be sure that he is telling us all the truth, and that he is not keeping back some vital secret. It is no doubt better so, and that it should

---

13   Carrie Parris, 'The Crimes Club: The Early Years of Our Society', Unpublished Ph.D. thesis (University of East Anglia, 2016), pp. 5–6.

be left to the writer of imagination to picture for us a man's inmost soul. The study of crime will help him to that end.[14]

As a 1925 press account of the club's dealings related, the activities of the club also had a utilitarian aspect: 'Several times during those debates, when the port has been circulating and the smoke of after-dinner cigars has been making the atmosphere blue, close scrutiny of the evidence of some great trial has ended in doubt as to the rightness of the verdict.'[15] In such instances, the club's members would work to quash the conviction that had resulted, as witness Conan Doyle's efforts on behalf of George Edalji, whose conviction for horse maiming would be overturned. This chapter will explore how the novelists associated with the Crimes Club, their female equivalents in the Detection Club, and their descendants in later fiction, offered a literary and creative engagement with the Crippen case which opened up alternative views of the story and began to liberate it from the 'classic' formation it had so emphatically received in 1910.

Somewhat disappointingly, the Crimes Club member who was to write most copiously on the Crippen case was unreliable raconteur and hack William le Queux, who consistently inflated his importance in the society, retailed apocryphal anecdotes regarding his encounters with classic cases (including claiming secret knowledge of the identity of Jack the Ripper) and propounded a view of the Crippen case more redolent of the old gothic sensations than of a modern, nuanced criminology. Thus, in both his memoirs, *Things I Know* of 1923 and a later short, sensational account of the Crippen case, Le Queux claims to have met Crippen on a number of occasions before he became notorious. The episodes are patently apocryphal and suggest Le Queux's limited imaginative engagement in the criminological nuances of the Crimes Club, given they are replete with the gothic tropes and melodramatic motifs that have been detailed in the previous chapter's account of 'classic Crippen'. Le Queux recounts how Crippen, under the alias of 'a certain Doctor Adams', contacted him from his Essex home (there is of course no evidence of Crippen's having lived anywhere outside London). Knowing Le Queux as a writer of 'mysteries of love and crime', Crippen allegedly requested an

14   H.B. Irving, *A Book of Remarkable Criminals* (London: Cassell, 1918), p. 27.
15   'The Crimes Club – One of the Queerest in the World', *Nottingham Evening Post*, 5 June 1925.

appointment with the writer so that he might suggest 'a new and exciting plot'. The Crippen who apparently arrived at a club to meet Le Queux is sketched with shades of the Ripper, 'a dapper, fair-haired man, of middle age, very well-dressed, with a tall hat and patent-leather boots.' The historical errors that give the lie to Le Queux's fabrications come thick and fast, even down to the suggestion that the two men smoked while they conversed (it is on record that Crippen avoided tobacco). In the putative conversation that followed, 'Crippen' comes across as a sub-Doylean 'doctor gone wrong, part Professor Moriarty, part Culverton-Smith, the doctor who deals in deadly toxins from the tropics in the late Holmes story 'The Dying Detective':

> "I suppose many people are deliberately poisoned and the murderer never traced?" I remarked.
>
> "Hundreds," he declared. "Since the days when Palmer poisoned thirteen people with his old-fashioned strychnine – in those days very hard to discover – hundreds of people of both sexes have been got rid of by poison or the bacteria of fatal diseases." ... He spoke of death calmly and coolly, as only medical men can.
>
> "Poisoners are always bunglers," he declared. "The fools use arsenic, antimony, alkaloidal and glucosidal poisons, under the delusion that they won't be found out. Sometimes they are not. The doctor, who has been attending the patient for some disorder, and the patient apparently dies from it, is often unsuspicious. He gives the certificate of death without even dreaming that poison is the cause."
>
> "Have you ever known such cases?" I asked.
>
> He hesitated, then with some little evasion, I thought, declared that there had, no doubt, been many.[16]

Le Queux claims to have had a further interview with the poisoner some time later in Devonshire. Patently apocryphal (Le Queux claims Crippen motored across Dartmoor to meet him, but he did not own a car), the tenor of this meeting is even more sinister, with Crippen describing means of administering undetectable poisons: 'He had weighed every detail and taken every precaution that there was no flaw by which the assassin could be traced.' Crippen's morbid preoccupations disturb Le Queux and, in a scene which appears to come directly

---

16 William le Queux, *Things I Know about Kings, Celebrities and Crooks* (London: Nash and Grayson, 1923), pp. 225–7.

from Doyle's 'The Adventure of the Dying Detective' (1913), where doctor-poisoner Culverton-Smith tries to dispatch Sherlock Holmes by sending the detective a package loaded with a poisoned spring, describes how he becomes wary of any correspondence sent by Crippen: 'whenever I received a letter from him, I opened it with the scissors, held it from me as I read it, and dropped it straight into the fire. I confess that I feared lest he might do me harm!'

Le Queux would later write a short history of the case published as *Dr Crippen: Lover and Poisoner*, but in its inaccuracies and speculations, and in the fact that it was prefaced with a reiteration of the claim to have met Crippen before he became notorious, it is barely more reliable than the overt inventions included in *Things I Know*.[17] Some reflection of the higher quality of discussion and debate that went on in the Crimes Club is however apparent in Le Queux's mention of some of the contradictions of the case, such as Crippen's purchasing of five grains of hyoscine when Crippen must have known that a fatal dose was the smallest fraction of that amount, and his audacity in taking Ethel to the Benevolent Fund Ball at the Criterion, which could only have encouraged the gossip and suspicions which did indeed ensue.

It is a pity that the Crimes Club member who wrote most copiously on the Crippen case was the unreliable Le Queux. Certain other members of the club had actually played a key role in the investigation and trial: barrister Ingleby Oddie had been on the prosecution team; Edward Marshall Hall had considered acting on Crippen's defence team before passing on the case; Bernard Spilsbury had deposed key forensic evidence. While the proceedings of the club's meetings were kept confidential, the club's recent chronicler has demonstrated from meeting agendas and records of papers presented that the Crippen case was much discussed and debated by the society's members. Insights on the different views presented can be gleaned from members' biographies and historical accounts published elsewhere. From Edward Marjoribanks's *Life of Sir Edward Marshall Hall*, for example, we know that the line of defence the barrister would have argued at Crippen's trial, had the prisoner endorsed it, would have been that Crippen had administered the hyoscine not with

17   Given the eminence and integrity of so many of the other Crimes Club members, it is remarkable that Le Queux retained his membership, especially since he uses one of the society's meeting dates to lend authenticity to a demonstrably untrue claim to have met another poisoner, Major Herbert Rowse Armstrong. See Robin Odell, *Exhumation of A Murder: The Life and Trial of Major Armstrong* (London: Harrap, 1975), p. 225.

murderous intent but as a sedative so that he might smuggle Ethel into Hilldrop Crescent for nocturnal liaisons: 'To be on the safe side he gave her a large dose, which turned out to be an overdose' and thus the death was accidental.[18]

Likewise, from Westminster Coroner Ingleby Oddie's memoirs entitled *Inquest*, we learn that the line he likely argued in the Crimes Club's discussions of the Crippen case held that Crippen administered the hyoscine to Belle in a nightcap of whisky. When this prompted delirium and raving (an attested effect of hyoscine) rather than torpor, Crippen was obliged to adapt his modus operandi: 'I believe Crippen shot his wife in the head with a revolver (which nearly all Americans possess) to stifle her cries which were also likely to arouse the whole neighbourhood,' averred Oddie – which would account for the witness accounts of hearing gunshots in Hilldrop Crescent that last January night of 1910.[19]

Finally, Filson Young's 1920 edition of the Crippen trial proceedings for the Notable British Trials series again shows the influence of Crimes Club deliberations and debates. These include ruminations on Crippen's personality and psychological make-up, with Young casting the quiet doctor as both masochist and psychopath: 'he was of the type that loves to be dominated by [women] and in his love for showering presents upon his wife in public, and in spending a quite ridiculous proportion of his income in the adorning of her plump little person, he exhibited the symptoms of the psychopathic type to which he undoubtedly belonged.'[20] In addition to Young's characterisation of Crippen, it is notable that the long tradition of antipathy and even misogyny towards Cora Crippen largely originates with his preface to the trial proceedings (and one is prompted to reflect on how the all-male composition of the Crimes Club might have influenced the discussion of criminal and victim's relationship).

While these accounts provide some insights on the Crimes Club's discussion of the Crippen case, they surely represent only the tip of the iceberg of extensive medico-legal and criminological discussion. Given the club's eminent membership, one is left sorely wishing to know more of what Conan Doyle (whose seat at the Crippen trial had been secured by Marshall Hall), Bernard Spilsbury, or Lord Northcliffe contributed to discussion of the case. Certainly,

18   Edward Marjoribanks, *The Life of Sir Edward Marshall Hall* (London: Victor Gollancz, 1930), p. 281.
19   S. Ingleby Oddie, *Inquest* (London: Hutchinson and Son, 1941), p. 80.
20   *Trial*, p. xvi.

the inauguration of the Crimes Club and the appearance of Filson Young's edition of the trial proceedings bolstered literary interest in the case. By 1926 such texts as the pseudonymous J.J. Connington's *The Case with Nine Solutions* were delighting in echoes of the Crippen case, with popular knowledge of both the sedative and the murderous uses of hyoscine now assumed in the readership of this tale of triple death in a small town.[21]

A decade after the publication of Filson Young's edition of the Crippen trial proceedings in 1920, a second society dedicated to crime and detection was inaugurated. With a membership composed of writers of crime fiction, this society was to play a highly significant role in the reimagining of Crippen in popular modernity, generating texts which would liberate the narrative from the culturally nostalgic and traditional formation which had so characterised its reception in 1910. In contrast to the Crimes Club, the Detection Club's membership comprised both men and women writers – and indeed, two of the three prime movers of the club's early years were Dorothy L. Sayers and Agatha Christie. And while the discussion of Crimes Club members generally gave primacy to medico-legal and forensic aspects of the crimes they debated, the members of the Detection Club were first and foremost concerned with exploring the criminal mind and the complexities and contradictions of human psychology. Such an approach was a firm departure from the stylised and melodramatic traditions that had impinged on the 1910 formation of the Crippen case: indeed, in the view of an early president of the Detection Club, Dorothy L. Sayers, a principal purpose of the club was to free the detective story 'from the bad legacy of sensationalism, clap-trap and jargon' with which it had been encumbered hitherto.[22] This meant returning to Crippen in a new light, revisiting the story for psychological interest and character study.

The first of the Detection Club members to explore this psychological interest in literary form was Anthony Berkeley, whose 1926 novel *The Wychford*

21   J.J. Connington, *The Case with Nine Solutions* [1926] (Harmondsworth: Penguin, 1949). Connington's novel refers to the 'memory-blotting property of hyoscine' (p. 279), the awareness of which almost certainly derives from Filson Young. Other 'Crippenesque' features of the novel include the adoption of a disguise by the criminal (p. 234) and the discovery of a box of revolver ammunition in a household drawer (p. 96), mirroring Dew's find at Hilldrop Crescent.

22   As cited in Martin Edwards, *The Golden Age of Murder: The Mystery of the Writers who Invented the Detective Story* (London: Harper Collins, 2015), p. 8.

Poisoning Case features the novelist-detective Roger Sheringham investigating the apparent poisoning by arsenic of a successful businessman in the small titular town. Sheringham's interest in the criminal character and the psychological impulses behind crime prompts many a criminological excursus to his companions (likely anticipating the kind of discussions the Detection Club would embark upon from 1930) and this includes reminiscences and allusions to the 1910 Crippen drama. As early as the second chapter, Sheringham is compassing the name of Crippen with those of Seddon and Palmer and arguing that the endurance of their crimes in popular memory resides entirely in the psychological interest: 'the character of the criminal, the character of the victim, their reactions to violence, what they felt and thought and suffered over it all.'[23] The Crippen murder, he later argues, is the most compelling of all of these cases and likewise outdoes even the best efforts of the writer of crime fiction: 'Not a shadow of a doubt as to who murdered Belle Elmore, or whether Crippen was guilty or not. But tell me the detective story that can compete with the story of that case for sheer, breathless interest.'[24] In the course of the novel, Sheringham's encyclopaedic knowledge of prior criminal cases informs his deductions and prompts further recollections of Crippen, though largely as an exception to the rules evinced elsewhere in the annals of crime: 'Crippen, by the way, was a poisoner by force of circumstances; but then he's an exception to every rule that you could possibly formulate.'[25]

The influence of Filson Young's view of Cora and the Crippen marriage is also directly acknowledged in Sheringham's expression of sympathy for Crippen and his rather troubling assertion that Cora even deserved her fate:

> If ever a woman deserved murdering, Cora Crippen did, and it's my opinion that Crippen killed her because he was a coward; she had established a complete tyranny over him, and he simply hadn't got the moral courage to run away from her. That, and the fact that she had got control over all his savings, of course, as Mr Filson Young has very interestingly pointed out. An extraordinarily absorbing case from the psychological standpoint.[26]

23 Anthony Berkeley, *The Wychford Poisoning Case* (London: Collins Crime Club, 1926), p. 8.
24 *Wychford Poisoning Case*, p. 104.
25 Ibid., p. 22.
26 Ibid., p. 22. Filson Young's edition of the trial proceedings is much referenced in 'Crippeniana' and makes a physical appearance in at least two texts: *Satan Was a Man*

Five years later, Berkeley would move still closer to the Crippen story with his rendering of a domestic murder and sensational trial that closely mirrored many of those notorious events of 1910. Penned under the pseudonym Francis Iles, Berkeley's text was emphatically a *crime* novel as distinct from a *detective* novel. *Malice Aforethought* reveals the crime's perpetrator in the novel's first sentence with the declaration: 'It was not until several weeks after he had decided to murder his wife that Dr. Bickleigh took any active steps in the matter.'[27] In a manner hailed as revolutionary for the genre in 1931, this immediate spoiler stresses how the novel's emphasis is not on the detection of the crime but on the motivation and impulsion of the criminal; the text would be first and foremost a character study. The novel's indebtedness to the case of Armstrong, the 'Hay-on-Wye poisoner', has recently been revisited by Martin Edwards, who observes how Armstrong's decorous appeal 'Excuse fingers' as he passed his tea-party guest an arsenic-laced scone 'captures perfectly the genteel nature of the kind of murder for which the Golden Age is famous'.[28] Yet shades of Crippen are also unmistakeably present, from external characteristics such as Bickleigh's 'fish-like' eye and diminutive height, to such parallel personality traits as Bickleigh's careful composure and impassivity in court, and his idealisation of his adulterous liaison with village newcomer Madeleine Cranmere, the terms of which recall Crippen's letters on his exalted love for Ethel, misconstrued by a base world: 'how could the cloddish world ever understand the peculiar delicacy of his own feelings, or appreciate what Madeleine meant to him?' Given the synonymy of Crippen with a certain London waxworks emporium by this date, his presence is also obliquely felt in the novel's inevitable allusion to Madame Tussaud's: 'Dr Bickleigh had never been in the Chamber of Horrors before. He was much interested.'[29]

A subtle novel in which Bickleigh ironically emerges as one of the most sympathetic of the closely observed characters presented by Berkeley/Iles, *Malice Aforethought* concludes with a clever twist in which the criminal

(1935) and *The Man Who Did Not Hang* (1948), where Detective Inspector Sorrow regards it as core reading for all officers: 'Here is a full report of the Crippen case ... it is one of the *Notable British Trials* series, indispensable, in my opinion, to every police officer, and to every criminologist generally.' (p. 251).

27   Francis Iles, *Malice Aforethought* [1931] (London: Pan, 1999), p. 1.
28   *The Golden Age of Murder*, p. 135.
29   *Malice Aforethought*, p. 17, p. 130, p. 136.

is acquitted of the murder of his wife but is condemned to the scaffold all the same after wrongful conviction for another local death that was in fact accidental. These innovative touches, along with the extensive publicity caused by attempts in the press to unmask the author behind the pseudonym, secured high profile for this early literary rendition of elements of the Crippen story.

The next treatment of 'literary Crippen' would be produced outside the cosy circle of the Detection Club, flowing from the pen of novelist Ernest Raymond. When *We, The Accused* appeared in the summer of 1935 reviewers were quick to recognise how Raymond sought to bring readers further still into the mind of the murderer, not only in the period leading up to his crime, and in the tense episodes of manhunt, arrest, and trial, but on into the agonising last hours in the condemned cell and to the foot of the scaffold in the execution shed. The *Illustrated London News* reviewer considered the work 'a great piece of special pleading and a most impressive book'.[30] *The Tatler* was more hostile to 'this story of propaganda', rejecting the thesis that 'for every capital punishment we each of us stand guilty with the accused'.[31] The protagonist and proxy for Crippen for whom so much sympathy is garnered in the novel is school-teacher Paul Arthur Presset, unhappily married to Elinor and increasingly enamoured of fellow teacher Myra Bawne. The plot offers a close retelling of the Crippen story: the Pressets are resident in the same leafy enclave of North London as the Crippens, Elm Tree Road substituting for Hilldrop Crescent; Presset is considered an unassuming and 'mild little man', and conducts his out-of-character affair with Myra in 'cheap Bloomsbury hotels' until in his wife's failing health he spies an opportunity to hasten her death and seize the chance of happiness with his lover.[32] Presset is soon being doggedly hunted by Inspector Boltro, whose investigation in this scenario is not of a missing spouse but rather of a spouse's death under suspicious circumstances. When Elinor's body is exhumed and the presence of arsenic traced, Presset takes flight with the trusting and faithful Myra, who knows nothing of the crime: 'Goodbye, 23 Elm Tree Road.'[33]

In the ensuing pursuit of the fugitives cross-dressing is not enacted, but it is summoned to mind by allusion when Presset buys a rucksack 'for his young

---

30   'Notes for the Novel-Reader: Fiction of the Month', *Illustrated London News*, 6 July 1935.
31   'A Story of Propaganda', *Tatler*, 20 July 1935.
32   Ernest Raymond, *We, The Accused* [1935] (London: Corgi, 1980), p. 94.
33   *We, The Accused*, p. 272.

son'. Likewise, the 'stop press' column that circulates as the pair attempt to flee to the continent stays close to the Crippen exemplar: 'Sensational turn in the Presset case ... police have reason to believe he is attempting to leave the country. Scotland Yard has issued a full description of the wanted man to every police station in the kingdom, and ordered observation to be kept at all main line terminuses, ports and docks.'[34] As with the Crippen case, a plethora of spurious sightings are reported to the police, frustrating the tracing of the fugitives, who amend their plan and head to the Lake District, Presset disguised as a priest (one of the disguises the press had suspected Crippen of adopting in 1910).

Raymond's novel is astute on the newspaper editors' deep investment in this 'summer-time sensation' centred on a 'mild little man' and on the centrality of the press in framing the public's engagement with the case: 'the story ran in their heads in the very language of the newspaper correspondents.'[35] Raymond is also insightful on the drivers of class consciousness and personal ambition that might underlie a Scotland Yard inspector's determination to take personal credit for the apprehension of a criminal who might just as easily be run to ground by officers more local to his place of hiding – 'For the story to be perfect, he must be in at the death'; 'Supposing the Cumberland police got him before he could get there, and Inspector Boltro was not on the spot!'[36] The developing relationship between the fugitives is also subtly traced, with Myra increasing in resolve and resilience as Presset progressively weakens under the strain, and standing by her lover even when she learns that he did indeed poison Elinor with arsenic derived from garden weed-killer.

All of these elements make for a subtle literary evocation of the Crippen case, which likewise reverberates in Boltro's arresting words to the fugitive, 'I think you know me, Mr. Presset', and in the judge's summation when Presset is found guilty and condemned to death at the ensuing trial: 'On the ghastly and wicked nature of your crime I will not dwell.'[37] Yet it is in the novel's closing Parts Four and Five that the text offers a sustained imaginative engagement with the protagonist at the centre of this crime sensation, as he passes through the last phase of his life in the hands of the criminal justice system,

34   Ibid., p. 283, p. 287.
35   Ibid., p. 303, p. 336.
36   Ibid., p. 307, p. 351.
37   Ibid., p. 382, p. 442.

paradoxically ennobled by his love for Myra and, like Crippen before him, winning the respect and affection of his captors and warders. Raymond's abolitionist stance, which had so provoked the reviewer of *The Tatler*, is sometimes signalled overtly, as when Presset realises the force of circumstantial evidence against him is such that even if his wife's death really had been an accident, he 'must have hanged just the same'.[38] It also drives the compelling description of the agonies of the condemned man in his last days:

> These wasting hours, how fill them? Take a man in perfect health, keep him with the utmost care in perfect health so that he can really suffer, remove the future from him – cut out, that is to say, all aspiration, all hope of achievement, all necessity to earn, all desire to make the body fine and the mind strong, all pleasure in creative work – and how will he spend the hours?
>
> Drift, from one unrecoverable minute to the next. Drift, with a stupid, dropping draw. Talk for a minute, play for a minute, and then remember, and gape, and drift again.[39]

The novel thus follows, at much greater length, the same scenario explored immediately after the Crippen case in W.S. Gilbert's one-act drama *The Hooligan*, where the condemned man awaits news of a possible reprieve on the eve of his execution. When this comes at the very last minute, the sudden reverse is too much for the young man's strained heart to bear and he collapses and dies. Presset is likewise the subject of a petition for reprieve, but holds no hope for a positive outcome, as he vouchsafes to Myra during one of their last fraught interviews, closely modelled on Crippen and Ethel's final meeting. Myra, in turn, offers the novel's most powerful commentary on the compelling contradictions of the condemned man's character: 'I know that, ever since your arrest – whatever you were before – you have been good.' The same paradox strikes the prison's governor, who stands at his window morosely surveying the prison yard on the morning of Presset's execution: 'How on earth could that decent fellow, considerate for all, have done so shocking a deed? It defeated the imagination.' It is this paradox, and this overwhelming sense of the full scope of the human tragedy of the murder case, that closes the novel. When the sentence of the law is carried out, the body that swings

38   Ibid., p. 409.
39   Ibid., p. 456.

above the execution pit is presented not in the traditional terms of melodrama and censure but as 'the body of a man who had foundered'.[40]

Raymond's novel patently offered a more profound and distinctive engagement with the criminological and psychological themes of the Crippen drama than had previously been attempted, inscribing extended internal monologues and free indirect discourse to render the interiority of his variously troubled and guilt-ridden protagonist. Ever since Filson Young's 1920 edition of the trial proceedings, attention had increasingly been drawn to the contradictions in Crippen's character. Describing the letters penned from Crippen's death cell, a 1926 issue of *The Tatler* had remarked:

> But Crippen's letters to Miss Le Neve while he was awaiting the result of his appeal breathe a devotion, an unselfishness, a gentleness which literally attain to beauty. Not one thought in them is there of self-pity. Every moment of every day he thought only of her – of her future, of how he could save her from the consequences of his crime. You would say to yourself, as you read them, that here is a true and noble man writing to a woman who should be proud of such a lover. And that the sentiments in them are genuine is borne out by his untiring efforts on her behalf. Even when he protests that he is innocent, the protest sounds sincere. It is all very disconcerting – isn't it? If only people would keep all the time in their own categories life would be very much more simple. But good men suddenly fall for the vilest temptations, and bad men suddenly rise to heights of courage and unselfishness.[41]

The crime fiction of this period was increasingly willing to explore this moral ambivalence, offering a much more nuanced exploration of the criminal mind than sensational accounts of bloody murder could ever countenance. In the same year that *We, The Accused* appeared, C.S. Forester drafted a novel, unpublished in his lifetime, which explores the plight of killers driven to their crime by a context of domestic violence. The early chapters of *The Pursued* (1935) present protagonist Marjorie Grainger suffering the domestic tyranny of husband Ted. Marjorie's mother, alert to the situation, plans her own part in freeing her daughter from her intolerable situation, her mind ranging over 'vague newspaper readings about Crippen and Armstrong and Seddon'.[42] When a

---

40   Ibid., p. 490, p. 505, p. 509.
41   *Tatler*, 30 June 1926.
42   C.S. Forester, *The Pursued* (Harmondsworth: Penguin, 2012).

nascent relationship between Marjorie and Ted's young and sympathetic work colleague George Ely brings events to a crisis, mother and daughter act on their plan, enlisting George's help in a surprisingly brutal axe murder (no genteel poisonings over scones here – perhaps one reason why the book was not published in the 'Golden Age' window during which it was written). The pursued of the book's title, mother and daughter then go on the run in a Crippenesque scenario where police posters announce a 'HUNT FOR TWO WOMEN' and a watch on all the ports. Departing from the Crippen template, when the women separate to increase their chances of escape, the mother is arrested and the daughter resolves to return home to face the consequences of her crime. We learn in the book's last line that she is subsequently found not guilty of murder.

There was to be one further literary reimagining of Crippen in 1935, a year that saw a flurry of interest in the case and which may have played its part in prompting Walter Dew to take up his pen to produce his memoirs three years later. Catherine Meadows's rendition of the case, published as *Henbane* in the United Kingdom and as *Doctor Moon* in the United States, presents Caspar Moon, Flora Melrose, and Marion Lennard as the literary counterparts of Hawley, Cora, and Ethel. Ventimiglia Road substitutes for Hilldrop Crescent and it is here that Inspector Barnes, the Dew figure, comes to call when Flora goes missing, prompting the familiar flight and manhunt. Meadows's novel, for which she had Filson Young's edition of the trial proceedings to hand, was the closest and most faithful rendering of the Crippen case to date. Aside from changes of name and setting, elaborations and departures from the known facts are few, attesting to the inherent dramatic power of the Crippen story. This faithful rendering is enlivened by the insightful charting of the Moons' steadily declining relationship, from Flora's first arrival in England through to the moment of crisis in their marriage. Patently influenced by Filson Young's view of Cora/Flora as the nagging harridan, Meadows cleverly conveys her criticisms of her husband in free indirect speech, suggesting the ubiquity of her excoriating voice in the doctor's head: 'Clumsy fool. Couldn't he look what he was doing? Didn't he know how to behave himself in a decent restaurant?'[43]

---

43 Catherine Meadows, *Doctor Moon* (New York: G.P. Putnam, 1935), p. 54. A corrective, more sympathetic view of Belle was proffered only later by such memoirists as barrister Cecil Mercer, who noted: 'I have read that Mrs. Crippen led [Crippen] a dog's life. Of that, there was not a tittle of evidence.' He moreover noted that Belle was well esteemed by her friends in the guild. But by the time of his memoirs in 1952 the unfavourable view

Flora's traits are closely carried over from Filson Young and Adeline Harrison's descriptions, even down to her taste for pink décor, her thrifty accounting when shopping in the Caledonian market, and her relaxed and bohemian approach to housekeeping, epitomised in the 'jumble of incongruous objects' in the Moons' kitchen.[44] In the account of the declining relationship and the nascent affair with Marion, Meadows dwells suggestively on the significance of the jewellery that figures so significantly in the case history. Husband and wife alike are shown to be preoccupied with baubles as tokens not only of success but of the vanity and beauty of the one who sports them. Moon's objectification of his wife and the vain pleasure he takes in bedecking her with jewellery is constantly stressed over the course of the couple's many arguments as to who should be deemed the owner of the jewels.

This objectifying streak in Moon makes for a less romanticised view of his nascent relationship with Marion, an initial motive force for his advances being a similarly objectifying view of her as a body to be adorned with the jewellery he purchases:

> He thought of Marion Lennard, of her pale face, her plain clothes, her thin ringless hands. Did she, he wondered, love jewelry? Her eyes had shone with pleasure when he showed her the brooch. A jewel like that would be reflected, sparkling, in her eyes. To fasten it there, see it rise and fall as she breathed, ... to hang a necklace round that slender neck, to hold the fragile fingers in his own and slide rings on to them ... The idea was strongly attractive. He sat on his chair, gazing out into the room. His eyes grew vague and glassy as the thoughts drifted through his mind.[45]

Aptly, such brooding or 'mooning' is characteristic of the protagonist, whose daydreaming thoughts tend inevitably towards murder as the domestic tension increases. In the climactic scene in which Caspar poisons Flora, Meadows cleverly engages with the established imaginative repertory of iconography around Crippen, presenting Moon as if he has already become a notorious figure in the Chamber of Horrors:

of Belle appears to have stuck. Cecil Mercer writing as Dornford Yates, *As Berry and I Were Saying* (London: Ward Lock, 1952), p. 240.

44   *Doctor Moon*, p. 138.

45   Ibid., p. 152.

Caspar leaned back in his chair. Two incandescent mantle lights burned above him. They gave him the grotesque appearance of a bespectacled wax figure. His face shone with an opaque and waxy pallor, his hair and mustache stared lifelessly like the dull synthetic hair of Madame Tussaud's creations. Even his limbs, in their trappings of dark cloth looked wooden and immovable ... To one who could peep through the door or peer down through the ceiling it would seem incredible that this stiff recumbent figure could be impregnated with the usual contents of the human body, that in him was the power of movement, speech and thought.[46]

The remainder of the plot is sufficiently faithful to the details of the Crippen case for Dorothy L. Sayers to have described the novel as 'a transcript of actual facts' which renders the 'grotesque drama the terrible and inevitable thing it was'.[47] Moon and Lennard abscond aboard a ship and the same cross-dressed disguise is deployed – 'You're going to be my son till we get to America ... Now, son, dress up'[48] – and Captain Brierley substitutes for Captain Kendall in identifying the fugitives and raising the alarm. Again deploying free indirect discourse, the book's closing phase includes cogent commentary on the image of 'classic Crippen' that had obtained hitherto, noting its simplifications, distortions, and value as newspaper copy:

Caspar Moon was a villain and a scoundrel, a nightmare that might come after eating a late supper of lobsters and Welsh rarebit, a bogey to frighten naughty children with, and a man whom it would obviously never be safe to get within a yard of ... Newspaper sales rose enormously and dinner parties were almost certain to be a success as long as there was such a fruitful topic of conversation which was unlikely to cause any dissension. An obscure little doctor and his even more obscure mistress had suddenly burst from their obscurity into a limelight which made them the most widely known and talked of people in the kingdom. The most intimate details of their lives were routed out by indefatigable newspapermen for thousands of readers to shudder over and smile at. The lies the little man had told, his hypocrisy, his immorality with an abandoned hussy who had the temerity to earn her own living instead of staying quietly at home, gave them as pleasurable tremors of righteous indignation as the crime itself. That either of them might be

46   Ibid., pp. 238–9.
47   'Henbane: Crippen as Tragic Figure', *Sunday Times*, Sunday 14 October 1934.
48   *Doctor Moon*, p. 272.

innocent, that they were in any case wretched, suffering, tragic, even that they were human, apparently occurred to nobody.[49]

Twenty-five years after Crippen's trial and execution, literary re-imaginings of this kind were enabling the more nuanced and insightful criminological and psychological commentary that had been discouraged by the sensational view of the case that had been so powerfully urged in 1910. This notion that such murder sensations are largely played out in the press for the entertainment of the public is reasserted in the book's closing scene where, in one of the music halls in which Flora Melrose/Moon once sang, two audience members intersperse their viewing of the performance with scandalised comments on Moon's recent execution and on the lurid history of the case. The novel's last line draws attention to the way in which the sanguinary entertainment they speak of has become as much a performance as the sketches playing out on the stage before them: 'The curtain came down smartly, with finality. The performance was over.'[50]

The texts of this era had mixed success in bringing a more psychologically nuanced and criminologically complex modernity to the understanding of the Crippen case. The melodrama imprinted in the earliest reception of the case remained a potent attraction for later writers. Thus, Edward Hale Bierstadt's *Satan Was a Man* (1935) moves through tonal and thematic contortions in relating the fictional drama of Carrol Lindsay – a protagonist whose psychopathology drives him to recreate the murders of Jack the Ripper, Lizzie Borden, and Crippen while in the grip of a fugue state. Lindsay's well-thumbed copy of Filson Young is carefully described, as is his imaginative engagement with Crippen. This yields some interesting speculations, such as the suggestion that when Crippen purchased the hyoscine he was unsure 'whether it was for himself and Ethel or for Cora'.[51] Later, Lindsay imagines Crippen repeatedly tracing the 'six paces this way and six that' of the condemned cell.[52] Despite these imaginative leaps and the presence in the Lindsay family home of a retired professor of psychology, masquerading as a butler so that he might

---

49   Ibid., p. 292.
50   Ibid., p. 313.
51   Edward Hale Bierstadt, *Satan Was a Man* (New York: Doubleday, 1935, repr. Eagle Books, 1954), p. 117.
52   Ibid., p. 118.

undertake a case study of psychopathology at close quarters, the book offers no more insights on the criminal mind than its sensational title would lead us to expect.[53]

There is also some evidence of the interpenetration of literary and historical texts during this 1930s flurry of Crippen-related writing. The 1935 case history *Doctor Crippen* by journalist Max Constantine Quinn makes free association between historical and literary protagonists – 'The theme of Cora Crippen and Hawley Crippen, her husband, is as stupendous as that of Macbeth, has its roots and impulses in the same dark and tortuous caverns of the human mind'[54] – and is in many ways a literary rendition of the story, entering into Crippen's mind, speculating on motives and even rendering his thoughts as internal monologues. A year later, Harold Eaton's short case history attempted a more psychologically-oriented commentary, including application of Krafft-Ebing's definition of masochism to account for the dynamic at work in Crippen and Cora's relationship: 'He belonged to the type that likes to be ordered about and tyrannised over by women – what Krafft-Ebing would term a Masochist.'[55]

Crippen's profile remained high towards the end of the decade, with a 1938 *Daily Express* volume *Sixty Famous Trials* revisiting the case of 'The Quiet Little Doctor of Hilldrop Crescent' and, in the wake of Raymond and Meadows's novelisations, beginning to acknowledge the possibility of a more sympathetic view of the criminal: 'It might be possible to sympathize with Crippen, but for the cellar horror.'[56] In the same year, following serialisation in *Thomson's Weekly News*, Walter Dew's memoirs would appear as *I Caught Crippen* (1938). This work saw the former chief inspector adopting a literary style congruent with late Conan Doyle detective stories, including pitching criminal and detective as nemeses. Though Dew averred that his reason for writing was 'to leave behind an authoritative record of the biggest case I was privileged to handle while an officer at the Yard', the fact that he was writing largely from memory, and the more exclamatory than documentary style of the text,

---

53   F. Tennyson Jesse, *Murder and its Motives* (London: Heinemann, 1924).

54   M. Constantine Quinn, *Doctor Crippen* (London: Duckworth, 1935), p. 43.

55   Harold Eaton, 'The Case of the Century: Crippen and the Belle Elmore', in J.M. Parrish and John R. Crossland, eds, *The Fifty Most Amazing Cases of the Last 100 Years* (London: Odhams Press, 1936), pp. 102–19 (p. 102).

56   Richard Huson, ed., *Sixty Famous Trials* (London: Daily Express Publications, 1938), pp. 87–100 (p. 100).

suggest a relaxed approach to the mythology that had grown up around the story.[57]

Dew's memoirs appeared in the same year as a three-act drama based upon the Crippen story. Paul Dornhurst's *They Fly by Twilight* was staged at London's Aldywch Theatre in October 1938 before embarking on a national tour that extended into the autumn of the following year, keeping Crippen in the public mind on the eve of the Second World War. This dramatic rendering of 'the celebrated Crippen murder' offered protagonists George and Flo Martin and Mary Williams as the Crippen, Belle, and Ethel characters.[58] Staging constraints and the requirements of dramatic unity meant that the adaptation of the Crippen drama was necessarily much compressed, but the outline is all there: George and Flo live above the shop where they eke out a meagre living, Flo having resentfully abandoned her dreams of the music hall stage and George attempting imaginative escape from their existence by reading Shakespeare and Bacon in his armchair. It is from the latter that the play's title is drawn, quoted scornfully but with an unwitting dramatic irony by Flo as she mocks her husband's cultural aspirations: 'Suspicions among thoughts are like bats among birds. They ever fly by twilight.'[59] Given the static stage set there can be no transatlantic chase, but there remains the affair and the domestic murder (in this case conducted offstage with the body disposed of under the kitchen floor). The possibilities of dramatic form allow for a more subtle and searching exploration of the psychology of the Crippen protagonist than had been ventured hitherto, illustrated by George's confession to Mary and his resolution to give himself up since escape from the inner demons he has unleashed will never be possible:

> I'm an outcast Mary, I've made myself an outcast. And in time you would hate me because I've made you one too … Every fear of mine would be magnified in you a hundred times. You couldn't have a friend – every single person in the world would be your enemy. You would always be watching – watching

---

57   Walter Dew, *I Caught Crippen* (London: Blackie and Sons, 1938), p. 7. On the circumstances of Dew's production of the MS of *I Caught Crippen* see Nicholas Connell's recent edition of the text: *The Annotated I Caught Crippen* (London: Mango Books, 2018).

58   *Worthing Herald*, Friday 24 March 1939.

59   *They Fly by Twilight*, in *Five Plays of Our Time*, ed. Sydney Box (London: Thomas Nelson and Sons, 1939), p. 414.

in case somebody knew. Knew about a shabby house on the edge of London and what it contained ...[60]

Likewise, George's recovery of moral integrity in his decision to confess to the crime means that the audience is better disposed to hear his paean for a more sympathetic hearing (a plea underpinned by the abolitionist Dornhurst):

> Tomorrow morning on a million breakfast tables, the morning paper will be unfolded. It will be propped up against the tea-pot. Across it there will be headlines: 'Gruesome find in a Clapham House.' 'Husband Murders His Wife.' People will shudder and let their tea grow cold while they read it. They'll say to each other: 'How could he do it? He is such an ordinary-looking man, isn't he? Hanging is too good for people like him.' I wonder if they knew the whole truth – all about the little things – would they be so hasty to condemn? Or would they say to themselves – 'Thank God, it wasn't us!' But they never will know. The whole truth is never told.[61]

As a new decade began, a further novelisation of the story was published. Hilda Lewis's *Said Doctor Spendlove* (1940), also published as *The Little Doctor*, presents Charles and Dixie Spendlove as the Crippen and Cora characters, while Elsie Palmer occupies the place of Ethel. The rendering is harsher in tone than preceding treatments, with the impassivity of the Crippen character concealing a capacity for sadistic rage, witnessed early in the novel when, in a scene set in the couple's cluttered and dirty kitchen (the influence of Adeline Harrison's account once again), he directs a sudden burst of fury at one of Dixie's discarded dresses: 'With a sudden movement of rage he tore at the lovely frock, ripping madly at the flounces. Then, his anger spent in the wild act, he switched off the light and gently shut the door behind him.'[62] In this darker rendition Dixie is presented as a nymphomaniac and Lewis follows Marshall Hall's suggestion that the Crippen character Spendlove is seeking only to sedate his wife – 'subordinate this animal, this strong enraged animal' – rather than murder her. The details of the ensuing overdose are deliberately vague, the killer not even being certain himself how many drops of the drug he has dosed Dixie with when he finds that the remaining contents of the vial have dripped away into the bathroom

60   Ibid., p. 475.
61   Ibid., p. 476.
62   Hilda Lewis, *The Case of the Little Doctor* [1940] (New York: Permabooks, 1949), p. 46.

sink: 'He picked up the empty tube. It felt light in his hands. Had it been full when he put it down? Or nearly full? Or even half-full?' In the rendition of the flight, arrest, and trial that follows, the psychological interest is the deepest yet in re-imaginings of the Crippen case, with serious questions posed as to the limitations of the conscious mind: 'When my hand unknowing poured the dose', asks Spendlove in an internal monologue, 'didn't my unconscious self mean to kill her, mean to carry out a plan long conceived … conceived when I prepared the hyoscine? How can I know? Who can judge of the unconscious? With my thinking self, I never meant to kill her; I swear to God.'[63]

Like Meadows before her, Lewis alludes to the 'classic' version of the story from which her own rendition departs. In an early scene between Spendlove and Elsie (the Crippen and Ethel figures), the pair consider a visit to Madame Tussaud's. Elsie is keen to visit the main emporium: '"Not the Chamber of Horrors though! … Murderers!" She shuddered a trifle affectedly.'[64] And indeed, the text turns from the sensation and melodrama represented by the Chamber and the tradition of 'classic Crippen', instead exploring the story for psychological interest and, significantly, closing the narrative with Elsie's extended ruminations on the extraordinary events she has played a role in – and just how travestied those events have been in the popular rendition:

> When she looked at the papers – and she couldn't keep away from them – when she saw what was written about her, she just couldn't believe it was herself they were writing about. Because her life had always been so ordinary and they had made it sound like a movie … Sounds like a story you'd read or see in the films. But it didn't happen that way.[65]

Increased narrative focus on the Ethel character was to be a feature of literary renditions of the Crippen drama over the next decade. The extent to which 'Ethel was in it with him' was a consideration of one of Agatha Christie's urbane characters in her Poirot short story collection, *The Labours of Hercules*, published in 1947. While, as we shall see, this was her first sustained engagement with the Crippen story, Christie had already made extensive use of Crippen allusions and poisoning plots in her writing career and she had also

---

63   Ibid., p. 127; p. 136; p. 237.
64   Ibid., p. 29.
65   Ibid., pp. 371–2.

invoked a somewhat 'Crippenesque' quality to her mysterious ten-day disappearance in December 1926.[66] Likely prompted by a crisis in her first marriage to the unfaithful Colonel Archibald Christie, the novelist went missing from the couple's Surrey home, leaving her car abandoned on a lonely country road and only surfacing ten days later in a Harrogate hotel where she had registered under the name of her husband's lover. By this time the Surrey police had been dragging ponds and watercourses and searching undergrowth with dogs while the national press were asking 'Where is Mrs. Christie?'[67] There were pronounced echoes of Crippen in the episode: Christie's sudden disappearance recalled that of Cora, Archie Christie suggested his wife might have adopted a disguise and the papers carried artist's impressions of how she might appear when bespectacled and bewigged. Further cultivating the association between the cases, the *Daily Express* sought the insight of Chief Inspector Walter Dew, who had Crippen in the headlines that year by entering a brief piece, 'My Race with Crippen', in the paper's competition for best real-life story – and thereby winning the £100 prize.[68] Dew's retirement to Worthing had clearly not nurtured any pro-feminist sympathies in the former Scotland Yard official, his contribution being to pronounce: 'All women are subject to hysteria at times' and to speculate that Christie's artistic preoccupation with thinking about 'crooks and murder' all day had adversely affected her.[69]

When Christie came to draw the Crippen story into art rather than life, she turned first to Belgian detective Hercule Poirot to reference the story. Christie's Poirot story that makes overt reference to Crippen, 'The Lernean Hydra', is also a subtle re-imagining of the drama, supplying an alternative destiny for the

---

66   Earlier Crippen allusions in Christie's works include *Sleeping Murder* (published in 1976 but written in the early 1940s), where Giles refers to 'the old Crippen touch'; *Three Act Tragedy* (1935), where Mr Satterthwaite alleges that Crippen suffered from an inferiority complex; and *The Murder of Roger Ackroyd* (1926), where Caroline Sheppard, ever eager to compare the murder in her village to classic crimes, speculates that the suspect will attempt to make a transatlantic escape: 'That's what Crippen did.' *Sleeping Murder* (London: Collins, 1976), p. 68; *Three Act Tragedy* [1935] (London: Pan, 1964), p. 110; *The Murder of Roger Ackroyd* (London: Collins Crime Club, 1926), p. 257.

67   'Where is Mrs. Christie? Mystery of Missing Woman Novelist', *Daily Herald*, 7 December 1926.

68   *The Annotated I Caught Crippen*, ed. Nicholas Connell (London: Mango Books, 2018), p. 265.

69   *The Golden Age of Murder*, p. 35.

Crippen character. The story opens with an approach to Poirot from middle-aged, mild-mannered Dr Oldfield, who is being hounded by rumours that his wife's death the previous year was not an accident and that he poisoned her. His practice is suffering and he is either avoided completely as he walks the streets or made the subject of scandalous gossip; Poirot concurs that rumour is like the nine-headed hydra of the story's title and accepts the challenge 'to try my hand at destroying the many-headed monster'.[70] Oldfield relates a picture of his former domestic life which is evocative of the strained relationship between Crippen and Cora: 'There were days when nothing I could do was right.'[71] He explains that these strained relations, plus the well-documented similarity between the symptoms of the gastric disorder of the kind suffered by his wife and arsenic poisoning had led to the gossip that currently enfolds him. Poirot however, against the doctor's affronted protestations, insists that there must be a lady in the case: 'If a man poisons his wife in order to travel to the North Pole or to enjoy the peace of a bachelor existence – it would not interest his fellow-villagers for a minute! It is because they are convinced that the murder has been committed in order *that the man may marry another woman* that the talk grows and spreads. That is elemental psychology.'[72] Oldfield grudgingly admits a burgeoning relationship with his dispenser Jean Moncrieffe, to whom he would have proposed by now were the situation not so sensitive. Accepting the case, Poirot makes enquiries in Oldfield's village, interviewing, among others, village gossip Mrs Letherean, who inscribes the crime with a lineage of poisoners: 'There have been cases like it before, of course … Armstrong, for instance, and that other man – I can't remember his name – and then Crippen, of course. I've always wondered if Ethel Le Neve was in it with him or not.'[73]

The twist in Christie's brisk revisiting of the story is that neither the Crippen nor the Ethel character turn out to have been involved in the death of Oldfield's wife. Instead, the late invalid's carer, Nurse Harrison, is unmasked as the murderer, her guilt established by a forensic detail which closely mirrors the notorious pyjama jacket evidence in the Crippen case. Harrison attempts to frame Jean Moncrieffe (of whose burgeoning relationship with Oldfield she is jealous) by planting a compact full of arsenic in the younger woman's bureau

---

70   Agatha Christie, *The Labours of Hercules* [1947] (London: Harper, 2008), p. 41.
71   Ibid., p. 42.
72   Ibid., p. 43.
73   Ibid., p. 50.

drawer and then submitting a false witness statement to the effect that she had
seen the compact in Moncrieffe's possession shortly before Mrs Oldfield's
death. Poirot however establishes that the compact '*is of a pattern and colour
that has only been manufactured for the last three months*'.[74] Her false claims
exposed, Harrison admits responsibility for the murder. The story ends with
the Belgian detective surveying with satisfaction 'the happy-looking middle-
aged man and the eager-faced girl opposite him'.[75] It might be a portrait of
Crippen and Ethel, only this time in a different version of the story which ends
not on the scaffold but at the altar; Christie supplies an alternative ending to
the signature case that, over nearly forty years, had influenced so many crime
stories and prompted so many retellings.[76]

Poirot is also the protagonist of the second Christie work in which the
Crippen story is referenced at length: *Mrs McGinty's Dead*, published in 1952.
When the eponymous Mrs McGinty is found dead at the novel's opening, her
lodger is initially suspected. Yet Poirot's investigations suggest the recent
murder is in fact related to at least one notorious crime from the past and
that key figures associated with a number of historical cases are living under
assumed identities in the small village of Broadhinny where McGinty died.
One such historical case involved conscientious, nondescript town clerk Alfred
Craig (the Crippen figure), married to a temperamental and difficult spouse,
and his mistress, young nursery governess Eva Kane (the Ethel character).

> Then one day the neighbours heard that Mrs Craig had been 'ordered abroad'
> for her health. That had been Craig's story. He took her up to London, the

---

74   Ibid., p. 59.
75   Ibid., p. 62.
76   A contemporaneous novel by Sidney Horler, *The Man Who Did Not Hang*, follows a
     similar conceit of supplying the Crippen story with a different conclusion. Protagonist
     Horace Harvey Pring, a dealer in patent medicines, poisons his wife, the failed music
     hall soubrette Mai Hawthorne, but succeeds in getting away with the crime. Murder is
     detected but falsely ascribed to Mai's lover, who hangs himself in his cell before ever
     the case comes to trial. Pring goes free to continue his relationship with Elsie Dean,
     the Ethel character. Only in the novel's closing pages does Inspector Sorrow note the
     curious parallels between the Pring and Crippen cases, even drawing down a copy of
     Filson Young from the shelves as he realises that Pring, 'another meek and mild, down-
     trodden husband', was most likely his wife's murderer: *The Man Who Did Not Hang*
     (London: Quality Press, 1948), p. 253.

first stage of the journey, by car late one evening, and 'saw her off' to the
South of France. Then he returned to Parminster and at intervals mentioned
how his wife's health was no better by her accounts of it in letters. Eva Kane
remained to housekeep for him and tongues soon started wagging. Finally,
Craig received news of his wife's death abroad. He went away and returned
a week later, with an account of the funeral.[77]

Craig, who had in fact murdered his wife and buried her remains in the cellar,
becomes notorious during his trial and execution, his effigy taking a prominent
place in the Chamber of Horrors.[78] Poirot's official police counterpart Inspector
Traill is convinced that Eva Kane was equally complicit in the crime and was
indeed the driving force in its commission: 'Eva Kane was all innocence and
horror. Very well she did it too: a clever little actress.'[79]

Christie's repeated questioning, in both Poirot short story and novel, of
the extent of Ethel le Neve's knowledge and agency in the Crippen case was
to prove timely. Within two years of the appearance of *Mrs McGinty's Dead*,
journalist and novelist Ursula Bloom was also to take up the question of Ethel's
version of events. Bloom's *The Girl Who Loved Crippen* first appeared in the
spring of 1954 in serialised form in *The Sunday Dispatch*, for which Bloom was
chief crime reporter, and in book form the following year. Advertisements
characterised the work as 'based on fact but presented with all that vivid and
understanding imagination for which its gifted author is famous'.[80]

Bloom's imaginative engagement with the story was rendered in a somewhat
exclamatory and mawkish prose, but played its part in rewriting the popular
conception of Crippen some forty years after his execution. She follows the
exculpatory drift of Ethel's own reminiscences of 1910, casting her protagonist
as an innocent abroad, swept along by events and able to exert limited agency
in a hostile world of gossips, police, law courts, and other oppressors. This
approach extends to peppering the narrative with portents and omens that
surround the superstitious protagonist: Ethel's mother warns her daughter
that the class ambition she harbours has led others before her to the nearby
Holloway Prison; Ethel's first landlady discerns trials, vicissitudes, and death

---

77   Agatha Christie, *Mrs McGinty's Dead* [1952] (London: Pan, 1971), p. 56.
78   Ibid., p. 90.
79   Ibid., p. 86.
80   'The Girl Who Loved Crippen', *Norwood News*, 2 April 1954.

17.   Ursula Bloom's *The Girl Who Loved Crippen* (1955) which idealised Ethel and Crippen as lovers and solidified the negative depiction of Belle Elmore in the case's posterity.

in Ethel's tea leaves while her second (the historically-based Mrs Jackson) gifts her a pearl necklace despite the superstition 'pearls means tears';[81] at Hilldrop Crescent a sinister earthy smell forebodes ill of the house, particularly the cellar; the Crippens' cat meows portentously; and crossing the threshold of the house to live there after Belle's disappearance, Ethel's very heart cries out: 'Danger! Danger!'[82]

Against this backdrop of ominous portents, the developing relationship between Ethel and Crippen is set out at a fast-moving pace with Bloom drawing selectively on the historical record.[83] The years at the Drouet Institute are dispensed with and Crippen's homeopathic activities outside of his dentistry are downplayed. Instead, Ethel comes straight to the Yale Tooth Specialists as secretary and, in a compressed time-frame, meets both Crippen and Belle, even taking a mislaid theatrical appointments book to the latter shortly after starting with the firm and thus paying a visit to the mistress of Hilldrop Crescent where, in a somewhat contrived scene, she is dispatched by Belle to fetch coal from the cellar only to be overcome at the dread horror of the place: 'there was something about this place that she found quite terrifying … It was not a cellar; it was a tomb!'[84] Already beset with this premonitory dread of the cellar, Ethel proceeds to faint when Belle reveals her lover, De Courcy, who is upstairs in the house. The tenor is thus established early for a presentation of Ethel as the put-upon innocent, taking refuge in her doomed love for Crippen from a hostile and obtruding world. Bloom echoes a discursive move from Ethel's own 1910 account, making frequent use of demonstratives to distance and estrange the people and events of which she disavows knowledge and association. The historical Ethel had exclaimed, 'What do *these* people want?' of Mitchell and Dew's unwelcome call at Hilldrop Crescent; 'What was all *this* mystery?' she had asked in exasperation at their investigation of the cellar; and she had rejoiced at how, in her boy's disguise, she had escaped 'all *those* people who had been

81   Ursula Bloom, *The Girl Who Loved Crippen* (London: Hutchinson, 1955), p. 63.
82   Ibid., p. 95.
83   Bloom's major source material appears to have been the 1950 reprint of Filson Young's edition of the trial proceedings. Nicholas Connell has established that, surprisingly, Bloom appears not to have read Michael Gilbert's case history of 1953. Interestingly, the cover of Gilbert and the dust-jacket of Bloom both described Crippen as 'hen-pecked', suggesting the increasing dominance in the popular imagination of Filson Young's negative view of Cora Crippen.
84   *The Girl Who Loved Crippen*, p. 41.

prying upon my movements [emphases mine].[85] Both the internal monologues
and the direct speech of the fictional Ethel follow this same discursive signature
to exclaim first her delicate sensibility and later her indignant innocence. Belle
is 'this big pretentious woman', 'this large commanding woman', 'this blustering
and flamboyant woman'; while her friends at the Music Hall Ladies Guild are
'these busy-bodies' or 'these wretched women'; and Dew and Mitchell are
'those odious policemen who had disturbed her so'.[86]

While the cumulative effect of these distancing demonstratives may serve
Bloom's end of sustaining an image of an innocent, even unworldly, Ethel
(she is described as elf-like and sylvan towards the book's close), it is a
portrait which offers little insight or even rumination on the true nature of
the Crippen–Le Neve relationship, and stops far short of any speculation in
answer to Christie's question of how much Ethel must have known. While
allusion is made to a hypodermic of hyoscine being found by Ethel in Albion
House (somewhat illogically given the forensic pathologists established it was
administered by mouth), and to a bloodstain on the bathroom wall at Hilldrop
Crescent, the textual focus on Ethel's absolute innocence leaves little space for
speculation on Crippen's crime.

Bloom was to remain heavily invested in Ethel's story long after publication
of *The Girl Who Loved Crippen*. After the initial serialisation of the story in *The
Sunday Dispatch*, Bloom was contacted by a male relative of Le Neve (accounts
vary as to whether this was in fact Ethel's brother) who intimated that Ethel,
while she had indeed left England for a new life after Crippen's execution,
was still living and now resettled not far from London. After a tentative correspondence and some brokerage by family members, Bloom would eventually
find herself meeting and interviewing the notorious survivor of the Crippen
drama, now living in suburban anonymity with her family. The novelist made
notes at the meeting and would make much of the connection in subsequent
decades: as late as 1972, she would even claim to have escorted an elderly
Ethel on a visit to Pentonville shortly before her death: 'She wanted to go back
to see the prison where her lover was hanged.'[87]

Bloom's novel was instrumental in cementing the Filson Young view of Cora
as harridan and shrew and in elevating the view of Crippen as long-suffering,

85 *Ethel Le Neve: Her Life Story*, p. 30, p. 36, p. 45.
86 *The Girl Who Loved Crippen*, p. 36, p. 40, p. 50, p. 108, p. 119, p. 127.
87 *Guardian*, 12 July 1972.

hen-pecked, and a true and loyal lover to Ethel. In this and in other details of her novel, Bloom further unpicked the image of 'classic Crippen', the imaginative hold of which she acknowledges in Ethel's view of the doctor as 'a waxen statue, his face the colour of a candle and entirely expressionless, like one of those figures that she had seen at Madame Tussaud's'.[88] With details of the murder of Cora de-emphasised and narrative stress laid instead on the lovers' attempted escape to a new life (Ethel being in blissful ignorance of the crime of course), Bloom's *Girl Who Loved Crippen* is more a tragedy of true love and an apologia for Ethel than a criminological study.[89]

Within a few short years, this instinct to rehabilitate the reputations of the principals in this classic murder story would be extended to Crippen himself. Perhaps in reflection of the liberalising attitudes of the era, the early 1960s saw a group of re-imaginings of the case which took up Marshall Hall's theory that Crippen never sought to murder his wife, only to sedate her with hyoscine so that he might conduct his affair in safety. This was the line adopted in the ill-fated 1961 stage musical *Belle or The Ballad of Dr Crippen*. Based on a play by Beverley Cross, the production's book was provided by Wolf Mankowitz while music and lyrics were contributed by Monty Norman, who would shortly write the theme music for the James Bond series of films.

Between Dornhurst's *They Fly By Twilight* and *Belle*, there had been one further Crippen-themed drama; Ronald Adams's *The Little Doctor* had been banned by the Lord Chamberlain in 1954 on the premise that Ethel le Neve was still alive ('Miss Le Neve is now over 70 and lives away from London … it is understood both her children and grandchildren are unaware of her true identity')[90] but this objection was overcome six years later when the production was finally staged featuring Edward Woodward in the title role. It appears that two musicals were originally proposed to follow in its wake; concurrent with the development of *Belle*, Caryl Brahms and Ned Sherrin were developing a Crippen-themed libretto piece which ultimately took an alternative form as the novel *Rappel 1910*.[91] It is unclear what discouraged Brahms and Sherrin from

---

88   *The Girl Who Loved Crippen*, p. 71.
89   Bloom would toil further in this seam of apologias for women from history, going on to write an imaginative biography of Eva Braun.
90   'Crippen Play Banned', *The Stage*, 21 October 1954.
91   On Brahms and Sherrin's musical see Adrian Wright, *Must Close Saturday: The Decline and Fall of the British Musical Flop* (Woodbridge: The Boydell Press, 2017), p. 25.

pursuing their original design, but if they harboured unease as to the public's readiness for a stage representation of the Crippen drama this would appear to have been well justified by the reception of Mankowitz and Norman's effort.

With the subtitle 'A Music Hall Musical', *Belle* ostensibly sought to evoke the same music hall world in which the Crippens had moved fifty years previously. It also legitimately picked up certain elements of the case which could be deemed comedic without too great a stretch: Belle's persistence on the music hall stage despite the limitations of her musical talent and stage presence; Crippen's purchasing of a quantity of hyoscine in monstrous proportion to the amount needed to commit murder; Ethel's boy's trousers splitting up the back as she paced the decks of the *Montrose*; the hapless Crippen commenting on the wonders of wireless telegraphy while the ship's radio room taps out the message that will bring Scotland Yard in pursuit of him and lead him to the scaffold. This image of Crippen as a man out of place and time, 'a hapless fellow brought down by the powerful thunderbolt of technology,' brings this rendering of the story much closer to the sensibility of popular modernity.[92] Also congruent with this sensibility is the play's employment of a melange of dramatic and musical styles as part of its evocation of the Edwardian admixture of old and new. 'It relished its opportunity to mingle spectacle … with horror, knockabout comedy and sentiment,' notes Adrian Wright in one of the few critical discussions of the play: 'Norman's pastiche score roamed over all manner of styles of the period.'[93]

This spirit of bricolage and associative contrasts is summoned from the outset by the play's programme notes, which range from high to low culture, astral bodies to national politics and the price of a pint:

> It is 1910. Haley's Comet twinkles in the night sky like a prehistoric sputnik. Far below, along the Strand, sparkle the lights of Gatti's and Romano's, The Empire and The Criterion – illuminating the nightlife of London; electioneering for Lloyd George, the Salvation Army campaigning for the Lord.
>
> What a year! Beer a penny a pint, music hall never better, Oxford win the Boat Race, Jenkinstown wins the Grand National, a new Cunarder launched, aviation all the rage, Marconi sets up a transatlantic wireless, an airship

---

92 Julie English Early, 'Technology, Modernity and the "The Little Man": Crippen's Capture by Wireless', *Victorian Studies* 39:3 (1996), pp. 309–37 (p. 311).

93 *Must Close Saturday*, p. 23.

disaster, concern in the Commons over German battleship building, Balzac's "Droll Stories" confiscated as obscene literature and a glorious summer forecast. Everything is normal. In fact, life is very much as it will be fifty years from now.

Only one thing is missing – a good old headline-making, yards of reading British crime. But it is not missing for long. And when it comes it is a classic, well worth waiting for.[94]

In fairness to the much maligned (and rarely reprised) musical, it is largely this spirit of Edwardian colour, eccentricity, and innovation that *Belle* seeks to summon, rather than a morbid engagement with the details of the crime. A selection of the musical's song titles is illustrative: 'Bird of Paradise' treats of Belle's uncertain vocal talents; 'Meet me at the Strand' evokes an Edwardian world of promenade and polite courtship; 'Coldwater Michigan' provides an opportunity for exploration of the picaresque elements of the Crippen story and the lot of the expatriate medic. Critical reception of the play was generally hostile, many papers objecting to the burlesquing of true crime and others questioning the production's musical standard: one paper objected to 'a series of mawkishly sentimental duets' between Crippen and Le Neve and *The People* reached the conclusion, irrespective of subject matter, 'that it is just a bad musical'.[95] The production closed after just a six-week run at The Strand Theatre, Mankowitz making a personal loss of £20,000 and characterising the critics who had played their part in the early closure as 'butchers who slaughtered us out of hand'.[96]

Despite its short run, *Belle or The Ballad of Doctor Crippen* warrants fuller attention than it has hitherto received. Offering valuable insights on the changing cultural perception of Crippen in the early 1960s, the play might tenably be considered as the fullest artistic realisation of the case in a mode of popular modernism, strongly contrastive to the 'classic Crippen' rendition familiar from previous chapters. Elements of the infrastructure of the 'classic' account of the case remained in place, such as the suggestion that the audience might visit Crippen's effigy in Madame Tussauds: 'see him for a six-pence in

94   *Belle or The Ballad of Doctor Crippen*, Decca Record Co., 1961.
95   'Cracks in the Belle', *Kensington Post*, 26 May 1961; 'It's Just Murder', *The People*, 7 May 1961.
96   'Farewell Belle', *Daily Herald*, 31 May 1961.

18.   Wolf Mankowitz and Monty Norman's *Belle or The Ballad of Dr Crippen*
ran at London's Strand Theatre for just six weeks in the spring of 1961.
The attempt to render Belle as protagonist, and to re-imagine the case in a popular
modernist sensibility, perhaps warranted a longer run than the play enjoyed.

the hall of fame.'[97] Yet the Marshall Hall defence that the hapless doctor never meant to poison but only to incapacitate, taken alongside the burlesque and irreverent touches of music hall sensibility, make for a new form of engagement with the case, ranging far from the melodramatic and sensational overtones of 1910:

> Here's a little story,
> A touching tale of woe.
> Happened here in London
> 'Bout fifty years ago.
>
> A little Yankee doctor
> Created quite a din,
> All because he gave his
> Dear wife a Mickey-Finn.[98]

A mere four years before the death penalty would be suspended in England and Wales, it is interesting to note this renewed interest in the possibility that Crippen might have been innocent of wilful murder (while doubtless culpable of abusing both partner and profession if he was indeed covertly sedating his spouse).

This same notion forms the central premise in a highly sympathetic portrait of Crippen in a 1962 film and associated novelisation, *Dr. Crippen*. The film would star British actor Donald Pleasance, sinister enough to evoke the inheritance of classic Crippen, yet sympathetic enough to imply that the events which overtook the doctor in 1910 were not entirely of his own making. Film and novelisation also did their part in embedding in the Crippen mythology the notion that Belle was provocatively unfaithful with the Hilldrop Crescent lodgers, the long-suffering Crippen even polishing the boots of the men who were cuckolding him. In the liberalised climate of early 1960s cinema, the full implications of Marshall Hall's theory are explored. Embarked on his affair with Ethel, Crippen must find a way to repulse the sexual demands of Belle (even the lodgers' attentions are not sufficient it seems) without her becoming suspicious: 'Dose Belle with something! Of course. It was so simple he could

---

97   Wolf Mankowitz and Monty Norman, *Belle or The Ballad of Doctor Crippen* (London: Wolf Mankowitz Presentations, n.d.), p. 2.

98   Ibid., p. 1.

19. Donald Pleasance as Crippen in the 1962 film and associated novelisation of the screenplay. The film poster was reminiscent of the original 1910 police bill.

not imagine why he had not thought of it before.'[99] With the hyoscine procured purely for this sedative purpose, the resulting death of Belle is presented as misadventure. As Crippen prepares to lace Belle's night-time cup of tea with the sedative dose, she calls down to him, causing him to start: 'As he did so, his wrist slackened and the paper in his hand lowered so that some of the white crystals poured on to the top of the powdered sugar in the bowl.'[100] Belle's preference for sugar in her tea brings fatal results.

This new conception of a truly hen-pecked and hapless Crippen carries him a long way from the classic image of 1910, a contrast brought to mind in one of the last scenes from *Dr. Crippen*, when the Pentonville prisoner relates to the prison governor, 'I was a monster worse than Jack the Ripper according to the papers.'[101] This view of an unworldly, innocent Crippen also lends an additional emotional power to the depiction of the intertwined fates of Crippen

99   Michael Hooker, *Doctor Crippen* (London: Brown, Watson Ltd, 1963), p. 60.
100 Ibid., p. 78.
101 Ibid., p. 154.

and Ethel, now united in the shared secret of his innocence and in a sense of the unjustness of the reputation posterity has afforded him:

> The crowd sent up a ragged cheer. At last the country was purged of that monster, the inhuman fiend, Crippen – but somehow even the most violent among them felt no exultation. They broke up quietly, and began to drift away.
>
> None of them took particular notice of the young woman, small and heavily veiled, as she turned and stumbled down towards the busy street. Part of Ethel le Neve had died in the execution chamber too, as the clock struck eight, and she had to be away from this place; away, lost and anonymous among the crowds, to whatever the future might hold.[102]

The UK release of *Dr. Crippen* in late 1962, and subsequently worldwide in the spring of the following year, seems to have enjoyed only limited profile and to have attracted relatively scant press attention.[103] If the approach of the swinging sixties and a preoccupation with world events and the space race had dimmed creative interest in an Edwardian crime sensation, this relative waning of Crippeniana was to be sustained into the 1970s. By this time, popular criminological attention was drawn instead to the Ripper case, where theories involving royal Rippers and Masonic conspiracies were in the ascendant, as witness Michael Harrison's *Clarence* (1974), which explored whether Queen Victoria's grandson was the Ripper, or Stephen Knight's *Jack the Ripper: The Final Solution* (1976), which suggested high-ranking Freemasons in the legal and medical professions as being responsible for the crimes. The Crippen story promised little of the novelty and ongoing mystery of these invitations to 'hunt the Ripper' – though a 1975 trail in *The Guardian* for Tom Cullen's upcoming case history popularised the notion that hyoscine had been applied as an anaphrodisiac while Richard Crane's short 1975 play *Crippen: A Music Hall Melodrama* would even dramatise the hypothesis that Belle poisoned herself.[104] For the most part, 1970s engagement with the North London Cellar

---

102 Ibid., p. 156.

103 A search of the broadsheets over the period of the release yields no extended reviews and only cursory notices such as *The Observer* classing the film as 'a solidly made thriller' (6 October 1963).

104 'What's Up Doc?', *Guardian*, 24 February 1976. The article was prompted by the auction at Sotheby's that day of various relics in the case previously owned by friend of the

Murder was confined to occasional features in retrospectives and reminiscences, as when Alfred Hitchcock gave an interview to the *Los Angeles Times*, rehearsing every detail of the case. The unsettled interviewer noted that the director showed great relish in recounting the discovery of the remains in the cellar: 'Hitchcock smiled his most beatific smile.'[105]

Sustained literary engagement with Crippen resumed in 1981 with Richard Gordon's *A Question of Guilt: The Curious Case of Dr Crippen*. Gordon, medical practitioner and prolific author of the long-running series of 'Doctor' novels beginning with *Doctor in the House* (1952), revisited the case with an eye to the crucial question of Crippen's motive. The novel's approach creatively interweaves the historical details of the case with a fictional narrative centred on protagonists Dr Eliot Beckett and Nancy Grange. When Nancy's sister is afflicted with tuberculosis and receiving urgent care in a Swiss sanatorium, Nancy learns of a potential treatment associated with Munyon's Remedies, and thus she and Beckett travel to London in search of Crippen as Munyon's manager. The premise allows for much subtle interweaving of fact and fiction with key vignettes including the pair's visit to Albion House, where Crippen's bow-legged walk puts Beckett 'in mind of some music hall comedian' and the couple's own invitation to a 'pot luck' dinner at Hilldrop Crescent, where the fictional characters interact with the historical Martinettis among the pink décor of the North London townhouse.[106] Subsequently, on the morning of 31 January 1910 – the day of the final dinner party at Hilldrop Crescent to which Nancy and Beckett are also invited – Crippen confides in the fellow medic that he doses Belle with sedative amounts of hyoscine to allay her physical demands upon him and to enable his assignations with Ethel – the Marshall Hall account of the case. Accordingly, the 'question of guilt' in the death that follows that night is not the fact of the administration of the drug but the crucial factors of intention and motive. The climactic scene that leads to Belle's death

Crippens and Music Hall Ladies' Guild doctor John Burroughs. Crane's play debuted at Manchester University Theatre and was billed as 'Bizarre, comic entertainment about our most famous murder': *Guardian*, 16 September 1975.

105 'Killing Some Time with Alfred Hitchcock', *Los Angeles Times*, 23 July 1972.

106 Richard Gordon, *A Question of Guilt: The Curious Case of Dr Crippen* (New York: Athenaeum, 1981), p. 68. There was to be a UK television depiction of the Crippen story in the same year in an episode of the ITV drama *The Ladykillers* (broadcast Friday 10 July 1981).

contains sufficient ellipses for the exact moment of the overdose to remain undepicted, but the presence in the house of a copy of *Grey's Anatomy*, loaned from Beckett, and the calm and methodical manner of Crippen's disposal of the body (described in grim detail by the medically-qualified author) tend to suggest premeditation.

The novel's creative interweaving of the fictional Dr Beckett with historical episodes from the Crippen story include him receiving one of Crippen's diversionary letters announcing Belle's departure for America; meeting Dew and Mitchell in the Holborn restaurant where they are interviewing Crippen and compiling his statement; and discussing the forensic evidence in the case with Spilsbury in his laboratory at St Mary's Hospital. Throughout the novel it is Beckett as medic and psychologist who provides the thread of speculation on the degree of intentionality in the crime; the more qualified doctor also speculates that Crippen may simply have botched the dosage: 'He was so appallingly ignorant, he probably gave her a lethal dose by mistake.'[107]

Imaginative responses to Crippen continued in 1982 with Peter Lovesey's award-winning crime novel *The False Inspector Dew*. No mere retelling of the case, the novel instead draws upon the Crippen story as the thematic context for a highly innovative plot involving impersonation, murder, and fraud. Walter Baranov (the putative Crippen character) has a background in music hall, a current practice in dentistry, and a wife with whom relations are strained. Alma Webster (the Ethel character) largely lives in a fantasy world, inventing a lover whom she 'kills off' during the Great War when questioning from friends and associates becomes too difficult. The pair meet in 1921 when Alma attends Walter's dental surgery for treatment and is instantly drawn to him. Crippen's connection to dentistry prompts the pair to discuss the case, revealing a deep imaginative sympathy in Alma: 'She had felt nothing but pity for the two fugitives pacing the deck of that poky little steamer in their pathetic disguises for ten days, while thanks to a sharp-eyed ship's captain and the miracle of wireless every Tom, Dick and Harry who could read a newspaper knew that Inspector Dew would be waiting with the handcuffs in Toronto.'[108]

As a relationship between the pair develops, Baranov resolves to murder his Belle-like wife Lydia and plans to disguise the crime by throwing the body overboard during a passage to New York aboard the *Mauretania*. Alma is to

107 *A Question of Guilt*, p. 150.
108 Peter Lovesey, *The False Inspector Dew* [1982] (London: Macmillan, 1983), p. 25.

stow away on the same voyage and is to assume the identity of the murdered woman to divert suspicion. Baranov is to travel under the assumed name of Walter Dew. The couple are pleased with the ingenuity of their plan and consider that Crippen himself would have approved: 'No body in the cellar. No ridiculous disguises.'[109] Yet all does not go to plan when, shortly after Walter is to murder his wife, a woman's body is retrieved from the sea and the ship's captain presses Baranov as 'retired Inspector Dew' to investigate.

The ensuing sophisticated and innovative narrative engages closely with the established imaginative repertory of the Crippen drama, complete with an obligatory Chamber of Horrors scene courtesy of Alma's nightmare:

> She was in a brick-lined cavernous place filled with motionless figures. It was the Chamber of Horrors. Suddenly, one of the figures moved, a woman in a long black cloak. Her face was pallid and there were strips of seaweed in her hair. It was Lydia. She took Alma's arm and guided her across the stone-paved floor, past the effigies of infamous killers, Burke and Hare, William Palmer, Dr Pritchard and Neill Cream. There was one figure standing alone. A plaque in front of it said H.H. Crippen. Alma looked at the face and screamed.[110]

Replete with twists and reversals, the plot sees 'Inspector Dew' solve the murder, thereby uncovering an on-board gambling scam. It also sees Walter and Alma separate as they come to recognise the fantasy they have modelled their actions upon: 'what if Crippen had never been caught? What if Ethel had faced the rest of her life with him?' In the last of many reverses, when Walter returns to home port it transpires that Lydia Baranov has not in fact been murdered: she disembarked from the *Mauretania* before ever the ship set out across the Atlantic: 'Lydia squeezed his hand again. "My poor Walter! You must have been beside yourself with worry. Did you think I'd fallen over the side?".' A more positive tone is struck in the couple's relations in these closing pages, both laughing at the captain's assumption of Walter as the 'real' Inspector Dew and hinting at a new rapprochement: '"It's taught me something, darling. I'm married to a man who values me. I intend to keep him close to me forever."'[111] It is as if Walter's imaginative engagement in the Crippen affair, and his role-play

109 Ibid., p. 84.
110 Ibid., p. 190.
111 Ibid., p. 232, p. 250, p. 251.

as Dew, have created a salutary space of play and possibility, averting the crisis of the couple's marriage and the commission of a new murder.

Innovation of premise and plot are also to be found in Emlyn Williams's hybrid text of 1987, *Dr. Crippen's Diary: An Invention*. Presented as a recently discovered manuscript of a diary kept between 1888 and 1910 that has only recently come to the light, the book explores the central paradox of Crippen's character, bringing the monster of classic Crippen tradition into dialogue with the mild murderer of later tradition and what he called the incongruous double image of 'The Little Man and the Monster'.[112] Thus, the young Crippen of an 1891 entry is pictured reading one of the key intertexts which, as we have seen, influenced the reception of classic Crippen – 'I bought a cheap copy of *Dr Jekyll & Mr. Hyde*. I like a good shocker as well, they take you out of yourself.'[113] He later reads a Holmes story from a *Strand* magazine in which 'a chap who has (by all accounts) a v. nasty wife, gets rid of her in quite a clever manner'.[114] Likewise, in an entry for 1896, the young doctor reads up on a case which, as the previous chapters have shown, was instrumental in framing the reception of his own subsequent crime:

> I was sitting with the St Louis paper & having a quiet read, about those terrible goings-on in London a while back – my nice respectable London – with this Jack the Ripper that's a maniac who murdered these women in the East End, terrible to think there are such people about, & they say he's supposed to be a Doctor, like that Dr. Jekyll – but this one is real, I don't like that. A libel on my profession.[115]

A range of such arch allusions and ironic inclusions is to be found in Williams's rendition of Crippen. Reading of the fictional diary of the highly comparable Charles Pooter, Crippen characterises himself as 'a Nobody with a Diary, that's me';[116] he recounts evenings at the music hall watching crossed-dressed acts;[117] and suggests to Ethel that they spend an evening further revisiting one of the Crippen story's key intertexts: 'we'll have a night out, West End style, what do

---

112 Emlyn Williams, *Dr. Crippen's Diary: An Invention* (London: Futura, 1987), p. 169.
113 Ibid., p. 24.
114 Ibid., p. 119.
115 Ibid., p. 34.
116 Ibid., p. 47.
117 Ibid., p. 62.

you say to *Dr. Jekyll & Mr. Hyde*, with H.B. Irving?'[118] When the crisis comes in the Crippens' marriage, the Marshall Hall view of the poisoning is once more in evidence. 'I've *got* to give her something in her drink to calm her down' resolves Crippen and proceeds to administer small amounts of hyoscine in Belle's drinks to sedate her.[119] An entirely new scenario is posed by Williams as to events in Hilldrop Crescent on 31 January 1910. After the Martinettis head home from the dinner party, Belle complains of a headache and helps herself to what she takes to be painkillers from Crippen's bathroom medicine cabinet: 'she had staggered into the bathroom (in the half-dark, sozzled) & taken the hysoscin. Probably 100 times the safe dose.'[120]

The diary continues through the summer of 1910, charting the Scotland Yard interviews, the disguise, and the flight across the Atlantic, ending with an entry at Father Point after the arrest, Crippen reflecting on the 'cheap sensationalism' of the press treatment of his domestic tragedy: 'sheer vulgar horror at the gory details.'[121] A short coda from Williams returns to the question of Crippen's bungling and the curious inconsistencies and mis-steps made by a man who might otherwise have committed the perfect crime:

> Foolishness led to foolishness: such as his senseless insistence on Ethel Le Neve wearing his dead wife's jewellery and furs in public; his assumption that his wife's friends would accept the fact that a letter from her to them had been dictated to him and not even signed by her; his dismissal of their mounting suspicions; his inner conviction (until it was too late) that he was hoodwinking Scotland Yard; his asking a friend to shop for a boy's wardrobe (surely the most bizarre and foolhardy errand ever thought up by a guilty man trying to cover up his tracks) when he could so easily have waited and done his own shopping in Dieppe; his childlike trust in Captain Kendall's friendly overtures; all following (and fatally consonant with) the burying of the pyjama-top.[122]

While in Williams's version of Crippen, the doctor's principal crimes are the mutilation of Belle's corpse and her burial in the cellar following accidental death, in John Boyne's *Crippen* (2004) the protagonist is innocent even of those

---

118 Ibid., p. 99.
119 Ibid., p. 65.
120 Ibid., p. 74.
121 Ibid., p. 164.
122 Ibid., p. 246.

deeds. The highly inventive novel transposes the Jekyll and Hyde motif into entirely new territory, framing a Crippen universe in which the killer is not the mild-mannered doctor at all but the quietly spoken and inscrutable Ethel. Just as the retiring young typist will adopt cross-dressed disguise as Crippen's son Edmund Robinson aboard the *Montrose*, so, it transpires, she has earlier adopted the assertive, resolute persona of a London doctor who rescues Crippen from long-standing domestic violence at the hands of his wife. It was cross-dressed Ethel who purchased the hyoscine, Ethel who murdered Cora, mutilated her and buried her in the cellar, and Ethel who boards the *Montrose* with a hatbox containing Cora's head, in readiness for depositing overboard during the voyage.

This audacious re-imagining of the case de-centres Crippen as protagonist (despite the book's title) and instead opens up the wider masquerades of the Edwardian society in which Crippen and Ethel moved. The members of the Music Hall Ladies' Guild are revealed to be social climbers at pains to disguise their origins; those same gossipers at the scandal and horror of the Crippen murder intersperse their condemnation with private ruminations on the likelihood of rich relatives dying so that they might inherit wealth and titles, or 'sleeping with the bedroom windows open'[123] so that current husbands might be replaced with wealthier and more agreeable successors. The Edwardian prurience and heteronormative suspicion underlying the passengers' responses to Ethel's cross-dressing are also examined by the novel. Captain Kendall's preoccupation with the 'unnatural' physical contact of 'Mr. and Master Robinson' aboard the *Montrose* is revisited with a much greater insight than the commentators of 1910 had summoned.[124] The fictional Kendall's prurience and suspicion is depicted as a compensatory reaction as he silently and repressively pines for his own close male intimate – veteran first officer Sorenson, who is back in England on sick leave. Even the ship's barber is aware of the emotional intimacy between the officers, who are 'thick as thieves … always together'.[125] Indeed, when Kendall receives a telegram informing him that

---

123 John Boyne, *Crippen: A Novel of Murder* (Harmondsworth: Penguin, 2004), p. 497.

124 Kendall's response to the on-deck hand-squeezing was reflective of a wider social unease around Crippen and Le Neve's relationship. As Julie English Early has observed: 'No matter the slant, potential sexual irregularity was attached to them even before the father/son ruse of their escape was known: 'Technology, Modernity, and "The Little Man": Crippen's Capture by Wireless', *Victorian Studies* 39:3 (1996), pp. 309–37 (p. 319).

125 *Crippen: A Novel of Murder*, p. 45.

Sorenson has deteriorated and his illness is now life-threatening, he has a breakdown before his shipmates in the *Montrose*'s wireless room, reflecting a passionate concern and desire he can hardly acknowledge.

The novel is poignant in its rendering of a world of oft-thwarted homosociality where strict public limitations are imposed on the scope of emotional and physical intimacy between men. One of the quieter tragedies in Boyne's re-imagining of the case is the revelation that the middle-aged Inspector Dew is lonely, feeling he may have found a potential lifelong friend in Crippen. The famous Holborn lunch between the pair is depicted as a scene of burgeoning intimacy between the men, Crippen's tale of domestic isolation with Belle stirring the sympathy and affection of the Scotland Yard detective. This makes for a poignant climax to the London-based investigation: when Dew pays his follow-up visit to Hilldrop Crescent it is not to threaten Crippen with further enquiries but to reveal that the case is to be dropped.

Dew wants to relay the good news in person and brims with anticipation at his reunion with the doctor. In a bold and unexpected piece of characterisation, Boyne presents Dew's lightness of step and of heart as he wends his way to Hilldrop Crescent on that mid-July evening: 'Passing by the Thames, he had an unlikely urge to jump on to an empty bench and burst into song … He practically danced up the steps to the door.'[126] The scene is poignant prologue to a disappointment that is as much personal as professional; Crippen has flown and the Inspector has been deprived of both prime suspect and potential friend.[127]

The possibility of same sex intimacy and desire, implied by Ethel's cross-dressing but so readily passed over in the classic rendering of the case, is also finally liberated from the narrative in Boyne's retelling. Ethel is presented from the outset as androgynous, 'as if God had been unable to decide whether to make her a surprisingly masculine girl or an unusually pretty boy.'[128] During Ethel's stint in boy's clothes as Edmund Robinson aboard the *Montrose* she is pursued by young socialite Victoria Drake, whose romances to date have been driven by the urge to attract and then disappoint a string of suitors. Edmund/Ethel's apparent unattainability only encourages Victoria's pursuit of the youth

---

126 Ibid., pp. 330–1.

127 Boyne's rendering of Dew, quite aside from its considerable artistic cogency, supplies an interesting rationale for the Inspector's otherwise rather curiously sudden retirement immediately after the Crippen case.

128 *Crippen: A Novel of Murder*, p. 195.

and on the last night of the voyage the pair share a kiss. The subsequent discovery of 'Edmund's' gender awakens both a new form of desire and a new sense of purpose in the young socialite:

> The memory of the kiss they had shared behind the lifeboats on that dreadful night of violence remained in her head; no one had ever kissed her quite like that, either before or since. Nothing made her shiver when her skin was touched quite like the fingers of Ethel Le Neve.[129]

Boyne's interweaving of Crippen and Ethel with these varied protagonists cumulatively suggests that the fugitives' disguise and intrigue are as nothing next to the concerted social and sexual masquerades of late Edwardian culture. Sympathetic *Montrose* passenger Matthieu Zéla's counsel at the close of the work resonates with both protagonists and readers alike: 'But remember, society's opinion of you is as nothing compared to your own self-respect. When you do get to Canada, I urge you to be yourselves. And enjoy life as yourselves. Otherwise, what's the point in living at all?'[130] Equally sympathetic and insightful are Zéla's words when, following the arrest of the fugitives, he ponders the capacity for criminality harboured in each human soul: 'We don't know what we're capable of. Come the moment, come the man. Or the woman, pretending to be a man. We can do the strangest things in the name of love.'[131]

As the centenary of the Crippen case approached, a further novelistic treatment was afforded to the story, this time from the pen of present-day Detective Club president Martin Edwards. In *Dancing for the Hangman*, Edwards' detailed knowledge of both the genre of crime fiction and the particulars of the Crippen story are writ large throughout. Edwards attempts to bridge the gaps in the historical record, including speculations as to precisely what took place at 39 Hilldrop Crescent, and once more revisiting the dynamic at the heart of the complex and contradictory relationship between Crippen and Belle. Appropriately for a novel appearing close to the centenary of the case, the melodramatic and sensational traditions associated with 'classic' Crippen are evoked once more, from suggestions that Crippen's childhood reading included Poe's *Masque of the Red Death* (complete with corpse dismemberment

---

129 Ibid., p. 500. Boyne's Ethel uses the alias 'Edmund' rather than the historical 'John George'.
130 Ibid., p. 427.
131 Ibid., p. 499.

and concealment of a body under the floorboards) to vignettes of Crippen's early career stint in Victorian London, where he hears stories of the scaffold and 'patterers recited rhymes about wicked deeds and murder most foul in return for pennies from passers-by'.[132] The novel posits a sadomasochistic basis for the Crippen/Cora relationship which sours and darkens over the course of the years. As in Boyne's novelisation, Crippen ultimately becomes the subject of domestic violence, his relationship with Belle deteriorating as her scant opportunities on the music hall stage decline still further. The novel also presents the cruellest rendering yet of the (still most likely apocryphal) suggestion of Belle's infidelity with the German lodgers which, along with Crippen's affair with Ethel, forms the prelude to the final crisis of the Crippen marriage. Once more in line with Marshall Hall's hypothesis of events (a view which, as has been seen, dominates the tradition of fictional writing about Crippen), the doctor begins drugging his wife only for sedative purposes so that he and Ethel might begin to spend nights together 'as man and wife'. The doctor's overdosing of his wife is related in the first person:

> My hands shook as I poured the drug into the spirit glass. Perhaps it was nervous excitement, perhaps the effect of a glass of stout of which I had partaken earlier. A single thought kept coursing through my brain. *Before Saturday dawns Ethel will have stayed with me here – and Cora will not have the slightest idea.*[133]

The cover up and ensuing flight are presented once again in Edwards's novel as the aftermath of a tragic mistake rather than a cold-blooded murder. This time, the narration of Crippen's plight as first fugitive, then prisoner, then condemned man is conducted in the first person, enabling a powerful measuring of the distance between the broad brush-strokes of the 'classic' rendition of the case and the more messy and painful reality of the man at the heart of the maelstrom:

> How galling that the possibility of my innocence seemed not to have occurred to a single soul! Nowhere could I find any acknowledgement that Cora might have died by an unlucky chance. I had been tried and found guilty in my absence, with Fleet Street acting as judge and jury.[134]

132 Martin Edwards, *Dancing for the Hangman* (Hexham: Flambard Press, 2008), p. 30.
133 Ibid., p. 228.
134 Ibid., p. 299.

The last decade has also seen a renewed merging of the historical Crippen with literary characters, as demonstrated by two novellas in which Sherlock Holmes investigates the mystery of Hilldrop Crescent. Following the lead of Nicholas Meyer's *Seven Percent Solution* (1978), which paired the fictional Holmes with none other than Sigmund Freud, *Sherlock Holmes and Dr. Crippen* and *Sherlock Holmes and the Hilldrop Crescent Mystery* offer independent versions of how the master detective comes out of retirement to work alongside Dew, Mitchell, and the other historical personages to investigate the celebrated North London Cellar Murder, contriving some twists and novel sidelights on the case along the way.[135]

The rewriting of Crippen has thus extended over a century since the appearance of Filson Young's 1920 edition of the trial proceedings converged with new currents in criminology and crime writing to prompt radical re-engagement with the case. In a sometimes unlikely literary journey ranging from page to theatrical stage, attempts have been made to re-imagine the case and to render the tale of the inscrutable 'mild murderer' in subjectively ordered accounts that rebalance and re-examine the relationships between Crippen, Belle, and Ethel, revisiting the tragic events of 1910.

If the pace of these re-imaginings has slowed in recent decades, there arguably still remains untapped potential in the story, not least the case for a more sympathetic re-imagining of Belle Elmore. Depictions that stray from Filson Young's misogynistic view of Belle are still largely lacking in the Crippen-themed literature, as is any exploration of the anti-feminist assumptions embedded in early criminological commentary where Belle was variously characterised as harridan (Filson Young) or nymphomaniac (Marshall Hall). Given her abrupt disappearance from history on that last night of January 1910, the production by Crippen of bogus letters purporting to come from her, and even hoax letters in her name written by reward-seekers during the trial, the recovery of Belle Elmore's voice and perspective remains a poignant unfulfilled potential in the tradition of writing about Crippen.

---

135 Nicholas Meyer, *The Seven Percent Solution* (London: Hodder and Stoughton, 1975); Val Andrews, *Sherlock Holmes and the Hilldrop Crescent Mystery* (London: Breese Books, 2011); Donald MacLachlan, *Sherlock Holmes and Dr. Crippen* (London: Breese Books, 2019).

CHAPTER SEVEN

GOODBYE
HILLDROP CRESCENT

Glaswegian comic performer Sandy McNab bought 39 Hilldrop Crescent in late 1910 for £500. On taking possession of the house he found the walls that Cora had decorated pink now stripped of their wallpaper and, in some places, even of the plaster and lath. Missing floorboards and pierced ceilings also attested to the exhaustive police searches of the previous summer. While protesting that he had 'no intention of running the house as a peepshow',[1] McNab was not averse to penning some gothic press copy reporting his explorations of the deserted building in the last days of 1910:

> I made my way all over the premises, and at last I came to the fateful cellar. I will not attempt to hide the fact that as my foot stepped upon the concrete floor, hardly yet dried, I felt a queer sensation at the pit of my stomach and a choking sensation in my throat. In my mind's eye I could see again the culprit working with feverish haste to bury the last trace of the crime from the eyes of man. Then I imagined the officers of the law examining the dark, damp, dungeon-like cellar, while the culprit stood calmly upon the steps behind them. The detectives were probably wise to leave the cellar at that time without making further examinations, and I felt I could do no better than follow their example.[2]

Beyond his imaginative vision in that evocative coal cellar, McNab found no traces of Crippen, Belle, and Ethel in Hilldrop Crescent in those dark days

---

1 'Scotch Comedian's Story', *Music Hall and Theatre Review*, 15 December 1910.
2 *Thomson's Weekly News*, 19 November 1910.

CRIPPEN'S HOUSE, 39 Hilldrop Crescent, London, N.
With Sandy McNab, the new owner, standing at gate,

20.   Sandy McNab, the new owner of Hilldrop Crescent in late 1910.

before Christmas 1910. This vacuum at the centre of the notorious address seems appropriate; the empty house mirrored the impression that the enigmatic, and now forever mute, Crippen had taken his secrets to the grave.

This sense of a story to be fleshed out, and secrets yet to be unearthed, must surely have provided significant impetus for the many literary renditions and re-imaginings of Crippen explored in the previous chapter. If 'Crippen considered in isolation was something of a cipher',[3] it fell to the crime novelists, criminologists, and lay commentators to begin the work of inscription, a process which gathered momentum as the 'classic Crippen' conception of 1910 was gradually displaced and challenged by new forms of representation and understanding across the fields of literature, psychology, and criminology. On the eve of the Golden Age of crime fiction, a reader sitting down with a copy of Filson Young's trial proceedings and a selection from the burgeoning library of post-war criminology, might well feel that the Crippen story represented a rich site of speculation and imaginative engagement – an open invitation to hunt the mind of a murderer.[4]

As the previous chapters have shown, that impetus to re-inscribe and revisit Crippen has endured for over a century. Yet despite the continued appearance of Crippen-themed fiction in the last decade, there are signs that the case is gradually losing its purchase on the popular imagination. Madame Tussaud's Chamber of Horrors closed to the public on 11 April 2016 with no fanfare nor public acknowledgement of the disruption of a tradition of waxwork exhibition and criminal artefact curation which extended back to the French Revolution. The Crippen waxwork is no longer on display anywhere in the exhibition, but has been banished to storage outside of London, inaccessible to the public. Among the undergraduate audiences to whom I have lectured on Crippen during the preparation of this book, familiarity with the story is also waning, with only the occasional 'CSI'-themed documentary on the contested forensic evidence in the case prompting flickers of awakened interest.

---

3   Julie English Early, 'A New Man for a New Century: Dr Crippen and the Principles of Masculinity', in *Disorder in the Court: Trials and Sexual Conflict at the Turn of the Century*, ed. George Robb and Nancy Erber (London: Macmillan, 1999), pp. 209–30.

4   Sample works of post-war popular criminology include the aforementioned H.B. Irving's *A Book of Remarkable Criminals* (London: Cassell, 1918) and Tennyson Jesse's *Murder and Its Motives* (London: William Heinemann, 1924).

There are signs then of a rupture in the tradition that Orwell so famously writes of in his wry essay 'On the Decline of the English Murder': 'Our great period in murder, our Elizabethan period, so to speak, seems to have been between roughly 1850 and 1925, and the murderers whose reputation has stood the test of time are the following: Dr Palmer of Rugely, Jack the Ripper, Neill Cream, Mrs Maybrick, Dr Crippen.'[5] As the preceding chapters have shown, Crippen was a particularly powerful focus in this imaginative repertory of murder, sustaining the sensibility Orwell describes for a century beyond the close of this 'Elizabethan period'. In October 1910 a correspondent for the *Sheffield Evening Telegraph* relayed how, immediately prior to the Crippen drama, a recent gathering of popular criminologists had reached 'general agreement that it was impossible for a notable crime nowadays to absorb public attention to the extent to which it was concentrated on such crimes as those of Palmer, Pritchard, Peace, Wainwright, the unknown Whitechapel murderer, and other historic criminals'. The Crippen case changed all of that: 'The history of the last few months, culminating in the dread scene at the Old Bailey last week, has completely disproved these conclusions. Never has there been a crime which has attracted and sustained public interest more powerfully than that of which Crippen was convicted on Saturday.'[6]

The Crippen case came to define a particular discursive and imaginative field for depictions of domestic murder, for a period of some fifty years from the commission of the crime in 1910. Adapting a concept from sociologist Charles Taylor, we might even describe this field as a particular form of murder imaginary – a common repertory of concepts, images, and expectations through which individuals structure their criminological understanding.[7] At the heart of the imaginary stood the physical waxen effigy of Crippen in the bowels of Madame Tussaud's Chamber of Horrors, presiding there, in what for many years must have seemed set to be a permanent memorial of a particular mode of imagining and remembering domestic murder. This 'murder imaginary' doubtless brought its simplifications and distortions and was largely driven by the commercial instincts of newspaper editors, but, as we

5   George Orwell, 'Decline of the English Murder', in *Essays* (Harmondsworth: Penguin, 1984), p. 345.
6   *Sheffield Evening Telegraph*, 24 October 1910.
7   Charles Taylor, *Modern Social Imaginaries* (Durham and London: Duke University Press, 2004).

have seen, it likewise represented a point of continuity with Victorian literary and theatrical modes which had otherwise become largely redundant, even by 1910. Recourse to this murder imaginary was a feature of the press treatment of the Haigh 'acid-bath murders' of the late 1940s and of John Christie's 10 Rillington Place murders for which he was executed in 1953. Five years later, a Christie case history would observe how the press coverage of the trial and execution had revived an illaudable but unmistakeable tradition

> which has always regarded a good murder as a popular entertainment ... And being such, it revives echoes of old music that had seemed forgotten ... the Christie music is not played by a symphony orchestra, but on the penny tin-whistle and a drum; music of the old street ballads, the ballads the Londoners sang of everyone they hanged, from Jolly Jack Sheppard to the Mannings.[8]

Probably the gradual displacement of this murder imaginary was inevitable after the discontinuation of capital punishment in 1965. It was one thing to stand in the Chamber of Horrors to gaze on the effigies of murderers who had passed into history, their stories sealed off from the viewer's everyday experience by the abrupt narrative closure of an execution; it was something else to brood upon such effigies while the subject of the representation was alive and well, detained indefinitely at Her Majesty's Pleasure in Pentonville or Broadmoor. The more the criminal justice system countenanced narratives of rehabilitation or medicalised and pathologised views of criminality, the more incongruous became a waxworks emporium stocked with the effigies of the bogeymen figures of yesteryear. Between this societal shift, and the crime novelists' efforts to revisit the Crippen story in a more subtle and nuanced criminological frame of reference, the Crippenesque murder imaginary was gradually disassembled, bringing an accompanying diminution of the story's implication in cultural memory.

Anne-Marie Kilday and David Nash have stressed the ways in which criminals and villains are both *made* and *unmade* by the exposure of their story to the media of various historical periods: 'Crimes and criminals, as well as their policing and detection, are themselves rooted firmly in narrative. This

---

8   Molly Lefebure, *Murder with a Difference: The Cases of Haigh and Christie* (London: Heinemann, 1958), pp. 250–1.

appears in the conceptualization of them by police and legal authorities as "cases" for investigation, interpretation and resolution.[9] As we have seen, the story of Dr Crippen was first fashioned as a work of nostalgia, patterned on the crime sensations of the preceding century. In the years following the First World War, and coincident with the Golden Age of detective fiction, the creative imaginations of a distinguished line of crime fiction writers set about proposing counter-narratives, revisiting the story in the light of new cultural under-standings of crime and criminals. Bequeathed such a legacy, the enigmatic figure of Hawley Harvey Crippen remains forever refracted in the contrasting lenses of memory and modernity.

> The black cap is placed on the judge's head, and an usher calls through the court for silence! The judge leans forward with his arms spread out upon the little table before him. He looks steadfastly at the prisoner, and in a strong, earnest voice pronounces the dread sentence of death. He will not dilate upon the ghastly and wicked nature of the crime, but he implores the doomed man to harbour no thoughts of a reprieve, but to make his peace with God.
>
> "Amen."
>
> The word is uttered by the silver-haired priest standing with bowed head near the judge's chair. Dr. Crippen turns. The warders close in upon him, but he does not need their assistance.
>
> He walks steadily towards the stairway and passes for the last time from our sight, still impassive, still extremely calm, still inscrutable![10]

9   *Law, Crime and Deviance since 1700: Micro-Studies in the History of Crime*, ed. Anne-Marie Kilday and David Nash (London: Bloomsbury), p. 3.
10 *Daily Graphic*, 24 October 1910.

Bibliography

National Archive Papers

CRIM 1/117
DPP 1/13
HO144/1719/195492
MEPO 2/10996
MEPO 3/198
PCOM 8/30

Periodicals, Serials and Newspapers

Aberdeen Press and Journal
Ballymena Observer
Belfast Telegraph
Belfast Weekly News
Birmingham Daily Gazette
Bournemouth Daily Echo
Brighton Gazette
British Medical Journal
The Bystander
Caledonian Mercury
Chicago Daily Tribune
The Clarion
The Courier
Daily Express

Daily Graphic

Daily Herald

Daily Telegraph and Courier

Derbyshire Times and Chesterfield Herald

Dramatic Censor

Dundee Evening Telegraph

Ealing Gazette and West Middlesex Observer

East London Advertiser

East London Observer

The Era

The Evening News

The Evening World

The Field: The Country Gentleman's Newspaper

Fifeshire Advertiser

The Globe

Hampshire Telegraph

Hartlepool Northern Daily Mail

Illustrated London News

Illustrated Police News

Islington Daily Gazette and North London Tribune

John Bull

Kensington Post

Kilburn Times

Lake's Falmouth Packet and Cornwall Advertiser

Lancashire Evening News

Leeds Mercury

Leicester Chronicle

Lloyd's Weekly London Newspaper

London and Provincial Entr'acte

London Daily News

London Evening Standard

Morning Chronicle

Morning Post

Music Hall and Theatre Review

New York Herald

Newcastle Daily Journal

The News of the World

Northern Whig
Norwood News
Nottingham Evening Post
Omaha Daily Bee
Ottumwa Tri-weekly Courier
Pall Mall Gazette
Pearson's Weekly
Penny Illustrated Paper
The People
The Performer
Portsmouth Evening News
Punch
The Referee
Roxbury Times
Salt Lake Herald
Sevenoaks Chronicle and Kentish Advertiser
Sheffield Evening Telegraph
Shields Daily Gazette
Sporting Times
St James Gazette
Staffordshire Advertiser
The Stage
Stonehaven Journal
Surrey Mirror
The Tatler
Thomson's Weekly News
The Times
Tower Hamlets Independent and East End Local Advertiser
The True Northerner
Washington Times
Weekly Expositor
West Middlesex Herald
Western Mail
Worthing Herald
Yorkshire Post and Leeds Intelligencer

Police Memoirs

Anderson, Robert, *The Lighter Side of My Official Life* (New York and London: Hodder and Stoughton, 1910).

Dew, Walter, *I Caught Crippen* (London: Blackie, 1938).

Macnaghten, Sir Melville, *Days of My Years* (London: Edward Arnold, 1914).

Smith, Sir Henry, *From Constable to Commissioner: The Story of Sixty Years, Most of them Misspent* (London: Chatto and Windus, 1910).

Fiction Influenced by or Alluding to the Crippen Case

Andrews, Val, *Sherlock Holmes and the Hilldrop Crescent Mystery* (London: Breese Books, 2011).

Berkeley, Anthony, *The Wychford Poisoning Case* (London: Collins and Sons, 1926; Harper Collins, 2017).

Bierstadt, Edward Hale, *Satan Was a Man* (New York: Doubleday, 1935).

Bloom, Ursula, *The Girl Who Loved Crippen* (London: Arrow, 1965).

Brahms, Caryl and Ned Sherrin, *Rappel 1910* (London: WH Allen, 1964).

Christie, Agatha, *The Labours of Hercules* [1947] (London: Harper, 2008).

——, *Lord Edgware Dies* (London: Collins, 1933).

——, *Three Act Tragedy* [1935] (London: Pan, 1964).

——, *The Murder of Roger Ackroyd* (London: Collins, 1926).

——, *Mrs McGinty's Dead* [1952] (London: Pan, 1971).

——, *Sleeping Murder* (London: Collins, 1976).

Connington, J.J., *The Case with Nine Solutions* [1928] (Harmondsworth: Penguin, 1949).

Crane, Richard, *Crippen: A Music Hall Melodrama* (London: School Play Productions, 1990).

Dornhurst, Paul, 'They Fly by Twilight' in *Five Plays of Our Time*, ed. Sydney Box (London: Thomas Nelson and Sons, 1939).

Edwards, Martin, *Dancing for the Hangman* (Hexham: Flambard Press, 2008).

Forester, C.S., *The Pursued* (Harmondsworth: Penguin, 2012).

Gordon, Richard, *A Question of Guilt: The Curious Case of Dr Crippen* (New York: Atheneum, 1981).

Hooker, Michael, *Doctor Crippen* (London: Brown, Watson Ltd, 1963).

Horler, Sydney, *The Man Who Did Not Hang* (London: Quality Press, 1948).

Isles, Francis, *Malice Aforethought* [1931] (London: Pan, 1999).

Le Queux, William, *Dr Crippen: Lover and Poisoner and other True Tales of Suspense* (London: Newnes, n.d.).

Lewis, Hilda, *The Case of the Little Doctor* [1940] (New York: Permabooks, 1949).

MacLachlan, Donald, *Sherlock Holmes and Dr. Crippen* (Cambridge: Baker Street Studios, 2019).

Mankowitz, Wolf and Monty Norman, *Belle or The Ballad of Doctor Crippen* (London: Wolf Mankowitz Presentations, n.d.).

Meadows, Catherine, *Doctor Moon* (New York: G.P. Putnam's Sons, 1935).

Raymond, Ernest, *We, The Accused* (London: Cassell, 1935).

Williams, Emlyn, *Dr Crippen's Diary: An Invention* (London: Futura, 1988).

Books and Articles

Ackroyd, Peter, *T.S. Eliot: A Life* (New York: Simon and Schuster, 1984).

——, *London: The Biography* (London: Vintage, 2001).

——, *London Under* (London: Vintage, 2012).

Altick, Richard D., *Victorian Studies in Scarlet: Murders and Manners in the Age of Victoria* (London: JM Dent and Sons, 1970).

Appleby, Louis, 'The Doctor and the Classic Crime', *British Medical Journal* 299:6691 (1989), p. 132.

Arata, Stephen, 'The Occidental Tourist: Dracula and the Anxiety of Reverse Colonization', *Victorian Studies* 33:4 (1990), 621–45.

Arnold, Catharine, *Bedlam: London and Its Mad* (London: Simon and Schuster, 2008).

——, *Underworld London: Crime and Punishment in the Capital City* (London: Simon and Schuster, 2012).

Bailey, Peter, 'Conspiracies of Meaning: Music-Hall and the Knowingness of Popular Culture', *Past and Present* 144 (1994), 138–70: 167.

Begg, Paul, Martin Fido and Keith Skinner, *The Complete Jack the Ripper A to Z* (London: John Blake, 2010).

Bell, Karl, *Spring-Heeled Jack: Victorian Urban Folklore and Popular Cultures* (Woodbridge: Boydell Press, 2012).

Belloc Lowndes, Marie, *The Lodger: A Story of the London Fog* (Oxford: Oxford University Press, 1996).

Benson, J., 'Calculation, Celebrity and Scandal: The Provincial Press in Edwardian England', *Journalism Studies* 10 (2009), 837–50.

Bernthal, J.C., *Queering Agatha Christie: Revisiting the Golden Age of Detective Fiction* (London: Palgrave Macmillan, 2016).

Biber, Katherine, *In Crime's Archive: The Cultural Afterlife of Evidence* (London: Routledge, 2018).

Birkenhead, Earl of, *Famous Trials* (London: Hutchinson, 1926).

Bondeson, Jan, *The London Monster: Terror on the Streets in 1790* (Stroud: Sutton Publishing, 2003).

Boyne, John, *Crippen: A Novel of Murder* (Harmondsworth: Penguin, 2004).

Brereton, Austin, *H.B. and Laurence Irving* (London: Grant Richards, 1922).

British Medical Journal, 'The Vegetable Alkaloids', *British Medical Journal* 2:2601 (1910), 1451–2.

Browne, Douglas G., *Sir Travers Humphreys: A Biography* (London: George G. Harrap and Co, 1960).

Browne, Douglas G. and E.V. Tullett, *Bernard Spilsbury: His Life and Cases* (London: Harrap, 1951).

Burney, Ian A., 'A Poisoning of No Substance: the Trials of Medico-Legal Proof in Mid-Victorian England', *Journal of British Studies* 38:1 (1999), 59–92.

Burrows, Jon, 'Melodrama of the Dear Old Kind: Sentimentalising British Action Heroines in the 1910s', *Film History* 18:2, 163–73.

Butler, Judith, *Bodies that Matter: On the Discursive Limits of 'Sex'* (New York: Routledge, 1993).

Caputi, Jane, *The Age of Sex Crime* (London: The Women's Press, 1987).

Carey, John, *The Violent Effigy: A Study of Dickens' Imagination* (London: Faber, 1973).

Carr, John Dickson, *The Waxworks Murder* (Harmondsworth: Penguin, 1932).

Chapman, Pauline, *Madame Tussaud's Chamber of Horrors: Two Hundred Years of Crime* (London: Constable, 1984).

Cohen, Ed, *Talk on the Wilde Side: Toward a Genealogy of a Discourse of Male Sexualities* (London: Routledge, 1993).

Connell, Nicholas, *Walter Dew: The Man Who Caught Crippen* (Stroud: Sutton Publishing, 2005).

——, *Doctor Crippen* (Stroud: Amberley, 2013).

—— (ed.), *The Annotated I Caught Crippen* (London: Mango Books, 2018).

Crippen, Hawley Harvey, 'A study of clinical experience with remedies relating to the left ovary', *Homeopathic Journal of Obstetrics, Gynaecology and Paedology* 1:1 (1889), 212–5.

——, 'Foetal Nutrition', *American Homeopathic Journal of Gynaecology and Obstetrics* 1:6 June 1885, 164–71.

Crone, Rosalind, *Violent Victorians: Popular Entertainment in Nineteenth-Century London* (Manchester: Manchester University Press, 2012).

Cullen, Tom, *The Mild Murderer: The True Story of the Dr. Crippen Case* (Boston: Houghton Mifflin, 1977).

Curtis, L. Perry, *Jack the Ripper and the London Press* (Yale: Yale University Press, 2001).

Dalrymple, Theodore, 'A Villainous Doctor', *British Medical Journal* 342:7794 (2011), p. 445.

Dickens, Charles, *The Old Curiosity Shop* [1841] (London: Vintage, 2010).

Doyle, Sir Arthur Conan, *The Adventures of Sherlock Holmes* [1892] (Harmondsworth: Penguin, 1981).

——, *Memories and Adventures* [1924] (Ware: Wordsworth, 2007).

Early, Julie English, 'Modernity and "The Little Man": Crippen's Capture by Wireless', *Victorian Studies* 39:3 (1996), pp. 309–37.

——, 'A New Man for a New Century: Dr Crippen and the Principles of Masculinity', in *Disorder in the Court: Trials and Sexual Conflict at the Turn of the Century*, ed. George Robb and Nancy Erber (London: Macmillan, 1999), pp. 209–30.

Eaton, Harold, *Famous Poison Trials* (London: Collins and Sons, 1923).

——, 'The Case of the Century: Crippen and the Belle Elmore', in *The Fifty Most Amazing Crimes of the Last 100 Years*, ed. J.M. Parrish and John R. Crossland (London: Odhams Press, 1936), pp. 102–19.

Eddy, J.P., *Scarlet and Ermine: Famous Trials as I Saw Them from Crippen to Podola* (London: William Kimber, 1960).

Edwards, Martin, *The Golden Age of Murder: The Mystery of the Writers who Invented the Modern Detective Story* (London: Harper Collins, 2016).

Ellis, J.C., *Black Fame: Stories of Crime and Criminals* (London: Hutchinson and Co, 1930).

Ellis, John, *Diary of a Hangman* (London: True Crime Library, 1996).

Engel, Matthew, *Tickle the Public: One Hundred Years of the Popular Press* (London: Indigo, 1997).

Evans, Stewart P. and Paul Gainey, *The Lodger: The Arrest and Escape of Jack the Ripper* (London: Century, 1995).

Felstead, Sidney Theodore, *Sir Richard Muir: A Memoir of a Public Prosecutor* (London: The Bodley Head, 1927).

Fido, Martin, *Murder Guide to London* (London: Weidenfeld and Nicolson, 1986).

——, *A Passion for Killing* [Audiobook] (Watford: MCI Spoken Word, 1998).

Flanders, Judith, *The Invention of Murder* (London: Harper Press, 2011).

Gardiner, D. and K. Sorley Walker, *Raymond Chandler Speaking* (Berkeley: University of California Press, 1997).

Gilbert, Michael, *Doctor Crippen* (London: Odhams Press, 1953).

Gilbert, W.S., 'The Hooligan', in *Original Plays by W.S. Gilbert* (London: Chatto and Windus, 1926), pp. 477–86.

Goodman, Jonathan, *The Crippen File* (London: Allison and Busby, 1985).

——, 'Much Ado About Crippen', *New Law Journal* 1997.

Harkup, Kathryn, *A is for Arsenic: The Poisons of Agatha Christie* (London: Bloomsbury, 2015).

Harris, Ruth, *Murders and Madness: Medicine, Law and Society in the fin de siècle* (Oxford: Clarendon Press, 1989).

Harrison, Michael, *Clarence: Was He Jack the Ripper?* (New York: Drake, 1974).

Hattersley, Roy, *The Edwardians* (London: Abacus, 2004).

Heppenstal, Rayner, *Tales from the Newgate Calendar: True Stories of Crime and Punishment* (London: Futura, 1983).

Hilton, James, *Goodbye Mr Chips* (London: Hodder and Stoughton, 1934, rep. 1958).

Hollander, Bernard, *Hypnotism and Suggestion in Daily Life, Education and Medical Practice* (London: Pitman, 1910).

Honeycombe, Gordon, *The Murders of the Black Museum* (London: Hutchinson and Co, 1982).

Humphreys, Travers, *Criminal Days* (London: Hodder and Stoughton, 1946).

Huson, Richard, *Sixty Famous Trials* (London: Daily Express Publications, 1938).

Irving, H.B., *A Book of Remarkable Criminals* (London: Cassell, 1918).

——, *Last Studies in Criminology* (London: Collins and Sons, 1921).

Jakubowski, Maxim and Nathan Braund (eds), *The Mammoth Book of Jack the Ripper* (London: Robinson Publishing, 1999).

Janes, Diane, *Edwardian Murder: Ightham and the Morpeth Train Robbery* (Stroud: Sutton Publishing, 2007).

Jewkes, Yvonne, *Media and Crime*, 3rd edition (London: Sage, 2015).

Keily, Jackie and Julia Hoffbrand, *The Crime Museum Uncovered: Inside Scotland Yard's Special Collection* (London: Museum of London, 2015).

Kelly, Alexander, *Jack the Ripper: A Bibliography and Review of the Literature* (London: Association of Assistant Librarians, 1973).

Kent, Arthur, *The Death Doctors* (London: New English Library, 1974).

Kilday, Anne-Marie and David Nash (eds), *Law, Crime and Deviance Since 1700: Micro-Studies in the History of Crime* (London: Bloomsbury).

Kinnell, Herbert, 'Agatha Christie's Doctors', *British Medical Journal* 341:7786 (2010), pp. 1324–5.

Knight, Stephen, *Jack the Ripper: The Final Solution* (London: Harrap, 1976).

– *Crime Fiction Since 1800*, 2nd edition (Basingstoke: Palgrave Macmillan, 2010).

Larson, Erik, *Thunderstruck* (London: Doubleday, 2006).

Le Neve, Ethel, *Ethel Le Neve: Her Life Story with the True Account of their Flight and Her Friendship for Dr Crippen Told by Herself* (London: Publishing Office, 1910).

Le Queux, William, *Things I Know About Kings, Celebrities and Crooks* (London: Eveleigh Nash and Grayson Ltd, 1923).

Lefebure, Molly, *Murder with a Difference: The Cases of Haigh and Christie* (London: Heinemann, 1958).

London, Jack, *The People of the Abyss* (London: The Journeyman Press, 1977).

Marjoribanks, Edward, *The Life of Sir Edward Marshall Hall* (London: Victor Gollancz, 1930).

Mayhew, Henry, *Mayhew's London – Being Selections from 'London Labour and the London Poor'*, ed. Peter Quennell (London: The Pilot Press, 1949).

McClaren, Angus, *A Prescription for Murder: The Victorian Serial Killings of Dr Thomas Neill Cream* (Chicago: University of Chicago Press, 1995).

McKay, Sinclair, *The Lady in the Cellar: Murder, Scandal and Insanity in Victorian Bloomsbury* (London: White Lion).

Menges, Jonathan, 'Connective Tissue: Belle Elmore, H.H. Crippen and the Death of Charlotte Bell', *Ripperologist* 158 (2017), 11–16.

Meyer, Nicholas, *The Seven Percent Solution* (London: Hodder and Stoughton, 1975).

Muddock, J.E., *A Wingless Angel* (London: Virtue and Co, 1875).

Napley, David, *The Camden Town Murder (Great Murder Trials of the Twentieth Century)* (London: Weidenfeld and Nicholson, 1987).

Oddie, S. Ingleby, *Inquest* (London: Hutchinson and Son, 1941).

Odell, Robin, *Exhumation of A Murder: The Life and Trial of Major Armstrong* (London: Harrap, 1975).

Orwell, George, 'Decline of the English Murder', in *Essays* (Harmondsworth: Penguin, 1994), pp. 345–8.

Ousby, Ian, *Bloodhounds of Heaven: The Detective in English Fictions from Godwin to Doyle* (Cambridge, Mass: Harvard University Press, 1976).

Packer, Sharon, *Movies and the Modern Psyche* (Westport, CT: Praeger, 2007).

Parker, Richard, *The Whip: Novelized from Cecil Raleigh's Great Drury Lane Melodrama* (New York: Macaulay, 1913).

Parris, Carrie Selina, 'The Crimes Club: The Early Years of Our Society', Unpublished Ph.D. Thesis (University of East Anglia, 2016).

Parrish, J.M. and John R. Crossland (eds), *The Fifty Most Amazing Cases of the Last 100 Years* (London: Odhams Press, 1936).

Pearson, Hesketh, *Modern Men and Mummers* (London: Allen and Unwin, 1921).

Pember, Ron and Denis de Marne, *Jack the Ripper: A Musical Play* (London: Samuel French, 1976).

Pilbeam, Pamela, *Madame Tussaud and the History of Waxwork* (London and New York: Hambledon, 2003).

Priestley, J.B., *The Edwardians* (London: Heinemann, 1970).

Quinn, Max Constantine, *Doctor Crippen* (London: Duckworth, 1935).

Read, Donald, *Edwardian England, 1901–15* (London: Harrap, 1972).

Ridley, Jane, *Bertie: A Life of Edward VII* (London: Vintage, 2013).

Ritschel, Nelson, *Bernard Shaw, W.T. Stead, and the New Journalism* (London: Palgrave Macmillan, 2017).

Robins, Jane, *The Magnificent Spilsbury and the case of the Brides in the Bath* (London: John Murray, 2010).

Rogers, Naomi, 'The Proper Place of Homeopathy: Hahnemann Medical College and Hospital in an Age of Scientific Medicine', *The Pennsylvania Magazine of History and Biography* 108:2 (1984), 179–201.

Saward, Joe, *The Extraordinary Life of the Man Who Caught Crippen* (Milton Keynes: Lightning Source, 2010).

Scott, Harold, *The Early Doors: Origins of the Music Hall* (London: Nicholson and Watson, 1946).

Scull, Andrew (ed.), *Madhouses, Mad-Doctors and Madmen: The Social History of Psychiatry in the Victorian Era* (Philadelphia: University of Pennsylvania Press, 1981).

Sedgewick, Eve Kosofsky, *Epistemology of the Closet*, 2nd rev edn (Berkeley: University of California Press, 2008).

Shew, E. Spencer, *A Companion to Murder: A Dictionary of Death by Poison, Death by Shooting, Death by Suffocation and Drowning, Death by the Strangler's Hand* (London: Cassell, 1960).

Showalter, Elaine, *Sexual Anarchy: Gender and Culture at the Fin de Siècle* (London: Virago, 1992).

Shpayer-Makov, Haia, *The Ascent of the Detective: Police Sleuths in Victorian and Edwardian England* (Oxford: Oxford University Press, 2011).

Sims, George R., *Mysteries of Modern London* (London: C. Arthur Pearson Ltd, 1906).

——, *My Life: Sixty Years' Recollections of Bohemian London* (London: Eveleigh Nash Co., 1917).

Singer, Ben, *Melodrama and Modernity: Early Sensational Cinema and Its Contexts* (New York: Columbia University Press, 2001).

Smith, David James, *Supper with the Crippens* (London: Orion, 2005).

Springhall, John, '"Pernicious Reading?" The Penny Dreadful as Scapegoat for Late-Victorian Juvenile Crime', *Victorian Periodicals Review* 27:4 (1994), 326–49.

——, '"Disseminating Impure Literature": The "Penny Dreadful" Publishing Business Since 1860', *Economic History Review*, n.s. 47:3, 567–84.

Stapleton, Susannah, *The Adventures of Maud West, Lady Detective* (London: Pan Macmillan, 2019).

Symons, Julian, *Bloody Murder – From the Detective Story to the Crime Novel: A History* (Harmondsworth: Penguin, 1974).

Taylor, Charles, *Modern Social Imaginaries* (Durham, N.C.: Duke, 2004).

Taylor, Seymour, 'Unqualified Practice and Crime', *British Medical Journal* 2:2604 (1910), 1747–8.

Thurston, Katherine Cecil, *Max: A Novel* (London: Hutchinson and Co, 1909).

Waddington, Keir, 'Mayhem and Medical Students: Image, Conduct, and Control in the Victorian and Edwardian Teaching Hospital', *Social History of Medicine* 15:1 (2002), 45–64.

Walkowitz, Judith, *City of Dreadful Delight: Narratives of Sexual Danger in Late-Victorian London* (London: Virago, 1992).

Wallace, Edgar, *The Four Just Men* (London: George Newnes, 1905).

Watson, Eric R. (ed.), *The Trial of George Joseph Smith* (London, Edinburgh and Glasgow: William Hodge and Co, 1922, repr. 1949).

Watson, Katherine D., *Dr Crippen* (London: The National Archives, 2007).

Wells, H.G., *Toro Bungay* [1909] (London: Pan, 1982).

——, 'The Red Room', in *The Oxford Book of English Ghost Stories*, selected by Michael Cox and R.A. Gilbert (Oxford: Oxford University Press, 1986), pp. 172–89.

Whittington-Egan, Richard, *Mr Atherstone Leaves the Stage: The Battersea Murder Mystery* (Stroud: Amberley Publishing, 2015).

Wiener, Joel H. (ed.), *Papers for the Millions: The New Journalism in Britain, 1850s to 1914* (London: Greenwood, 1988).

Wilson, A.N., *After the Victorians: The World Our Parents Knew* (London: Arrow, 2006).

Winslow, L. Forbes, *The Suggestive Power of Hypnotism* (London: Rebman Ltd, 1910).

Wood, Walter (ed.), *Survivors' Tales of Famous Crimes* (London: Cassell, 1916).

Woolf, Virginia, 'Character in Fiction', *The Criteron* II (1924), 409–30.

Wright, Adrian, *Must Close Saturday: The Decline and Fall of the British Musical Flop* (Woodbridge: Boydell Press, 2017).

Wright, David, 'Getting out of the Asylum: Understanding the Confinement of the Insane in the Nineteenth Century', *Social History of Medicine* 10 (1997), 137–55.

Yates, Donford, *As Berry and I Were Saying* (London: Ward Lock, 1952).

Yellon, Evan, *Surdus in Search of His Hearing: An Exposure of Aural Quacks and a Guide to Genuine Treatments and Remedies, Electrical Aids, Lip-reading and Employments for the Deaf Etc Etc* (London: The Celtic Press, 1906).

Young, Filson (ed.), *Trial of the Seddons* (London: William Hodge, 1914).

—— (ed.), *The Trial of Hawley Harvey Crippen* (London: William Hodge, 1920).

Index

Page numbers in *italic* refer to illustrations; page numbers followed by 'n' indicate footnotes. The abbreviation HHC refers to Hawley Harvey Crippen.